PROSE STYLE: A Handbook for Writers

PROSE STYLE
A Handbook for Writers
Third Edition

Wilfred Stone
Stanford University

J. G. Bell
Stanford University Press

McGraw-Hill Book Company

New York   St. Louis   San Francisco   Auckland   Bogotá   Düsseldorf
Johannesburg   London   Madrid   Mexico   Montreal   New Delhi
Panama   Paris   São Paulo   Singapore   Sydney   Tokyo   Toronto

PROSE STYLE: A Handbook for Writers

1 2 3 4 5 6 7 8 9 0   MUMU   7 8 3 2 1 0 9 8 7 6

See Acknowledgments on pages 304–306. Copyrights included on this page by reference.

This book was set in Caledonia by Rocappi, Inc. The editors were Ellen B. Fuchs, Donald W. Burden, and Phyllis T. Dulan; the cover was designed by Nicholas Krenitsky; the production supervisor was Judi Allen. The Murray Printing Company was printer and binder.

Cover painting: "Departure" by Vivienne Andres, 1972.

Library of Congress Cataloging in Publication Data

Stone, Wilfred Healy, date
    Prose style, a handbook for writers.

    Includes index.
    1. English language—Rhetoric. I. Bell, J. G., joint author. II. Title.
PE1408.S766   1977   808′.042   76-25158
ISBN 0-07-061732-5

CONTENTS

PART 3 MECHANICS

PREFACE

The warm reception of earlier editions of this book has borne out our belief in the need for a short, readable, informal approach to the problems of writing. Though apparently many teachers have used the book as a straight reference rather than (as we had hoped) a book to be read and *then* used as a reference, we still believe in our original design. This third edition, like its predecessors, is a book to be read—a useful review for the student who is already familiar with the fundamentals, a useful guide to the student who wants to become a better writer.

Users of the second edition will note several changes. We have extensively revised Chapters 1, 2, 6, and 8. Elsewhere we have done the usual updating, notably of the research paper in Chapter 14 and the Index to Current Usage, and made such other changes as users have persuasively recommended. We have corrected what some teachers justly considered an excessive emphasis on errors and fallacies. Finally, we have done our utmost to modify our linguistic and literary inclinations and to address our comments and examples to a more general audience. We trust that these changes have brought this edition closer than any of its predecessors to the needs and expectations of its users.

For help in preparing this edition we are indebted to Fred W. Alvarez, Jenifer Angel, Betty Brereton, Helen Brooks, Andrea Hammer, Janice Haney, Donald Lazere, John McClure, Colleen McGrath, John F. Pfeil, Susan Squier, and Keith A. Tandy. A number of our improvements are the result of thoughtful reviews of the second edition by Doris Betts, John Doggett, H. Leon Gatlin, James A. Gowen, W. Georg Isaak, Ralph M. Wirfs, George Wolff, and Peter T. Zoller.

Wilfred Stone
J. G. Bell

PROSE STYLE: A Handbook for Writers

PART 1
THE WRITER AND
HIS MESSAGE

1

ABOUT WRITING

Often the beginning writer thinks of good writing as something to imitate rather than something to create. Surrounded as he is by handbooks, anthologies, and other weighty repositories of precept and example, he often feels frustrated, even despairing. Do people really think he can learn overnight to write like George Orwell or Mary McCarthy? If they do, he can see only one hope: rote learning and imitation. To be a writer he must set aside the Joe Smith he is and write like some Joseph W. Smith he is not, never was, but vaguely supposes he ought to be. From this point of view, writing is not saying what one thinks or feels; it is more like acting in a play written by others.

We think this point of view is mistaken. In our opinion, learning to write well is first of all a matter of finding your own voice and using it—*your* voice, not someone else's. If Joe Smith is who you are, then Joe Smith is the one your reader wants to hear from. A writer should put himself into the act, write his own part. Nothing less in the long run makes writing worth reading.

Of course most of us draw on more than one voice, depending on our audience: we speak one way to children, another way to our peers. Just so does writing take place in a context: a writer must not only find his own authentic voice, but learn to adjust that voice to his readers' capacities if he is not to end up talking to himself. Let us examine the elements of that context—the writer, his readers (or audience), and his writing.

THE WRITER

Writing starts with the writer. He must have something to say, must want to say it, and must learn how to say it clearly and well. The easiest of these three requirements is the last: the techniques and conventions of good writing. They can be learned, and a good part of this book is given over to instruction in them. What cannot be learned, at least in the same way, is self-confidence: belief in yourself and in the importance and authenticity of what you write.

Many beginning writers contemplate that blank sheet of paper in despair. "But I don't have anything to write about!" "Who cares what I have to say?" Finding a subject is sometimes difficult, but more basic may be your belief that, compared with professional writers, you're just no good.

Don't believe it. You can learn a lot about writing from reading professional writers (there is a close connection between liking to read and liking to write), but they are not fundamentally different from you. Your experience, like theirs, is unique; so are your feelings and thoughts. If you are asked to write about something your class has been reading, don't just panic and fake something. Think it over. There is bound to be some point where your personal experience intersects with what you are reading. That point of intersection is where *you* come in, where you can speak with the authority of your unique experience. You may address only a tiny corner of a large issue, but authority is none the less real for being asserted in a small matter. Writing about Shakespeare or the Second World War is inherently no more interesting than writing about your roommate or your uncle's webbed feet. The interest depends not on the size or the grandness of the subject, but on whether you have entered it and made it your own.

Let us assume that you are Joe Smith. For several weeks your class has been reading essays on the role of women in Western life, and you have now been asked to write about something in those readings that moved or stimulated you. At first the succession of pieces by

Strindberg, Freud, Shaw, and a selection of feminists ranging from Simone de Beauvoir to Betty and Theodore Roszak left you cold. All this talk about women being dominated by men didn't square with your experience. Wasn't your mother the boss in your family? Wasn't your sister studying to be a lawyer? Weren't you an accomplished dishwasher? What was all the fuss about? You were all for equal pay for equal work, and so were most of the people you knew. Perhaps there had been injustices in the past—especially in foreign countries—but weren't they being taken care of? Certainly when Gunnar Myrdal, in his essay "Women, Servants, Mules, and Other Property," compared women to slaves, he was going too far.

But then things got more complicated. One day a classmate called you a "sexist" for snickering at her remark that a lot of men treated women as sex objects. You were skeptical. Didn't women *want* to be sex objects? Weren't the cosmetic and bra advertisements clear evidence of what women wanted? No, said your critics, women don't want to be sex objects, they want to be human beings. It is only men who want them to be sex objects; this viewpoint, along with the ads and other props that support it, is part of a male plot to keep women emotionally and financially dependent. Some of these arguments seemed to you excessive, but you gradually began to see things from a new angle—with strong reinforcement from Una Stannard's essay "The Mask of Beauty":

> Women are not free to stop playing the beauty game. . . . Every day, in every way, the billion-dollar beauty business tells women they are monsters in disguise. Every ad for bras tells a woman that her breasts need lifting, every ad for padded bras that what she's got isn't big enough, every ad for girdles that her belly sags and her hips are too wide, every ad for high heels that her legs need propping, every ad for cosmetics that her skin is too dry, too oily, too pale, or too ruddy, or her lips are not bright enough, or her lashes not long enough, every ad for deodorants and perfumes that her natural odors all need disguising, every ad for hair dye, curlers, and permanents that the hair she was born with is the wrong color or too straight or too curly, and lately ads for wigs tell her that she would be better off covering up nature's mistake completely. . . .
>
> Glittering and smiling in the media, looked at by millions, envied and ogled, . . . these ideal beauties teach women their role in society. They teach them that women are articles of conspicuous consumption in the male market. . . .
>
> The ideal beauties teach women that their looks are a commodity to be bartered in exchange for a man, not only for food, clothing, and

shelter, but for love. Women learn early that if you are unlovely, you are unloved. The homely girl prepares to be an old maid, because beauty is what makes a man fall in love.

Males, you have to admit, have fewer such worries. You even begin to see the parallel with slavery: the adopting of a false self, the turning of the self into a commodity, is to enslave that self. You begin to see how strictly masculine, and how self-serving, were a lot of the old arguments about the nature of woman and a woman's place—such pronouncements as "Man's biological function is to do; woman's is to be" (Robert Graves), such hypotheses as Freud's "penis envy." You bring a new skepticism to Freud's comments on John Stuart Mill's "The Subjection of Women":

> In his whole presentation [writes Freud] it never emerges that women are different beings—we will not say lesser, rather the opposite—from men. He finds the suppression of women an analogy to that of negroes. Any girl, even without a suffrage or legal competence, whose hand a man kisses and for whose love he is prepared to dare all, could have set him right. It is really a stillborn thought to send women into the struggle for existence exactly as men. If, for instance, I imagined my gentle sweet girl [his wife] as a competitor it would only end in my telling her, as I did seventeen months ago, that I am fond of her and that I implore her to withdraw from the strife into the calm uncompetitive activity of my home.

But is it such a "stillborn thought" to think of women as equal competitors in the struggle for existence? Why shouldn't women themselves be asked whether or not they want to "withdraw from the strife"? Is not this insistence that women stay in the doll's house or on the pedestal tantamount to saying "Let her mind go to seed" or "Let her talents atrophy"? And are women really, after all, such "different beings"? Betty Roszak argues exactly the contrary:

> This male habit of setting up boundary lines between imagined polarities has been the impetus for untold hatred and destruction. Masculine/feminine is just one of such polarities among many, including body/mind, organism/environment, plant/animal, good/evil, black/white, feeling/intellect, passive/active, sane/insane, living/dead. Such language hardens what is in reality a continuum and a unity into separate mental images always in opposition to one another.

Well, what are you going to make of all this? Your initial position, roughly that of *Playboy*, has now been pretty well shaken. The woman who called you a sexist was no flatterer, but she did put you into the act; thanks to her, you and your feelings became related to a larger issue. You are now beginning to have something to write about. Where to start?

Our advice is to look for a place where the issue intersects with your own experience, where it touches you to the quick. With this help from your classmates, these readings have begun to penetrate your defenses and some of your unconscious prejudices: the familiar male arguments about a woman's "place" being in the home are beginning to strike you as rather childish and naïve. Still, something troubles you. Have you been too easily convinced? Are you being conned into accepting a female chauvinism that is as one-sided as the male chauvinism you are accused of? As you ponder this question, the words begin to flow. You remember something out of your own experience. Do women have any idea, you wonder, how hard it is to be a man? Here is the essay you finally produce:

> When I was a kid about twelve years old, I once got jumped by a kid a lot smaller than me. It happened in a slum district not too far from where I lived. He rabbit-punched me a couple of times from behind and then jumped around in front and sneered up at me: "Think you're a wise guy, don'ya?" The funny thing was, I wanted to argue with him: "How can you think I'm a wise guy (whatever that means) if you don't even know me?" But I didn't say anything. I couldn't think of anything to say.
>
> Then suddenly I remembered with a shock who he was. He was a caddy at the golf course where I sometimes worked. His name was Lulu, and somebody had told me that he was head of a street gang and had done time on the county farm. He was a little guy, but I knew the routine: if I laid a finger on him there'd be a dozen of his buddies coming out of the bushes after me. They were probably watching the action right now from somewhere across the street. Guys like this never worked alone. I was scared. Finally, he gave me two hard kicks and warned me to stay away from the caddy house. I never said a word. In some strange way, I was scared stiff.
>
> For years afterward that incident haunted me. I had been a coward. My manhood had been tested and I hadn't measured up. I was fairly big and could have licked that kid, but something held my arms. Was I scared of the others who might have been hiding across the street? Was I scared of something in myself? Or was I just scared of my own shame if I hit a guy half my size? I don't know, but I know I was scared.
>
> At this time in my life a coward was just about the worst thing people could call you. Women's libbers despise and ridicule men for taking such things seriously, and in a way I think they're right. But they are wrong when they suppose that all men *enjoy* being aggressive. It's not

so. I for one hated it. I didn't want to hit that guy. More than that, I didn't want to be in a position where I had to feel ashamed if I *didn't* hit him! What I think is that men are trapped in their roles just as women are in theirs. We do what we think is expected of us. But it is a mistake to talk about the problem as if there were a male conspiracy to keep women in their place. I just don't think Robert Graves and the others are right when they say that men are out to dominate women. In fact, I think most men would love to be unaggressive if they thought they could get away with it.

Anyway, I'm certainly willing to see things changed if they can be. But I don't think a lot of yelling at men by the women's movement (or vice versa) is going to help. What's needed is that men and women have got to learn to talk to each other in a new way. The women's cause has a lot of justice in it, but not much will be accomplished unless their spokesmen—spokeswomen? spokespersons?— realize that it isn't all that much fun being a man either.

Is this a good essay? It could be improved in various ways, but in its essentials it is good writing. First, the writer is on the level. His essay begins where he lives, in an experience he can discuss with some authority, and moves out into larger issues from that sound base. Second, he is using his reading knowledge to supplement what he honestly feels and thinks; he is not using that knowledge as a substitute for his own thought. The result is an intelligent response, deeply felt, to a serious issue. It is perhaps still too defensive, not far enough from the *Playboy* philosophy, to please a discerning feminist; but it is the kind of writing and thinking that invites respect.

Good writing, in short, begins with some knowledge of one's self and of the world. We are not saying that every essay should begin with a personal anecdote, though much writing does, or even that there is anything inherently good about writing in the first person. We are saying only that what you write should be as authentic as you can make it, true to your vision of the way things are—not your parents' vision, not your teacher's vision, not your political party's vision, *your* vision. Obviously that vision should be matured by as much knowledge, from whatever sources, as you can acquire; but that knowledge is dead unless you care about what you say. The beginning writer who makes "as you desire me" his working motto gives his game away. The perceptive reader knows when you are saying only what you think you ought to say, or what you hope will sound profound. When your concern turns off, so will his.

Not all subjects are controversial, and not all lend themselves to personal involvement or moral concern. But whatever your subject— even if you are only describing the objective process of beating an egg—honest reporting is your most important resource. Sight, in the sense of seeing clearly, differs only in degree from insight.

THE AUDIENCE

Without an audience or the hope of an audience, most writers would have no motive for writing. Writing is a medium of communication. It carries your thought not only out from you, but in to some-one else. How you write will depend on who that someone else is: you write one way in a letter to a child, another way in a business letter, still another way in a love letter. The differences are not only in what you want to say, but in what will interest your reader, and in what ideas and words you think the reader can grasp.

What is true of a letter is equally true of an essay or report. If you are a scientist writing for scientists, a clergyman for clergymen, a labor leader for union members, you will feel free to use terms that a lay audience would not understand without an explanation. Similar assumptions about the educational and intellectual level of your read-ers will govern other decisions as well. For example, those assump-tions may determine the length of your sentences and paragraphs (inexperienced readers like them short), the complexity of syntax, the level of detail.

If you are addressing a general audience—as, let us say, a writer for *Reader's Digest* or The *New York Review of Books*—you will adjust your writing to the presumed capacities of a much wider range of readers. If you use technical language, you will explain what you mean in clear and simple terms; if you take a position on a controver-sial topic, you will go out of your way to be persuasive. If, by con-trast, you ignore your readers' capacities, or even if you overestimate or underestimate them, your words will be imperfectly understood at best, and will probably go unread.

Nor can you safely ignore your readers' sensibilities, as this excerpt from another student essay shows:

> I was really turned on by Vivian Gornick's essay "Woman as Out-sider," especially by her remark that "there isn't a woman alive who is not obsessed with her sexual desirability. Not her sexual *desire*. Her

sexual *desirability.*" A woman's life, Ms. Gornick goes on to say, is "ruled by the continual measure she is taking of her ability—on a scale of one to ninety million—to attract men."

Now I don't know about that "scale"—that seems an awful lot of men to keep your eye on at the same time—but on the point of sexual desirability Ms. Gornick is dead right. I've done some of my own research in the matter. For some years now I've been testing that old adage "Men seldom make passes at girls who wear glasses" by making passes at intellectual types. The results have been satisfying beyond my wildest dreams. They *were* worried about their desirability, and I've been able to help put their worries to rest. I've discovered, like the Frenchman I read about in Charles McCabe's column, that "Brainy broads are groovy."

This writer is addressing that most narrow and parochial of audiences, his own classmates, and is probably misjudging even that audience. Vivian Gornick's essay raises a serious issue; in making sport of it the writer invites the scorn we accord those who whistle in church. Some readers will laugh, but most will be bored or put off by the writer's bad manners. If you aspire to entertain, make sure you know your readers.

To say that a writer must think constantly of his readers, must anticipate their reactions and choose his words accordingly, is not to contradict what we said earlier about the need for honesty and courage. The purpose of writing is to say something, not to get published. If you temporize or compromise your principles, if you oversimplify to the point of misrepresenting, if you pander to the prejudices of an editor or teacher, you will not be the kind of writer we are asking you to admire. Your integrity as a writer comes first. When we place attention to your reader's capacities as a very close second, it is only because a writer's integrity has no meaning if his writing is not read.

We have spoken here in terms of publication, and of a wide range of readers. Though you doubtless are not literally writing for publication, it is helpful to imagine that you are—and that your teacher is not your audience so much as your editor, receiving and judging a manuscript you have sent him at his request.° If the manuscript is some-

---

° With apologies to those who prefer *he or she* (etc.) where either sex is possible, we shall use in this book the conventional and less cumbersome *he.* An erudite and illuminating discussion of this question can be found in Ann Bodine, "Androcentrism in prescriptive grammar: Singular 'they,' sex-indefinite 'he,' and 'he or she,' " *Language in Society,* 4:129–146 (August 1975).

thing that he thinks would interest the readers of his magazine, he will accept it; if not, he will send it back. Your teacher, to be sure, is an audience too, and since he may be your most attentive and critical reader you can hardly be indifferent to his reactions. But his personal reactions are secondary to his views on how your imaginary audience will react, and on what revisions might make its reaction more favorable. In short, you should think of such a critic as an editor, helping you to ask useful questions about the effect of your words.

THE WRITING

We come finally to the third element in our three-way relationship, writing itself. The rules or conventions that make for clear writing are only part of the story. To approach the task of writing only through rules—through learning what is proper and improper, grammatical and ungrammatical, conventional and vulgar—is, we feel, a dead end. The rules are important, but there is a big difference between knowing the rules and knowing how to write, and an even bigger difference between writing "correctly" and writing well.

The best writers tend to be people with something on their minds, curious people who want to discover things, or think things through, and tell others what they have come up with. The heart of writing is not rules but this motivation. Even if most of what you write has been assigned, you cannot do your best work without this spark. If the writer is not motivated, what he writes will probably not be worth reading; if he is, he will find out where to put his commas and how to write good paragraphs almost as a by-product of his motivation.

There are many varieties of writing, ranging from formal through informal and colloquial to slangy, varieties that reflect both the writer's approach and his assumptions about his audience. There is nothing "wrong" or "right" about any of these varieties as such; each has its place, each its charm. Our concern in this book will be with so-called standard English, the kind that most educated people write for publication, or public attention, on subjects they are serious about. This definition obviously covers a lot of ground, from the smooth professional journalism of *Time* and *Newsweek* to the academese of *Daedalus*, from the bright, empty cadences of a television commercial to the earnest exhortations of a Sunday sermon.

Standard English is a variety of usage, not an indication of quality; standard English is not necessarily good English. Indeed, a great deal of what passes for standard English in American writing is graceless and unclear. That is one reason why books like this one are needed. Consider the following examples of awful "standard" English.

An eminent engineer baffles us with "the advantage in wealth gains accruing through accelerated velocity of scrap recycling, in which each cycle represents an impress of sun-free energy into the cumulative commonwealth standard of efficiency advance." A sociologist, in leaden jargon, criticizes other sociologists: "They make suggestions about the types of environmental intervention that might maximize the integration of formal academic instruction with student life beyond the classroom." An image-mad English teacher writes:

> Both the tangential and pivotal interventions in his novel of experimental ploys prevent him from being viewed as an anachronism emerging unchanged as belatedly as a seventeen-year locust from a late Victorian chrysalis, while they, moreover, offer an incidental confirmation of what the experimenters were finding important.

Finally, here is a history professor lamenting in lamentable prose the "feeble control of the English language" in undergraduate writing:

> On the one hand, there is often the need to compensate for the failings of secondary education, its emphasis on instrumental utility, social relevance, and civic consensus, and its low valuation of originality and of irrelevance or antagonism to prevailing social values, and especially of the skills of thought and communication.

Translation: "Unhappily, secondary education trains students to prefer social adjustment and practical skills to thinking for themselves and saying what they think." Those three- and four-syllable nouns tied together by *and*'s, that "on the one hand" without the other ever appearing, make a relatively simple idea appear difficult. The writer means well; he just doesn't know how to write.

In the pages that follow, we will have a lot to say about tone, imagery, grammar, sentence structure, and diction. We will invoke rules and conventions. But it should not be forgotten that these rules and conventions are means, not ends. The aim of writing may be defined as follows: to spare your reader the error of misunderstanding your message, and the bother of figuring it out, by making it as clear as possible from the outset. Rules and conventions are useful only to the extent that they serve this end.

Writing, as a transaction between writer, subject matter, and audience, begins and ends with the writer. His integrity, his perception, his tact, and his goals—in short, his qualities of character—are what finally make the difference between worthwhile writing and junk. Intelligence, education, and maturity help; so does a mastery of technique, a capacity to choose the more effective way of getting a message across. But the writer's first order of priority is to understand and come to terms with himself—that self which is the inescapable underwriter of everything he says.

SUBJECT AND THEME

The first practical step in doing a piece of writing is finding a subject. The second is finding what you want to say about that subject, or what your "theme" will be. For example, the subject of George Orwell's well-known essay "Politics and the English Language" is stated in the title. The theme is established in the first few paragraphs, and can be paraphrased as follows: "When a civilization is decadent, as ours is, the language of that civilization becomes decadent too. By cleaning up the language—ridding it of its bad habits— we can reverse the process of political decay." Behind all of Orwell's examples of stale and corrupted language lies this theme; indeed, this theme is the point of the essay, its reason for being. In a formal argument the theme is the proposition or contention to be proved. In an informal essay no proof as such may be called for, but the theme must be backed up by example and reasoning.

Finding a Subject

In earlier editions of this book we talked of "choosing" a subject, but "finding" now seems to us the better word. "Choosing" implies that the writer has before him a clear-cut array of topics or ideas to choose from, like so many prepackaged meats in a supermarket. Few writers—especially inexperienced writers—are so lucky, or so organized. For many, perhaps most, the problem of writing is not so much what to write about as how to get anything at all down on paper. For such writers the techniques of prewriting and "freewriting," discussed below, may be the necessary first steps in finding a subject. But for now let us suppose that you are ready enough to put words on paper if only you could think what to say.

As we have seen, you will write best about something you respond to, something that hits you where you live. If your teacher offers a choice of subjects none of which interests you, or one broad subject on which you feel you have nothing to say, the problem is a little harder. But one thing is sure: you like what you know something about, and the best way to relieve boredom or indifference is to gather some information. How can you gather information? There are many ways, but four come to mind. (1) Open your eyes and look for telling details in the people, events, or whatever you are investigating. (2) Interview people or solicit answers to a home-made or professional questionnaire. (3) Ransack your experience for relevant memories. (4) Go to the library and find out what other people have had to say about something that interests you.

Finding a Theme

Once you have your information in hand, your problem is how to limit your subject, how to focus on some aspect of it that interests you. No one could write meaningfully on "Racism in America" or "The Drug Problem" or "The Rise of the Computer"—especially in a short essay. Subjects at that level of generality are simply not very interesting to most people; they get interesting only when you get down to details. Once you have your subject, you must *narrow the area* of that subject, and, after that, go after *one main point* (or thesis) within that area.

This is a critical stage: a quick, what-the-hell decision may lead to hours of frustration or tedium, whereas another ten minutes' thought might turn up an angle or aspect of the subject that you would really enjoy looking into. Play with the possibilities, let your imagination loose, do some "brainstorming." It doesn't much matter what the subject is: the problem is to get below the surface to that point of intimacy where affection and sympathy—or maybe rage and indignation—come into play. Bored by baseball? Go to a Little League game: observe the nervous kid in right field, the hyperactive coach, the exaltation and despair of the parents in the stands. There's a story there if you zero in on it. No taste for classical music? Read a short biography of Mozart and listen to a few records, if only to hear what it was that made such a stir in 1769 or 1787. You may end up loving classical music; at the very least, you will never again listen to Mozart with your old indifference. Although familiarity can breed contempt, it more often works the other way: people often dislike things only because they know nothing about them. If one aspect of a subject bores you, probe for another. You'll find one if you keep looking.

Getting from subject to theme is often a matter of narrowing one's focus, perhaps not once but several times. The process goes something like this:

Subject: Racism in America

Focus 1: Racism in the media

Focus 2: Racism on television

Focus 3: Racism in *Star Trek*

Racism in America is too big a subject to deal with in an essay. Only when we narrow such a subject, reduce it to workable size, can we really say anything important—or interesting—about it. To show, as one student we know has done, that the producers of *Star Trek*, though priding themselves on their freedom from sexism and racism, are open to criticism on both scores is to deal with a subject like racism at a level where people care what you say.

Finding a theme usually takes more thought than finding a subject. Some people bring to serious subjects a built-in point of view: that of a Christian, a Marxist, an anti-vivisectionist, or whatever. But others, perhaps most, have to search for what they can say with assurance. Finding a theme is always an exercise in thinking, and nearly always an exercise in self-discovery. Learning what you want to say is part of learning who you are.

We recommend taking some chances, crawling out on intellectual limbs even though they may be sawed off. We think people who approach writing this way make the best writers. If you don't know what you think about a subject (and most people don't at first), try thinking about it from two or three points of view; or compare what others have written and argue for the point of view you think nearest the truth. But, whatever you do, be yourself. Your teacher's opinion of computers, or of baseball, or of Mozart, is finally irrelevant to what you write. You are writing not to please or spite your teacher, but to make a reasoned presentation of your views to a wider, if hypothetical, audience.

Prewriting

What of the writer who has no opinions, even rudimentary ones, and who can't seem to develop any? What of the student whose response to a blank sheet of paper is despair? An able and creative teacher named Peter Elbow has addressed this common problem in his book *Writing Without Teachers*. The gist of his program is given in his opening paragraph:

> The most effective way I know to improve your writing is to do freewriting exercises regularly. At least three times a week. They are sometimes called "automatic writing," "babbling," or "jabbering" exercises. The idea is simply to write for ten minutes (later on, perhaps fifteen or twenty). Don't stop for anything. Go quickly without rushing. Never stop to look back, to cross something out, to wonder how to spell something, to wonder what word or thought to use, or to think about what you are doing. If you can't think of a word or a spelling, just use a squiggle or else write, "I can't think of it." Just put down something. The easiest thing is just to put down whatever is in your mind. If you get stuck it's fine to write "I can't think of what to say, I can't think what to say" as many times as you want; or repeat the last word you wrote over and over again; or anything else. The only requirement is that you *never* stop.

These are writing calisthenics, warm-up exercises that make the real event less forbidding and more natural. When some people try to write, they automatically begin to worry: about sounding stupid or childish, about making errors in spelling or grammar, about having nothing to say. They think of good writing as something *others* do—teachers, professional writers, whoever—not hapless klutzes like themselves. Nonsense, says Elbow; let the words flow and worry about all that other stuff later.

The freewriting exercise described above is obviously just a beginning, something to get the words flowing. The next stage is to freewrite *about* something: describe a person, write a dialogue or a letter, voice a pet peeve or prejudice, discuss a film. The possibilities are limitless. Much of what you write will be garbage and will go into the wastebasket. But don't stop; keep your pencil or typewriter moving.

Next take one of your more successful efforts and red-circle any passages or ideas that seem worth saving. Gradually a sense of priority among your ideas will begin to emerge, a sense of what you might usefully say in a paper and how you might say it. Next arrange your material in some sequence. If it seems to work fairly well, throw out any redundant, irrelevant, or contradictory passages, and fill in any obvious holes in reasoning and evidence.

Up to this point you have done no editing whatever. Your paper may be—indeed probably is—as full of slang and bad grammar as your everyday speech, as full of muddled syntax and wasted words as one might expect in any uncensored and uncorrected utterance. Well and good: first things first. Only now, at the very end, with your argument as good as you can make it, are you ready for such secondary concerns as grammar and spelling. Now the editing begins.

Obviously, this process may take more time than you feel you can afford. But it works, and as you gain confidence from success your warm-up time gets shorter. The great value of Elbow's approach, it seems to us, is not so much in his total method (to which this brief description does scant justice) as in his techniques for loosening up, for throwing caution to the winds and getting something down on that blank sheet of paper. The way to start writing, says Elbow, is to start writing. His advice is certainly worth a try.

Freewriting is not the only way to get started. Some writers like to work from an outline, casual or formal; some like to build around "bright ideas" that come to them in moments of inspiration. But whatever your approach, some sort of first draft is essential. Very few writers can produce a finished product at the first crack, and even the most gifted professional writers typically go through two or more drafts before they have something they are satisfied with. The nature of those drafts is not so important as the advice to revise, revise, revise. Prewrite in the way you find most easy or effective, but remember that revision is what makes the final product. Editing (see pp. 127–138) comes later. It is important, but it makes no sense unless you have a draft whose content and sequence you are happy with, a draft saying what you want to say and needing only some last touches to make it clearer and more effective.

2
EXPOSITION, ARGUMENT, LOGIC

In this book we are concerned mainly with one form of writing, the essay, which Frederick Crews defines as "a fairly brief piece of nonfiction that tries to make a point in an interesting way." By this definition most term papers and love letters are essays—*attempts* (French, *essais*) to get a point across and to be interesting. By contrast, freewriting and answers to so-called essay questions on examinations are not essays, since freewriting by definition has no point and answers to essay questions usually make little effort to win the reader's interest. An essay, then, is not just so many hundreds or thousands of words. It has other basic requirements, some of which we explore in this chapter.

The two main forms of nonfiction are exposition (explaining something) and argument (urging a course of action or a point of view). Most serious thinking in prose is cast into one or both of these forms. Simpler modes, like narration and description, offer the writer no special problems beyond what to emphasize, what to leave out, and how to maintain chronological or spatial sequence. Exposition and argument, by contrast, involve the writer in difficult problems not only of emphasis and sequence, but of logic and evidence. In this chapter we shall see what some of these problems are.

EXPOSITION

When you tell someone how to play bridge or how to make a carrot cake, how to proofread a manuscript or how to work a physics problem, you are doing what writers inevitably spend a lot of time doing—explaining. Explaining is exposition: telling somebody else something you know. Here is Lee Strout White explaining how to start a Model T Ford:

> The trick was to leave the ignition switch off, proceed to the animal's head, pull the choke (which was a little wire protruding through the radiator), and give the crank two or three nonchalant upward lifts. Then, whistling as though thinking about something else, you would saunter back to the driver's cabin, turn the ignition on, return to the crank, and this time, catching it on the down stroke, give it a quick spin with plenty of That.

Here is Oscar Lewis explaining—via another's verbatim account—what life in a *barrio* is like:

> But I have always been a brother to my sisters. I have never punished them without a reason, like if they didn't obey me, or because they talked back to my *papá*, or called me "lousy black." I am heartbroken at the thought of how many times I have beaten them. I want to ask their pardon, but when I see them I lose my courage. It makes me suffer, because a man shouldn't beat a woman. But I only slapped them with the palm or back of my hand. And when I slapped, it was only on the arm or the back, or the head.

The White passage is pure exposition; the Lewis passage is exposition edging over into argument. In fact, it has been claimed that in the broadest sense all rhetorical forms, all organizations of words, are arguments. If you are explaining how to start a motor, you are in a sense arguing that one starts it this way and not another way, that you know the right from the wrong of it. If you describe how something looks to you, you are arguing that it looks this way and not that way—and perhaps, by implication, that its reality is of this sort and not another. At the extreme, a description can be deliberately polemical, deliberately argumentative, as in this portrait of Ronald Reagan, then Governor of California, by Gore Vidal:

> Ronald Reagan is a well-preserved not young man. Close to, the painted face is webbed with delicate lines while the dyed hair, eye-

brows, and eyelashes contrast oddly with the sagging muscle beneath the as yet unlifted chin, soft earnest of wattle soon-to-be. The effect, in repose, suggests the work of a skillful embalmer. Animated, the face is quite attractive and at a distance youthful; particularly engaging is the crooked smile full of large porcelain-capped teeth. The eyes are the only interesting feature: small, narrow, apparently dark, they glitter in the hot light, alert to every move, for this is enemy country—the liberal Eastern press who are so notoriously immune to that warm and folksy performance which Reagan quite deliberately projects over their heads to some legendary constituency at the far end of the tube, some shining Carverville where good Lewis Stone forever lectures Andy Hardy on the virtues of thrift and the wisdom of the contract system at Metro-Goldwyn-Mayer.

Here the writer has deliberately selected only those details that will spell artificiality and duplicity; aiming as he is at caricature, he has made no attempt to see his subject in a balanced focus. But even when a writer is striving hard for objectivity, the subjective has a way of creeping in. Nor is this necessarily bad. Things happen, people come into our lives, that make objectivity impossible or inappropriate. We are pained or thrilled or frightened and want to say why. To convey our emotions is often the only way to serve the truth, to humanize the cold facts. Certainly there is no stronger argument, in capable hands, than the detailed picture, in word or film, of a human being with whom we can identify, as opposed to the abstract statistic. Take, for example, this passage from Seymour Hersh's classic account of the events at My Lai:

Do Chuc is a gnarled forty-eight-year-old Vietnamese peasant whose two daughters and an aunt were killed by the GIs in My Lai that day. He and his family were eating breakfast when the GIs entered the hamlet and ordered them out of their homes. Together with other villagers, they were marched a few hundred meters into the plaza, where they were told to squat. "Still we had no reason to be afraid," Chuc recalls. "Everyone was calm." He watched as the GIs set up a machine gun. The calm ended. The people began crying and begging. One monk showed his identification papers to a soldier, but the American simply said, "Sorry." Then shooting started. Chuc was wounded in the leg, but he was covered by dead bodies and thus spared. After waiting an hour, he fled the hamlet. Nguyen Bat, a Viet Cong hamlet chief who later defected, said that many of the villagers who were eating breakfast outdoors when the GIs marched in greeted them without fear. They were gathered together and shot. Other villagers who were breakfasting indoors were killed inside their homes.

This is nominally pure exposition or narration, but the facts stir an urgent call for more—for an inquest, for conclusions, for changes in whatever awful system made this awful thing happen. What happened at My Lai? Hersh tells us. How did it happen? Why did it happen? Such questions follow insistently and carry the exposition quickly into the realm of argument. Argument and exposition, though identifiable as separate forms, are never long divorced. That is because all argument depends upon evidence, and exposition is the form evidence usually takes.

THE LOGIC OF ARGUMENT

By argument we mean the act of presenting evidence for or against a proposition. If you argue that pizza is better than hamburgers because it tastes better, you are not really arguing at all; you are merely voicing your opinion. If you argue that pizza is better than hamburgers because it has more nutritional value, or equal nutritional value for less money per ounce, you are offering an argument in the valid sense. The difference is that your nutrition argument is capable of being objectively tested by means that you and your audience can agree on. You have, in other words, some *common ground*. Without such common ground an "argument" quickly deteriorates into an empty wrangle.

Argument, even the most low-keyed argument, engages your emotions as well as your reason: you want to be right, but you also want to win, and these desires sometimes work at cross-purposes. The problem is to keep the emotions in harness and to give reason its head. There is no simple formula for such horsemanship, but here are some practical suggestions that might help.

Avoid Rationalization

Rationalizers (as distinct from reasoners) are people who invent reasons for believing what they already believe or what they want to believe. As James Harvey Robinson says, "We are incredibly heedless in the formation of our beliefs, but find ourselves filled with an illicit passion for them when anyone proposes to rob us of their companionship." We all harbor partially conflicting beliefs that we cannot bear to modify. With your conscious mind you are for peace, yet war movies excite you; you hate smog, yet you love your automobile; you believe in racial tolerance, yet you distrust Turks. Such conflicts lead people into rationalizing, into making up, as Robinson says, "good" reasons for believing as they do rather than facing the conflict, finding the real reasons behind it, and resolving it. Virtually all the rules that follow are devices for putting real reasons ahead of "good" reasons.

Watch Your Reasoning

Most written and spoken arguments do not aim at proof in any formal way, but simply seek to win assent to a proposition by giving reasons in support of it. Those reasons are important, as we shall see next, but equally important is the structure—the chain of reasoning—in which they are found. Consider, for example, this argument from George Orwell's *Down and Out in Paris and London:*

> Take the generally accepted idea that tramps are dangerous characters. Quite apart from experience, one can say *a priori* that very few tramps are dangerous, because if they were dangerous they would be treated accordingly. A casual ward will often admit a hundred tramps in one night, and these are handled by a staff of at most three porters. A hundred ruffians could not be controlled by three unarmed men. Indeed, when one sees how tramps let themselves be bullied by the workhouse officials, it is obvious that they are the most docile, broken-spirited creatures imaginable.

Such an argument has a structure that Stephen Toulmin, working changes on Aristotle, has broken down into three parts: claim, warrant, and evidence:

Claim: Tramps are not dangerous characters.

Warrant: If they were, they would be treated like dangerous characters.

Evidence: But they are not treated like dangerous characters; on the contrary, a staff of three unarmed men often controls as many as one hundred tramps.

The claim is the proposition to be proved (and when it is proved it can be called a "conclusion"). The warrant asserts some link between that proposition and the evidence. The evidence is the list of reasons why the person addressed should accept the claim.°

As a practicing writer you may not often have occasion to analyze an argument in logical terms—and many arguments will not break down so neatly—but occasionally you need such an analytic instrument and need it badly. Just as an outline can help chart a writer's course, so can this kind of check on a chain of reasoning.

Examine Your Evidence

Most of us have a fair working sense of what is good evidence and what is not. At a high school rap session a student says, "If Paula wants to be an airline stewardess, why should she take algebra or United States history?" If we can assume that Paula has found her vocation at sixteen and will have time for nothing but her job and her social life until she dies, the answer is "Why indeed?" But unless we make these silly assumptions, the implied equating of training with education—of a job with a life—is kid stuff. Even in strictly vocational terms the argument is no good: if Paula doesn't make it as a stewardess, she may well find a little algebra handy in some other job. In short, the questioner's "evidence" is mere rhetoric.

There are many other logical fallacies, from equivocation to false analogy, some of which we shall discuss later.† But at the heart of all these fallacies is one primary error: the misuse of evidence. Either no evidence at all is advanced, as in the claim that pizza tastes better than hamburgers, or "facts" are set forth, as by Paula's champion, that do not logically support the writer's argument and thus remain mere facts or information, not evidence.

The best way to detect such errors, in others' writing or one's own, is by horse sense. Consider the following two passages, the first from

---

° From *The Uses of Argument* (Cambridge, Eng. 1958), as cited in Douglas Ehinger, *Influence, Belief, and Argument: An Introduction to Responsible Persuasion* (Glenview, Ill., 1974), pp. 10-26.

† Those interested in further investigation of argument and logical fallacies should consult a good elementary logic text, e.g. Howard Kahane, *Logic and Contemporary Rhetoric* (Belmont, Calif., 1971), or Monroe Beardsley, *Thinking Straight*, 4th ed. (Englewood Cliffs, N.J., 1975). An excellent chapter on logic, geared to the needs of the writer, is Chapter 5 of Richard D. Altick, *Preface to Critical Reading*, 5th ed. (New York, 1968); another is Chapter 11 of Richard E. Young, Alton L. Becker, and Kenneth L. Pike, *Rhetoric: Discovery and Change* (New York, 1970).

a student paper, the second from Philip Slater's *The Pursuit of Loneliness*:

> A big problem at Hanford is the lack of interest in providing an adequate budget for safety systems.[1] For example, a study made in 1968 by the General Accounting Office showed that a majority of the storage tanks at the facility were past the time of replacement and were vulnerable to leaks, and yet the only spare tanks available were also old and had been classified as unusable.[2] This sort of thing is what makes me wonder if the Atomic Energy Commission is capable of running the complicated system of waste storage plants that will be required when nuclear power is in full operation.

> If the body can be used as a working machine, and a consuming machine, why not an experience machine? The drug user makes precisely the same assumption as do other Americans—that the body is some sort of appliance. Hence they must "turn on" and "tune in" in their unsuccessful effort to drop out. They may be enjoying the current more, but they are still plugged into the same machinery that drives other Americans on their weary and joyless round.

The first argument clearly passes muster. The writer has not claimed more than she can document: she is talking about "a big problem," not "the biggest problem." She has backed her claim with hard evidence (the two footnotes cite official reports). If you should seek to prove her wrong, your evidence would have to be at least as good as hers. Slater, by contrast, offers us no hard evidence at all. Even if we accept his analogy between people and machines, we can only wonder at his sweeping assertion that all drug users, and most or all other Americans, regard the body as "some sort of appliance." Maybe they do; maybe this is a brilliant insight. But where no evidence is offered, the wise reader is skeptical.

Define Your Terms

What do you mean by that term? In what sense are you using that word? Such questions are often heard in arguments. And for good reason: unless we agree on the meaning of our words, we have no possibility whatsoever of finding a common ground.

We are here concerned primarily not with formal definitions but with working definitions—short, necessary clarifications of terms or concepts in the context of a specific argument. In the following passage a sensitive student makes it clear that she will use "success" in a rather different sense from the usual one:

> People often look at an intelligent youngster and say, "One day he/she is going to be a success." Why do these people say "one day" when the child is succeeding today? It is when people begin speaking of the word success as though it were a profession itself that my understanding of it becomes unclear. It seems that one must *seek* success rather than happen upon it naturally through doing what one wants to do in life.

And here the historian Barton J. Bernstein explores the reality behind the talk about "defensive" and "offensive" missiles during the Cuban missile crisis of 1962:

> It is clear that the Kennedy administration's own distinctions between offensive and defensive weaponry were arbitrary, unilateral, and somewhat self-righteous. After all, when is a missile offensive, and when is it defensive? For America, it turned out, her missiles in Turkey were defensive, but Russia's missiles in Cuba were offensive. The distinction, at least for the United States, did not always seem to rest upon the nature of the weapon—all surface-to-surface missiles can be used for aggression—but sometimes upon the administration's presumptions about the intention of the possessor. To other interpreters, however, a nation's likely intention is judged, and also influenced, by its overall strategic capabilities, as well as those of its potential adversary. The distinction employed by the United States was never accepted by the Soviets, who continued throughout the crisis, as before, to call the weapons in Cuba defensive.

Had this kind of obvious clarification been made at the time and agreed to by both sides as a reasonable basis for further discussion, the dispute might have been resolved short of the brink of war.

Learn to Spot Defective Arguments

We are bombarded daily by arguments urging us to buy prestige in the form of rugs, youth in the form of soap, health in the form of snake oil. The writer who would argue honestly does well to sharpen his wits on these less-than-honest efforts, so as not to go wrong in the same ways they do.

Consider, for example, the following advertisement by an oil company. Beginning with the boast that this company's men were "willing to go almost anywhere to get the oil you need—even as deep as 1,000 feet under the Gulf of Mexico," it continued in these words:

> America needs energy. We're working to see that you get it.
>
> But first, we've got to look for it.
>
> And looking for oil requires a lot of looking around, even when you're on dry land.
>
> Imagine how difficult it becomes when you're looking for it under water—in depths that can go as deep as a thousand feet.
>
> But America does need oil, and experts agree there's plenty of it right here in this country. Buried offshore.
>
> So far, the oil industry has paid the U.S. Government close to 10 billion dollars for offshore leases. Just for the right to look for oil.
>
> [Our company] alone, since December 15, 1970, has paid the U.S. Government over 800 million dollars. And has 77 very promising off-shore properties—owned fully or partially—to show for it. That's more than 200,000 acres.
>
> With this much underwater acreage, we look forward to finding large new reserves of crude oil, and of natural gas, too, to meet your energy needs.

Here special pleading is carried to the point of melodrama: the oil company as hero, braving all odds to "see that you get it," the self-sacrifice (going "almost anywhere to get the oil you need"), the altruism (giving ten billion to the U.S. Government "just for the right to look for oil"). Students who were read this passage laughed, never doubting that an oil company's main motive for going anywhere or doing anything is profit. They also noted the things that weren't said: that oil is a nonrenewable resource in short supply, that offshore drilling is a serious source of pollution, that much of the money spent on exploration comes from a tax break, the so-called oil-depletion allowance. An argument, properly considered, seeks the truth, the whole truth, and nothing but the truth. Here no such aim is evident; the oil company is peddling a fiction. One would like to think that most Americans are too smart to be taken in by an "argument" like this, yet for some reason we seem to go right on buying oil, snake as well as regular.

STRATEGIES OF ARGUMENT

In argument, strategy can be almost as important as truth. Here are some good rules to keep in mind:

Open with an Attention-Getting Statement

Your first objective is to get the attention of your audience, without which you will argue your case in vain. A human-interest anecdote is a good opener. So is a provocative question: "How many more people must be murdered before the arguments of the gun lobby are seen for what they are?" Or consider this editorial opener by a newspaper writer warning his fellow townspeople about their water supply: "If the people of this town don't wake up soon, they will wake up later to find that the water in their faucets is fit for nothing but flushing toilets." An opener like that, followed by hard evidence and sound reasoning, is hard to beat.

Anticipate Your Opponent's Arguments

Arguing in writing is like arguing in a debate except that your opponent is not physically present. That is no reason to ignore him. Indeed, the best thing you can do is put yourself in his place, go over the evidence favoring his side of the argument, try to see things his way. If space permits, you might even include in your paper a paragraph or two setting forth his position as persuasively as he would if he were given the opportunity.

Some writers shy away from such practices lest the appeal of their opponent's arguments detract from the appeal of their own. We think they are wrong. A good defense is always based on a knowledge of your opponent's strengths as well as his weaknesses. And if you seek truth rather than merely victory, it is essential that you think through the whole issue rather than just your side of it.

Emphasize the Positive

If you can, dwell on the good points of your position rather than the bad points of the opposing position. If you call the advocates of capital punishment cruel, bloodthirsty, and uncivilized, or if you call readers of pornography sex-mad perverts, you will convert none of those you criticize and your tone may well alienate the undecided. Suppose your experience leads you to argue that English people are more lovable than French people. If you emphasize that the English are genial, helpful, and honorable, giving examples to support your claims, your readers will feel good not only about the English but about you. If, by contrast, you devote most of your essay to attacking the French as a bunch of greedy, mean-spirited second-raters, your readers will wince at your ferocity, sympathize with its victims, and very possibly conclude that you are too emotional on the subject to be trusted.

That is just the way people are. Your logic may be impeccable, your evidence unassailable, but if you alienate your audience your logic and evidence go for naught. In a class discussion of two reviews of a film, an unfavorable one by Pauline Kael in the *New Yorker* and a rather neutral one by Vincent Canby in the *New York Times*, the class found Kael's argument the stronger but they *liked* Canby's better. Why? They were put off by Kael's intensity, her relentless insistence on her own point of view and resistance to all others. And they were won over by Canby's capacity to find something to praise (chiefly the acting) even in a film he didn't much like.

Beware, however, of going too far, of being so positive that you subvert your own integrity. Don't let politeness or eagerness to please prevent you from doing justice to your argument. The idea is to emphasize the positive, not exalt it mindlessly like Pollyanna; to de-emphasize the negative if you can, not to suppress it.

Save Your Best Arguments for Last

It is usually best to arrange your arguments or pieces of evidence in climax order, leading your audience from doubt to belief to overwhelming conviction. Let us say you are arguing that abortion should be legalized. You jot down the main arguments you plan to use:

    (a) the population explosion threatens human survival

    (b) the life of the mother should come first

    (c) the fetus up to a certain age is not a "person"

    (d) a woman has a proprietary right to her own body

What is climax order here? That is a matter for your careful judgment—judgment that will get better the more you know about the subject. But it might well be best to end with (d), since it is a "gut" argument likely to have a strong and immediate human appeal to at least some members of your audience. And you could perhaps begin with (a), since this is probably the argument most distant from people's immediate personal concerns.

Don't Oversimplify

People who say that there are "two sides to every question" are mistaken. There are more likely twenty. Even such a seemingly two-sided question as whether the English are more lovable than the French has its complications. The French may behave better abroad and the English at home; French adolescents may be more winning than English, but English old people more cheerful than French; the lovability quotient for factory workers may be different from the lovability quotient for farmers, and both quotients may be different today from what they were thirty years ago and what they will be thirty years hence.

The example is absurd, but the point is important. Argument in the maturest sense takes this kind of complexity into account.

LOGICAL FALLACIES

Modern logicians tend to substitute letter and number symbols for words and sentences, and with good reason: the written language is not as precise an instrument as they require. Words are symbols, imperfect symbols invented and used for the most part by non-logicians. A large part of the writer's job is fashioning clear and logically sound statements out of these imperfect materials. It is not an easy job.

But neither—given some basic common sense and reasonable care and thought—is it an impossible job. These qualities are not conspicuous in the following essay, which is an only slightly modified version of an actual paper submitted in an English class. The superscript numbers, indicating various logical fallacies committed by the writer, are keyed to the numbered headings in the subsequent discussion.

An American Myth

One of the most persistent American myths[1] I know is that all the poor people in the world,[1] the people to whom we shell out millions in aid every year, are unhappy[1] just because they are poor. Sitting where we are on our mountain of luxury, we feel that if people do not have television sets, two cars in the garage, paid vacations, and a nice house in the suburbs, they are unhappy.[9] It just is not so. I can say with absolute assurance—from personal observation in Turkey, Syria, Egypt, Lebanon, Greece, and Mexico[3]—that the poor are not unhappy if we leave them alone.[9] They do not enjoy themselves in the same way we do, but their lives are nevertheless full of pleasure. They have their own holidays and dances and rituals—which are entirely different from ours—but that is their own culture and they like it. Nor do the poor suffer or feel pain in the same way we would under similar conditions;[9] they have grown used to their lot and are happy in it if left alone. We forget that often the loveliest flowers grow on manure[4] heaps.[8]

To prove my thesis, look at what happened in 1965 after we sent millions of tons of wheat to India during the famine.[3] Instead of making the country contented, there were food riots all over North India and some fighting with Pakistan.[5] The people were more ungrateful, not less. And the same thing some years ago in Egypt; after all our help, Egypt let the Russians build the Aswan Dam and the country was overrun with "Yankee Go Home" signs.[5] We stirred the people up with our aid, with a vision of luxury to which they were not accustomed, and then nothing would satisfy them.

The same thesis applies to the poor at home. Our welfare rolls are filled on the one hand with deadbeats[2] too lazy to work and on the other with hopheads[2] who won't work on principle.[6] Why do we go on subsidizing whores[2] who have a child a year—each one by a different father? If we cut off the supplies, these people would straighten out and join the same civilized society that the rest of us live in and pay taxes in.[5] Why do we do it? Because we are infected[2] by the sentimental idea that these people cannot help themselves, and that if we do not help them we will be Bad Samaritans. Actually we are Bad Samaritans doing what we do now, for these people—once they get used to living on handouts—lose all pride and self-respect, like zoo animals.[8]

How many of our policy makers have actually been in a slum? They think it is terrible because it is so unlike the place *they* live. But my father has worked in embassies all over the Middle East and I have had plenty of opportunity to see slums. Actually slums are no worse than any other place once you get used to them; they are just different.[9] "There's no place like home" applies there just as much as anywhere. Instead of getting people out of slums, we should get the slums out of people.[4]

Jesus said "Blessed are the poor," and "The poor shall never cease out of the land." Yet here we are engaged in the absurd[2] effort of trying to eliminate what cannot be eliminated.[7] Moreover, it *should* not be eliminated, for the presence of those less fortunate than ourselves in this world brings out the best in us. When we give to our favorite charity, we are sharing part of our best selves. But we should not ever forget that charity begins at home.[10]

---

1. Undefined Terms

No clear communication is possible if we do not know what our words mean. Since words, unlike mathematical symbols, are not fixed in value but constantly changing, a writer who hopes to be understood must frequently pause to define his terms. A complete definition may be impossible (such a simple, everyday word as *property*, for example, is subject enough for a book), but the writer should at least provide a working definition—some indication of which of a word's various possible meanings he is using. In the essay under discussion, for example, the word *myth* seems to be used in its secondary and derivative sense of "something untrue," but it could also have that richer meaning suggested by Mark Schorer: "Myths are the instruments by which we continually struggle to make our experience intelligible to ourselves." Does the writer have this meaning in mind as well as the more obvious meaning? We cannot know, for he has not told us.

Other problems of definition occur throughout this essay. Just what is meant by "poor people," and in particular by the phrase "all the poor people in the world"? That's a large number of poor people, and of different kinds of poor people—people with plenty of food and no money as well as people in danger of starvation, young people with big debts but bright prospects as well as old people with no debts but no prospects either. Which of these people is the writer talking about? All of them? But surely some are happy, some unhappy; some interested in help from abroad, some not. Is he talking about only some of them? Then which ones?

And what about that word *unhappy*? It is hard enough to define happiness in the abstract; it is far harder to say with assurance whether someone else is or is not "happy." Is happiness the same as pleasure? Then what about those Christian martyrs who claimed to find ecstasy in their self-sacrifice—so much so that the early church inveighed against the seeking of martyrdom? Are brides happy, as the greeting cards say? If so, are the fainting fits, cold sweats, and hysteria that often accompany a bride to the altar part of her happiness? To see the concept in these terms is to see the word *unhappy* as mixed and relative, connected to the human condition, and not as absolute.

What should our writer have done? Probably he should have said, early in the paper, something like this: "By happiness I do not mean bliss or uninterrupted satisfaction, but simply a feeling that things are going reasonably well." This is no formal definition of happiness, but it is a good working definition for our writer's purposes. It will make his argument clearer to his readers, and his competence to expound it more apparent.

Obviously, most of the words in any essay have more than one possible meaning, and no one stops to define them all. How far should a writer go in defining terms? He should define all key words in his argument whose definition is not self-evident—words like *unhappy*, on which the argument of "An American Myth" pivots. He should define any other abstract terms—*myth, the poor*—that are not clear in context. He should define or explain all strange words. In the interests of style, he should present his definitions as gracefully and unobtrusively as possible; but if the claims of precision and the claims of grace conflict, the former should prevail.

2. Name-calling

Name-calling is an appeal to prejudice by false or invidious labeling. Words have connotations: some are neutral, some favorable, some unfavorable. A few years ago there was a popular parlor game in which people were asked to describe a given condition successively in the first, second, and third persons with increasing acerbity as the focus shifted away from themselves: "I am intelligent, you are clever, he is a smart aleck"; "I am enjoying myself, you should slow down, he is dead drunk." It is an old trick to place what you dislike in a class of things that all respectable people dislike, and the writer of this essay has indulged it freely. Obvious examples are his use of the words *deadbeats* and *hopheads* to describe people on relief. Are there no old women, no cripples, no unemployed who would work if they could? Three other instances of name-calling in the essay, not all of them nouns, are indicated by the same number.

3. Inadequate Sampling

One of the commonest errors in amateur argument is that of generalizing from too small a sample. The writer of "An American Myth" claims to "prove" his thesis by citing what happened during one year in India. But it does not follow from that one instance (see 5 below) that the poor are happy if left alone or even that they riot and start wars whenever anyone gives them a little wheat. Even the one instance itself leaves something to be desired. What part of India are we talking about, for example, and what was the connection between the wheat and the outbreaks of violence? Not only is this instance no proof of the general case; it is itself unacceptable as evidence.

Another error in sampling appears in the list of countries—Turkey, Syria, Egypt, and so on—that the author provides. At first glance this list seems impressive; the author has been around and seen things. But then doubts creep in. Has he seen enough to make generalizations about "all poor people"? Of course not. Has he even really *seen* what he says he has seen? Looking and seeing are two different things, as different as tourism and research. "Personal observation" could mean occasional glances out the back window of the embassy limousine. Is that a big enough sampling to make generalizations about the poor in the Middle East and Mexico? Few would think it was.

4. Equivocation

To equivocate is to use a term in two or more senses without making the shift in sense clear. In "An American Myth" the most obvious equivocation is the play on the word *slums* in the next-to-last paragraph: "Instead of getting people out of slums, we should get the slums out of people." This sounds fine, but what does it mean? The argument rests on our equating run-down areas like Harlem or Watts with an internal psychological condition of which we know only that it is offensive to the writer. Can such disparate things be equated? Almost certainly not. But they are equated here anyway by the equivocal use of the word *slums*. Similarly, the word *manure* in the first paragraph is used simultaneously to mean filth and fertilizer.

There is also another and opposite kind of equivocation, in which different words are used for essentially the same thing, so that what is one thing in nature is made to appear two. A clever mystery novel was once published in which everything depended on the identity of one narrator, "I," with a "Mr. Taylor" frequently mentioned by another narrator; the reader was allowed to infer the twoness of this onesome right up to the last sentence of the book. Most such equivocations, however, are less deliberate. Thus the writer of "An American Myth" distinguishes between *aid*, which is no good, and *charity*, which is good. But what is foreign aid except charity on a large scale? If our writer objects to one and supports the other, let him speak of small-scale and large-scale charity, or of public and private aid. To do otherwise is to transform a difference in degree into a difference in kind.

5. *Post Hoc* Reasoning and *Non Sequitur*

If one of two associated events happened before the other, it may be wrongly argued that the first caused the second: *post hoc ergo propter hoc*, "after this, therefore because of this." Thus Philip Wylie writes of the effect of giving the vote to women: "Mom's first gracious presence at the ballot-box was roughly concomitant with the start toward a new all-time low in political scurviness, hoodlumism, gangsterism, labor strife, monopolistic thuggery, moral degeneration, civic corruption, smuggling, bribery, theft, murder, homosexuality, drunkenness, financial depression, chaos, and war." The implied assumption is that votes for women caused all the trouble. Wylie's facetious intent is plain, but this same fallacy is frequently found in more serious arguments. In "An American Myth," for example, the appearance of riots in India and "Yankee Go Home" signs in Egypt after these countries received American aid shipments does not prove that the aid *caused* the riots and the signs. Maybe it did, but the case is yet to be proved; our author provides no evidence whatever.

Post hoc is closely related to a more general fallacy known as *non sequitur*, "it does not follow." It is a good idea to be careful in using words like *because, since, thus,* and *therefore.* "I bought Lucy a Christmas present because I like her better than Eileen" is a *non sequitur* unless it has been established that you were in a position to buy only one present.

In the following dialogue from the film script of Jean Renoir's *Grand Illusion* there is a veritable escalation of *non sequiturs*:

> THE LOCKSMITH: A good-looking blonde . . . big blue eyes. . . . An angel! Well, three days later I had to go and see the doctor. Don't trust a blonde!
>
> ROSENTHAL: The same thing happened to me with a brunette.
>
> MARÉCHAL: You can't trust anyone!

Based on an utterly illogical connection between hair color and venereal disease, the argument leaps from two unfortunate experiences to the supremely illogical conclusion that no one can be trusted. "Thinking" of this sort is all too common. The author of "An American Myth" is guilty of just such thinking when he claims that cutting off American aid would be a boon to its present recipients. How can he predict so simple and universal an outcome from so complex a set of conditions?

6. False Disjunction

To be caught on the horns of a dilemma is to be forced to choose between two equally undesirable alternatives. A dilemma is an either-or situation. If we take the highway, we will encounter traffic; if we take the bypass, we will be on a rough road. If we vote Republican, we will get a reactionary; if we vote Democratic, we will get a leftist. We must choose—or so at least we are told. But are these the only alternatives, and are they accurately and honestly defined? Often they are not. In "An American Myth," for example, we are told that everyone on relief is either a deadbeat or a hophead. A moment's thought will demolish this assertion. Elsewhere we have a subtler disjunction: between leaving the poor alone and trying to give every poor family television sets, two cars, and a house in the suburbs. If this is the choice we must make, there is much to be said for the author's recommendation that we leave the poor alone. But are these really the only alternatives? Surely the most starry-eyed dreamer favors more modest and realistic benefits for the roadless and suburbless peasant farmers of India.

The worst disjunction of all in this essay is the persistent separation of the poor ("they" or "these people") from the writer and his audience ("we" or "the rest of us"). This kind of simplification is one of the ways of prejudice. If one can somehow regard another person as a thing or a statistic, one is relieved of the necessity of understanding him, sympathizing with him, treating him with respect. According to the United States government, a non-farm family of four with an income of under $5,050 a year is poor. According to our writer, such a family is not only poor but radically different, which is tantamount to claiming that the $2 difference between $5,049 and $5,051 is some sort of unbridgeable chasm. F. Scott Fitzgerald was experimenting with the same distinction in reverse when he remarked to Ernest Hemingway, "The very rich are different from you and me." "Yes," Hemingway replied. "They have more money."

7. Argument to Authority

Writers who have no evidence for their views often resort to citing some authority whose pronouncements they assume the reader will accept as sufficient. How do you know there is no serious smog problem in the city? Mayor Schultz says so. How do you know that the Chinese Communists are evil? General Baker says so, and he has spent thirty years in the Far East. This is all very well if the so-called authority does in fact know what he is talking about, but he may not. Especially in matters as complex and controversial as the smog problem and the future behavior of China, a discriminating reader is likely to want something more convincing than the opinion of Mayor Schultz or General Baker.

The all-time champion in the list of authorities cited, ranking just above Aristotle and Benjamin Franklin, is the Bible. If the Bible says something, it must be true, or so millions of Christians have believed. Thus, in "An American Myth," we find Jesus cited to support the argument that it is pointless to talk about eliminating poverty. A deeply religious person might be swayed by this argument; but most people today would find the use of Jesus's name here a way of removing the discussion of poverty from the rational to the emotional level.

8. False Analogy

The writer of "An American Myth" is particularly addicted to the fallacy of false analogy. Consider, for example, his claim that some of the loveliest flowers grow on manure heaps. This is intended to suggest not only that some of the loveliest people come from slums, which may be true, but (as is clear from the context) that these people are lovely *because* they live in slums, which is doubtful. The intended analogy may be stated as follows: Slums are to the growth of lovely people as manure is to the growth of lovely flowers. As we have seen, the force of this metaphor depends heavily on equivocation in the use of the word *manure.*

The analogy between poor people on welfare and zoo animals is equally false. Basically it asserts that poor people and zoo animals are the same in one particular: if they are given the necessities of life and not forced to work for them, they will grow lazy and decadent. But zoo animals have no choice; they cannot hunt their food, they must eat what they are brought or starve. And as for people, some of the most energetic people in history, from Plato to John F. Kennedy, have not been deterred from achievement by having the necessities of life assured them from birth. The writer might reply that the very poor are different from John F. Kennedy, but this, as we have seen, remains to be proved. It would seem more likely on the face of it that they are different from zoo animals.

A discussion of false analogy in another context will be found in Chapter 7, pp. 117–118.

9. Undocumented Assertion

"An American Myth" is full of undocumented assertions. We must again and again ask this writer questions. How do you *know* what you say you know? How do you *know* that the poor in Egypt and those other countries don't feel pain the same way you do? How do you *know* what our policy makers think about slums? These generalizations appear here sometimes as premises and sometimes as conclusions, but in either case they are for the most part inadmissible. This writer has not learned much about evidence or its use. Slums are no worse than any other place once you get used to them, he says. How close has he been to one? We gather that he has frequented embassies, not slums. If he knows nothing about them from this kind of experience, then what other kind of experience is he drawing on: interviews, polls, books, other authorities? He does not tell us.

Bacon once wrote, "If we begin with certainties, we shall end in doubts; but if we begin with doubts, and we are patient with them, we shall end in certainties." A serious inquirer may take either path and find truth at the end, but not our writer. Beginning with certainties, and heedless of the most obvious objections, he proves (to himself) what he wants to prove and ends where he began. Whatever appeal this method may have, there is no truth in it, and less learning. Truth is a matter of keeping your mind open and adjusting what you think to accord with what you learn, a matter of weighing all the evidence you can find before deciding where you stand. The more evidence you invoke, no matter which way it points, the better your judgment is likely to be.

There is another undocumented assertion that runs through "An American Myth": the assertion of the writer's superiority. This is implicit rather than explicit and thus not strictly a logical fallacy in the sense of this chapter, but it is more damaging to his credibility than many of the other fallacies discussed in these pages. Indeed, it invites attention to them, since people are quick to look for flaws in snobs.

10. Argument *ad Hominem* and *ad Populum*

An *ad hominem* argument is directed "at the person," thus diverting attention from the issues at stake to the character of their advocates. An *ad populum* argument ("at the people") is one that appeals to the emotions of a group rather than to its reason. Both are diversionary, question-evading tactics used to shore up weak arguments. At their lowest, they are mere mudslinging.

If the issue is your opponent's administrative ability, but you call people's attention to his churchgoing habits or his political ideas or his feebleminded brother, you are resorting to an *ad hominem* argument—a logically irrelevant appeal to your hearers' passions and prejudices. At its lowest, *ad hominem* is a mere smear tactic; thus we find J. Edgar Hoover trying to discredit Martin Luther King with his own followers by revealing that King had once registered at a "white" motel.

The *ad populum* argument often depends on a logically doubtful but emotionally compelling distinction between *we* and *they*: we the noble Roman people, they the base slayers of Caesar; we the Aryan master race, they the vile Jews; we the people's republic, they the capitalist warmongers. A form of *ad populum* argument is a staple of the television commercial: you, being a person of taste and discrimination, will want to smoke *our* brand of cigar or use *our* soap. Don't use your mind; use ours.

In "An American Myth" the reader is repeatedly invited to see himself as part of an elite "we" who send wheat to India, subsidize the poor, and pay the country's taxes. The writer instinctively feels that if he can get his readers to identify with this "we," they will accept the separation between "we" and "they" on which his argument depends. The tactic flatters the reader, tells him he is a superior person who keeps superior company; but on the issue of foreign aid versus charity at home, which is after all the writer's subject, it says exactly nothing.

The ten fallacies enumerated in this chapter, and the dozen-odd others discussed in books on logic, have a peculiar characteristic: they tend to merge into each other. Thus the manure-heap image is an instance not only of false analogy and equivocation, but of name-calling, false disjunction, and undocumented assertion. The appeal to Jesus is not only an argument to authority but an *ad populum* argument, not to mention an instance of "poisoning the wells," a logical fallacy in which the other party, though not demonstrably dishonorable, is deprived of all opportunity to reply with honor, as in the celebrated question "Have you stopped beating your wife?" It is also a fair case of suppressed evidence, since Jesus had a few remarks on the other side of the question as well, notably "Go and sell that thou hast, and give to the poor."

Most of the other examples discussed above could also be classified under two or more of the fallacy headings. What does this mean? It means, as we might expect, that illogicality is more a general state of mind than a series of particular fallacies with neat little names. Far from being the monster of unreason that our bill of particulars makes him out, the author of "An American Myth" is just a slightly more than ordinarily sloppy thinker, a slightly more than ordinarily hasty writer, and a slightly more than ordinarily passionate partisan. The way to avoid logical fallacies is to stop and think. Are you telling the reader no more than you can prove? Are you telling him everything he has to know if he is to judge matters for himself? Have you used words unequivocally and defined your terms? Are your premises clearly related to each other and to your conclusion? In a word, have you been honest and thorough? If you have, you have probably also been logical.

3

TONE

Tone is the quality that conveys a writer's attitude, and perhaps something of his intentions. "When you say that, smile!" said Owen Wister's cowboy to the stranger; unless the words came with the right tone, they were fighting words. Our culture hangs together partly because we know its idiom, know what tone to adopt in given situations. It also hangs together because at least some of us have an ear for tones that lie below the surface: the malarkey in the politician's promises, the hostility in the peace lover's sermon, the lie in the advertiser's "truth."

What is true of speaking is equally true of writing. In every written statement there is an implied voice, a tonal quality that reveals the writer's attitude toward his subject matter and toward his audience. Is he objective, angry, contemptuous, indifferent, amused, cynical, ironic, sentimental? The list of possible tones is almost endless. Indeed, a one-word description can rarely do justice to the tone of a piece of writing, for the tone can be as subtle and complex as the personality of the writer.

Here is a scientist writing for students of science: "Proteins are long-chain molecules built up of hundreds of molecular subunits: the 20 amino acids." The tone is calm, unimpassioned, explanatory; the writer's purpose is not to urge or persuade, but simply to put known quantities together into an objective exposition, and that purpose governs his attitude both toward his subject and toward his audience. If the same scientist were addressing a lay audience, his tone might be quite different. Here is the biologist Loren Eiseley writing for a popular audience on "How Flowers Changed the World":

> Before the coming of the flowering plants our own ancestral stock, the warm-blooded mammals, consisted of a few mousy little creatures hidden in trees and underbrush. A few lizard-like birds with carnivorous teeth flapped awkwardly on ill-aimed flights among archaic shrubbery. None of these insignificant creatures gave evidence of any remarkable talents. The mammals in particular had been around for some millions of years, but had remained well lost in the shadow of the mighty reptiles. Truth to tell, man was still, like the genie in the bottle, encased in the body of a creature about the size of a rat.

What makes the difference in tone? The fact that Eiseley, though objective in the sense that he never departs from what biologists accept as true, has another motive as well: the desire to be vivid and entertaining. Adjectives with immediate visual appeal like *mousy* and *lizard-like*, familiar turns of speech like *some millions of years*, familiar analogies like *the genie in the bottle*, all indicate that this author is writing to stimulate the interest and imagination of readers who know little about his subject. If he had addressed a professional audience in such terms, he would have seemed patronizing if not ridiculous.

KINDS OF TONE

Writers' tones are as various as human temperaments and moods. But some tones occur frequently enough in student writing, and give enough trouble, to be worth a few words.

Invective

Invective is name-calling, the expression of undisguised anger or passion in writing. Here is a letter to a college newspaper lamenting the treatment a speaker received at the hands of a crowd:

> In any community—even an academic community, I suppose—there will always be those fearful, ignorant, sadistic people who feel their smelly little existence to be somehow threatened by ideas different from

their own. Usually, though, the university tradition of free inquiry man-
ages to keep their neurotic tendencies toward anti-intellectual, sheep-
like orthodoxy and violence in check, at least until they get out of college.

But now I watched a mob of these mental pygmies whose sick and
unpatriotic intolerance had found a seemingly "legitimate" outlet in
two-bit patriotism. They threw various objects at ———— and then
ducked behind each other (that's the old American way for you!).

Writers of invective let you have it. They in no way disguise their
righteous indignation or hate or disgust; they are not calm analysts
but passionate partisans. As persuasion, this kind of writing is rarely
effective. An angry writer usually has one of two effects on his readers. If they agree with him, his lack of restraint embarrasses them:
fine, fine, but why beat a dead horse? If they disagree, his lack of
restraint confirms their disagreement: loudmouths, after all, are never
right. Be wary of invective if you want to win an argument. Even if
people happen to be "mental pygmies," they will not thank you for
telling them so.

Invective for comic or satiric effect is another matter; witness its
appeal to gifted writers of all eras, from Rabelais to Shaw. The Irish
are among its most gifted practitioners, as in this genial harangue by
the artist Gulley Jimson in Joyce Cary's novel *The Horse's Mouth*:

"And what is a government individually, a hatful of prophets and mur-
derers dreaming of bloody glories and trembling at the grin of the grave.
I forgive it, the belly-ripping abortionist, the batter-brained, cak-handed,
wall-eyed welsher, the club-foot trampler, the block-eared raper that
would sell its sister for a cheer, the brick-faced hypocrite that would
wipe art and artists off the face of the earth as it would skin an orange,
and cut the balls off the genius of the Lord to make a tame gee-gee for
the morning Park. I forgive it," I said, as we got on to the bus. "I forgive
government, with all its works, because it can't rise out of its damnation,
which is to be a figment."

"That's rather strong," said a gentleman in shammy-gloves, opposite.

And so it is, but not as strong as it is funny. Cary, like all good writers
of comic invective, is a prodigal with words, flinging them at a target
like so many custard pies. Though the words are savage enough, the
effect is good-natured, more akin to the art of showing-off than the art
of combat. If you want to cut down an enemy, there are better ways
than this.

Exhortation

Exhortation can be close to invective. It is the voice of the preacher or the moralist, hammering home his values and opinions; its intention is to convince. Here is Philip Wylie on the subject of war:

> There is no other way to look at war than as the final proof of the infantilism of man—the revelation of his inherent lack of civilization, his serfdom to his instincts, and, therefore, his failure to achieve adulthood. War proves how wholly dependent we are upon the instinctual plane for our motives and what a thin tissue our repressive brain—our reason—has stretched between us and other animals.

Although a step beyond mere invective, this passionately opinionated statement contains as much heat as it does light. Note the unqualified assertions ("there is *no other way* to look at war," "war *proves*") and the denunciatory tone ("infantilism," "serfdom to his instincts"). This writer is not sitting down to reason with you; he is letting you know what's what. As the reader, you are placed in the irritating position of being talked at: Wylie is doing all the speaking and you all the listening. A writer's tone says a great deal about what he thinks of his readers—whether he considers them intellectuals or boobs, reasonable men or fanatics, friends or enemies. Be careful not to insult your readers unless that is your intention.

Exhortation need not be so strident. In "The Moral Equivalent of War," William James took an antiwar position in many ways similar to Wylie's, but listen to the difference in tone:

> It is plain that on this subject civilized man has developed a sort of double personality. If we take European nations, no legitimate interest of any one of them would seem to justify the tremendous destructions which a war to compass it would necessarily entail. It would seem as though common sense and reason ought to find a way to reach agreement in every conflict of honest interests. I myself think it our bounden duty to believe in such international rationality as possible.

We are here a long way from invective; James keeps his temper, does not raise his voice. He is practicing some of the reasonableness he preaches, and in doing so he is tacitly saying to the reader, "You are the kind of person who can be reached by reason." Note the qualifications ("it would seem," "reason ought to"); our assent is invited, not commanded or presumed.

Is James's approach as effective as Wylie's? Probably more so. When James's article appeared in 1910, some thirty thousand copies of it were distributed, and it has been often reprinted since. It is still one of the most honored arguments against war in our literature.

Narrative

Narrative does not overtly argue or editorialize, but simply presents a set of events or conditions. Consider the following paragraph from Dee Brown's *Bury My Heart at Wounded Knee*:

> As Crazy Horse walked between them, letting the soldier chief and Little Big Man lead him to wherever they were taking him, he must have tried to dream himself into the real world, to escape the darkness of the shadow world in which all was madness. They walked past a soldier with a bayoneted rifle on his shoulder, and then they were standing in the doorway of a building. The windows were barred with iron, and he could see men behind the bars with chains on their legs. It was a trap for an animal, and Crazy Horse lunged away like a trapped animal, with Little Big Man holding on to his arm. The scuffling went on for only a few seconds. Someone shouted a command, and then the soldier guard, Private William Gentles, thrust his bayonet deep into Crazy Horse's abdomen.

There is no editorializing here, yet the writer of narrative is every bit as concerned with his reader's response as a writer of invective or exhortation. His method is simply less direct. Rather than telling us what to think, he presents a set of selected details that control our response—in this case pity and outrage. The narrative tone tends to be neutral, dispassionate, distanced. These are the facts, it seems to say; respond to them as you will. Though the response is in fact manipulated by the writer's selection and use of detail, the reader responds as if to a personal experience. He knows this is the way it was: he was there.

This tactic of dispassionately presenting material that speaks for itself is equally effective in nonfiction. A good example is the Seymour Hersh passage on Vietnam (p. 21). Here is another, in which the black writer James Baldwin recounts an experience in a Swiss village:

There is a custom in the village—I am told it is repeated in many villages—of "buying" African natives for the purpose of converting them to Christianity. There stands in the church all year round a small box with a slot for money, decorated with a black figurine, and into this box the villagers drop their francs. During the *carnaval* which precedes Lent, two village children have their faces blackened—out of which bloodless darkness their blue eyes shine like ice—and fantastic horsehair wigs are placed on their blond heads; thus disguised, they solicit among the villages for money for the missionaries in Africa. Between the box in the church and the blackened children, the village "bought" last year six or eight African natives. This was reported to me with pride by the wife of one of the *bistro* owners and I was careful to express astonishment and pleasure at the solicitude shown by the village for the souls of black folk. The *bistro* owner's wife beamed with a pleasure far more genuine than my own and seemed to feel that I might now breathe more easily concerning the souls of at least six of my kinsmen.

Satire

Satire is a form of ridicule aimed at correcting some folly or abuse. Here, for example, is part of a satirical book review by Thomas Reed Powell. After lamenting that most books on the Constitution of the United States "are very hard to read" and make you "think very hard all the time," Powell goes on to say:

> The new book which Mr. Beck has written about the Constitution is a very different kind of book. You can read it without thinking. If you have got tired trying to read the other kind of books, you will be glad of the nice restful book that Mr. Beck has written. It runs along like a story in a very interesting way. Most of the story is about how the Constitution got made. This is really history, but it is written in a very lively way like a novel, with a great many characters, almost all male, and plenty of conversation and a very exciting plot. . . . Besides the story there are many quotations from Shakespeare, Beethoven, Horace, Isaiah, Euripides, Beard, and other famous men. Many of these quotations are quite old, but some of them seem fairly new.

The book is made ridiculous. Why? Because by pretending to be a fool who admires it Powell persuades us that no one but a fool *could* admire it, and hence that it must be a foolish book. As his satirical device Powell has adopted the tone and tastes of a twelve-year-old. Note the incidence of the schoolboy word *very*, the jumbled chronology that puts Isaiah after Shakespeare and the historian Beard cheek by jowl with Euripides, the writer's simpleminded taste in novels (which he reads because they are lively, having exciting plots, and are above all easy), and the devastatingly feeble "seem fairly new." The writer is clearly immature, half-educated, and uninteresting; a book he likes must be awful.

Satire, more than most other tones, requires a sensitivity to the tone of others. Indeed, in parody, which is what Powell is writing, the satirist actually takes the tone of the person or piece of writing that he is satirizing—pompous, childish, inarticulate, or whatever. Although satire can be biting, it is just as often gentle: fun to write and fun to read. Unlike invective, satire usually invites the reader in and asks him to join the fun.

Irony

The dictionary defines irony as "a sort of humor, ridicule, or light sarcasm, the intended implication of which is the opposite of the literal sense of the word." This is an imperfect definition. Irony is by no means always funny, nor is it the same as sarcasm; sarcasm comes from a Greek word meaning "to tear flesh," a kind of direct assault, as when one says, "You think you're pretty damned smart, don't you?" One thing is said and another meant, but there is no real deception. Irony, by contrast, is oblique, subtle, and indirect in its working; the deception is not just a gimmick but an essential part of the writer's message.

It is the last part of the dictionary definition that gets to the heart of the matter. Irony always sets up a tension between opposites: between the ideal and the real, the seen and the unseen, the literal and the implied, the achieved and the intended. This duality must always exist. An elementary form of it was displayed some years ago by a San Francisco entrepreneur who marketed 29-cent cans of "fresh air" to be sent as gifts to people in Los Angeles. The directions on the can went something like this: "Punch a small hole in the top and inhale slowly. Do not gulp the air; breathing air can be habit-forming. Increase your intake by degrees. Ten cans a day can be safely consumed. If excessive euphoria is experienced, see your doctor." Where is the irony? In the contrast between the giver's ostensible motivation, benevolence, and his actual motivation, self-congratulation; and in the receiver's awareness of that contrast.

This is a low form of the genre, hardly more than a practical joke. At the other extreme is Jonathan Swift's famous "Modest Proposal," which sets forth in sober, businesslike language a proposal that the children of Ireland be slaughtered and used as a source of food for that starving land. The irony here comes from Swift's implied message: that even the most outrageous brutalities must now seem commonplace alongside the horrors wrought by England's exploitation of Ireland. He is ostensibly saying to the English, "As a conscientious student of English administrative practice, I have come up with a plan that I think you will admire." He is in effect saying "You are monsters."

In desperate situations, irony sometimes seems the only possible mode of redress. Most Negro jazz has irony at its base; thus, for example, Louis Armstrong's classic "What Did I Do to Be So Black and Blue?" plays profound changes on the cliché "black and blue." Lenny Bruce's quip "Toilet, you're lucky you're white!" evokes the "Negro" problem in five words. In the following exchange reported in the *New York Times* between a South African judge and a political prisoner up for retrial, the prisoner is aware that any expression of dissatisfaction with his lot will be taken as evidence of criminal revolutionary sentiment:

> "You have no objection to being ordered around by whites?"
> "I have become satisfied to such an extent that my health keeps improving."
> "Are you satisfied with your wages?"
> "I have never complained—not on a single day."
> "Do you want better wages?"
> "No, your worship."
> "Are you satisfied with your house?"
> "It's a very beautiful house."
> "Are you satisfied with the pass laws?"
> "Yes, entirely."

Who could be taken in by this irony? If the judge was, he was a fool. If he wasn't, he was powerless to act, since the prisoner's words were scrupulously inoffensive. The judge was caught in that ironic situation known as the double-bind; there was no way he could win.

Similar circumstances evoked a celebrated piece of irony from Sigmund Freud. In May 1938, after intense harassment by the notorious Nazi secret police unit known as the Gestapo, the 82-year-old Freud was at last granted an exit visa from Vienna on the condition that he sign a document attesting that his treatment by the Germans had been irreproachable. He asked permission to add a few words below his signature, and this being granted, he wrote: "I can heartily recommend the Gestapo to anyone."

Irony can take many forms. There is dramatic irony (where a theater audience or a reader knows something a character does not know), there is Socratic irony (the pose of ignorance that Socrates assumed to bait his opponents), and there is verbal irony—some forms of which we have illustrated. Irony is one of the sharpest instruments of criticism available; thanks to its unique balance between intelligence and feeling, it can probe into the deepest aspects of existence. The ironic tone is not easy to master, but it is worth the effort.

ERRORS IN TONE

Tone is what establishes the rapport between writer and reader, the emotional premises of their relationship. But often a writer, without intending to adopt any particular tone, alienates his reader through sheer inadvertence, clumsiness, or insensitivity. Even simple slips can be devastating, as in this overexplicit telegram to a union official who had suffered a heart attack: "The board of Local 1245 last night passed a resolution wishing you a speedy recovery by a vote of 18-17." Most errors in tone, however, are not accidental. Rather they reflect a deep, if usually temporary, misreading of a writer's subject, or his audience, or both. In our remarks on invective and exhortation we pointed out some other pitfalls to be avoided; in the following pages we discuss still others.

Sentimentality

If irony is difficult for the beginning writer to master, sentimentality is difficult for him to avoid. By sentimentality we mean not just maudlin or gushy writing, but the whole range of counterfeit emotions. Here is a football player describing a visit to a hospital for crippled children:

> When I held Gracie in my arms, I knew then the meaning of the phrase "Strong legs run that weak legs may walk." She was about seven years old, and when I picked her up and held her close to me I could hear her

heart beat, and when she smiled she brought tears to my eyes in spite of myself. I somehow knew, as I held her, that this was the happiest moment of her life. And seeing her suffering, I was filled with rage at all those ungrateful bums in Harlem and Berkeley who were out rioting and raising hell because they didn't think they were getting enough for nothing out of this life.

In a class discussion of this paragraph, one student put her finger on something puzzling: "I don't see how the writer could be so full of love in the first part of the paragraph and so full of hate in the last." When asked if the hate in any way discredited the love, made it seem fake or insincere, the class was almost unanimous in saying yes. What the class detected was the presence of sentimentality.

Sentimentality is often defined as "emotion in excess of the fact," the fact being a human situation—the death of a loved one, the election of a president, the birth of a baby—that legitimately evokes emotion. The sentimentalist squeezes more emotion out of such an occasion than discriminating people regard as proper or decent. He enjoys the emotion for its own sake, as a kind of narcotic, and he does not shrink from the stalest clichés when the fit is upon him. He invokes the patter of tiny feet, the love of a good woman, silver threads among the gold—all those prefabricated phrases that evoke stock emotional responses. During a recent political campaign a commentator reported a candidate's speech in these terms:

> He got his first rafter-ringing response by coming out foursquare for the Declaration of Independence and the Constitution. He rated another salvo for saying he would not bend before the breeze or run with the tide. . . . And [he] talked tough about sending out the Marines to win back our respect. "History shows us what happens to appeasers," he said as the militant ladies in the audience beat their white gloves together.

That candidate knows the tricks of the sentimentalists. He is talking from the emotions to the emotions with no mediation from the mind. Sentimental chichés defeat the possibility of thought. What specific policies does our candidate believe in? He does not tell us, and those ladies with the white gloves, being sentimentalists themselves, do not ask him.

Sentimentality is a way of not facing reality; it prettifies things rather than seeing them as they are. The sentimentalist believes not in love, but in "true love," an ideal absolute that exists only as a fantasy and has nothing to do with real relations between real people. What he hates above all else is the complexity, ambiguity, and mess of actual life. "All idealization makes life poorer," wrote the novelist Joseph Conrad. "To beautify it is to take away its character of complexity—it is to destroy it." This insight is beyond the sentimentalist's comprehension. He will say, with Edgar Guest, that "It takes a heap o' livin' to make a house a home," but he will not include in that "livin' " the dirty diapers, the family quarrels, or Grandpa's addiction to bourbon. He does not care about "livin' " in any real sense; he lives in a world of wish fulfillment and sees what he wants to see.

Holden Caulfield, in *The Catcher in the Rye*, describes the classic type as he observes a woman sitting next to him in the movies. Although the film is (to use one of Holden's favorite words) hopelessly "phoney," the woman is crying her eyes out; and the phonier the film gets, the more she cries. This action would seem to indicate a kind-hearted woman, whatever one might think about her taste. But Holden wasn't fooled; for sitting next to her was a small boy who, throughout the show, was bored and had to go to the bathroom. She wouldn't take him, but told him to shut up and behave himself. Holden comments: "She was about as kindhearted as a goddam wolf. You take somebody that cries their goddam eyes out over phoney stuff in the movies, and nine times out of ten they're mean bastards at heart. I'm not kidding."

Holden is perfectly right; moved by the secondhand suffering on the screen but indifferent to her boy's real distress, this woman is a mean bastard without even knowing it. So is Françoise, the cook of Proust's *Swann's Way*, who weeps over the childbirth symptoms she reads about in a medical book while ignoring a fellow servant in the agony of labor. Proust supplies a telling comment: "The sufferings of humanity inspired in her a pity which increased in direct ratio to the distance separating the sufferers from herself." Scratch a sentimentalist and you will usually find a person capable of cruelty, or at least an unlovely indifference to the distress of others.

This brings us to the illustration we began with. It was probably not just chance that brought hate and love into such uneasy juxtaposition in that football player's theme, but something more fundamental in his life, some deep-lying feeling of resentment or insecurity. His words described what he wished he felt or thought he ought to feel, not what he did feel. Sentimentality is a pretense, a masquerade, a protective device; it pretends to be full, but it is empty. As D. H. Lawrence said of John Galsworthy, "Sentimentalism is the working off on yourself of feelings you haven't really got."

Pomposity

Two pompous pronouncements follow, the first from a dean's welcoming address to a freshman class, the second from a professor's letter to a college newspaper:

> I would like to welcome you to X——— University and to express the hope that your educational work will be most productive and rewarding. I am sure you will find that members of the University community are most willing to help you receive the maximum benefit from the curriculum and to have an enjoyable and satisfying learning experience at X———. . . .
> This program, which is designed to facilitate learning, involves the imparting of knowledge through research. To maximize learning, the University has made provision for small classes, close student-faculty contacts, high-quality instruction, and personalized education.

> In this connection I received a letter from Provost ——— just recently asking that possible implementation of improved mechanisms for handling problems of faculty-student relations in teaching situations be brought up for consideration by the Steering Committee of the Senate of the Academic Council.

Such double-talk, such perverse inability to be simple and straightforward, is the antithesis of communication. What sort of welcome is there in words like *program* and *personalized education* and *learning experience*? What human problem is buried under all the *implementations* and *relations* and *situations* and *considerations*? Such language does not bring people together; it pushes them apart. It is language for computers, not human beings.

Few young people naturally talk or write like this, but with such examples all around, who can blame students for imitating them? It is natural, after all, to imitate one's seniors, and perhaps necessary to one's advancement in the world. And how pleasant it is to be able to sound impressive with no more labor than it takes to change the likes of *better ways* to the likes of *improved mechanisms*. The technique is soon mastered, and we find examples like this, from a report by an education student on an experiment in which music was piped into the corridors of a high school:

> The hypothesis, therefore, is that music can reduce the intensity dimension of the student so that he remains in the range of the effectiveness along the continuum. By remaining within the range of his greatest effectiveness he should be able to maximize his rewards and thus possess a positive attitude toward school.

Language like this cannot be read; it must be translated. What this passage seems to mean, though we cannot be sure, is: "Students seem calmer and happier when the music is on, and do better work." If that is what the writer meant, that is what he should have written. The idea of writing is to say clearly what you mean, not to stun people by your mastery of a charmless and impenetrable jargon.

Highbrowism

Highbrowism is close to pomposity as an error in tone, but it is usually more deliberate. The pompous writer indulges in "fine writing" out of insecurity or bad training, which leads him to a false notion of his own dignity and the dignity of the written word. The highbrow writer has a different motivation: he wants to show off. He cannot resist letting his teacher and classmates know that he is up on the latest fad or theory. His theme may begin as follows:

> "The Love Song of J. Alfred Prufrock" is a vision of the relativism of our time. "I should have been a pair of ragged claws" is but a distant paraphrase of Rilke's "Der Panther" and its "weiche Gang geschmeidig starker Schritte." To understand both works one profits immensely by an acquaintance with the Existentialist vision of Jean-Paul Sartre in "The Root of the Chestnut Tree" and Camus in "The Myth of Sisyphus."

What is wrong with this passage is not that Rilke, Camus, and Sartre are irrelevant, but that they are dragged in by the ears, introduced for self-advertising reasons rather than for what they contribute to the discussion.

The writer who cares about his readers will either suppress allusions of this sort or take care to explain them fully; he will be interested not in impressing but in instructing, not in widening the distance between himself and his readers but in narrowing it. The frequent use of unexplained allusions is a manifest error in tone.

Flippancy

Flippant writing is writing that takes a serious subject lightly, as in the "Brainy broads are groovy" essay discussed on pp. 9–10. Flippancy is a fault comparable to laughing at a funeral or making jokes about wooden legs to a cripple; it can be forgiven in the very young, but it is seldom appreciated. Here is a sample from a freshman theme:

> I thought themes on what I did last summer went out with model T's, but since they didn't, I'll dig right in, for there's no point in flunking out of this school before I've given it a whirl (or vice versa). I'll tell you what I did last summer: I worked in a canning factory. And I'll tell you what I did in that canning factory every chance I got (which wasn't often): I sat on my can.

Most teachers will react to themes like this with bored tolerance. Although writing like this can be funny, it more often fails of its own ingenuousness. Good writing takes time and effort. Flippant themes usually come from an unwillingness to accept the challenge of an assignment. This is a pity in the case of our young canner, who clearly has a way with words. A little more effort, a little more restraint, and he might have given his comic bent a more hopeful lease on life.

Some writers seem to think that whatever emerges from their gut is sacred and should be recorded without modification for posterity to ponder. Their teachers rarely agree, and hence a conflict arises—one only partly related, to be sure, to the question of tone. Here is the beginning of a theme on the assignment "Is it ever permissible to break a law?"

> I started to think. I thought, questions like that don't turn me on. I mean, how do you answer questions like that, when those questions don't really exist? I moved on to what was important. What was important was the music, and the music told me all about law that I needed to know. I just took the hand of that music and it led me right between the cliffs of right and wrong. It led me out, man, and it didn't matter whether the law said it was right or wrong.

Flippancy aside, this kind of psychedelic free-associating is likely to find few appreciative hearers. Writing should normally be intelligible to as many people as possible, but this writing is in a private lingo. Whatever it may mean to the writer's friends, it is opaque to the ordinary reader. Private lingos have their uses. But if you are trying to say something meaningful about the limits of the law—something a lawyer or a concerned citizen would listen to—you should say it in words we can understand, and in a tone that invites our attention.

Tone expresses the relationship that exists between writer and reader, the assumptions they share. The tone we use in discourse is a reminder of the kind of people we are, at least at the moment of speaking. If a conversation begins with "Listen, you son of a bitch," it is one sort of conversation; if it begins with "Is there anything I can do to help?" it is another sort. The same thing happens in writing. No matter how sure we are of our opinions, it is elementary courtesy and good sense to acknowledge the reader's existence, the possibility of his disagreement, the potential value of his criticism. No matter how indifferent we may be to our readers, it is elementary courtesy to put them at their ease. Unless we are bent on mayhem, it is elementary good sense to establish a basis for mutual respect.

PART 2
TECHNIQUE

4

PARAGRAPHS

 To know your subject and your audience, to have your material ready, to have made your basic strategic decisions, is not enough. You must also develop a talent for writing itself, an ability to reach and hold your readers. That is where technique comes in. Technique may be defined as a mastery of the psychology and the mechanics of good writing; it is what clears the static off the line from writer to reader. Always there is the reader to think of—the elusive reader with his unknown capacities and incapacities, his sophistication and his ignorance, his prejudices and his susceptibility to distraction. The pitfalls are many. Make what you write too long, and he will be bored. Make it too short, and he will be confused by your omissions. Add a comma, choose a word carelessly, and he may misunderstand you. Get a fact wrong, misspell a word, and he may write you off as an ignoramus.

There is still another pitfall: make him work too hard, and he will give you up for the boob tube. The educated American today is accustomed to skillful writing—in newspaper stories and magazine articles, in national advertising, and even on network television, where scarcely a sentence is uttered that has not first been written down and revised to exacting standards by a professional writer. To be sure, much of this writing is shallow and unmemorable, devoted to conveying routine news or selling detergents; but for better or for worse it has taught the educated American reader to expect economy, clarity, and directness in what he reads. To get a hearing from readers so conditioned, you must not only say what you mean, but say it well.

The next five chapters are concerned with the technique of writing effectively. In Chapters 4-7 we progress from larger units of thought to smaller ones: paragraphs first, followed by sentences, then words, and finally an important special use of words, namely imagery. Chapter 8, "Editing," shows how the lessons of Chapters 4-7 are applied in practice.

ASPECTS OF THE PARAGRAPH

Paragraphs are not just hunks of prose marked by indentations; they are the basic units of thought out of which an essay is composed. They are building stones, parts of a larger whole. Though we shall necessarily in this chapter discuss paragraphs without reference to their context, they are in fact inseparable from that context. To put this another way, the problem is not so much to write an effective paragraph, let alone a dazzling paragraph, as to write your paragraphs in such a way as to make an effective—and integrated—essay.

The Thesis and the Thesis Sentence

Being a single unit of thought, a paragraph often contains a topic sentence or thesis sentence in which the thought in question is stated in capsule form. Not every paragraph contains a thesis sentence as such, but every good paragraph contains a thesis. In this paragraph from the magazine *Ramparts,* the thesis (of both the paragraph and the essay) is stated with unusual explicitness in the first sentence:

> It is the thesis of this essay that the reasonable man has become the enemy of this society at this time. His reason has been soured by compromise and his moral conscience traded for a conscience of conciliation. The capacity to ask fundamental questions appears to have been lost. The criticism of the war, in the mass media and in Congress, has been generally marginal and directed to practical, tactical techniques.

The worst thing that reasonable men seem capable of saying about our attempt to control another people's destiny is that it is not working out very well; if we were winning, it would no doubt be considered a good war.

Here, by contrast, is a paragraph from Thoreau's *Walden* in which the thesis is not explicit but implicit:

Why should we be in such desperate haste to succeed and in such desperate enterprises? If a man does not keep pace with his companions, perhaps it is because he hears a different drummer. Let him step to the music which he hears, however measured or far away. It is not important that he should mature as soon as an apple-tree or an oak. Shall he turn his spring into summer? If the condition of things which we were made for is not yet, what were any reality which we can substitute? We will not be shipwrecked on a vain reality. Shall we with pains erect a heaven of blue glass over ourselves, though when it is done we shall be sure to gaze still at the true ethereal heaven far above, as if the former were not?

Thoreau's rhetorical questions, metaphors, and poetic style require more of the reader than the *Ramparts* passage; we are asked not just to follow a line of argument, but to participate imaginatively in the writer's meaning. Yet the single idea, the thesis, is there as surely in this paragraph as in the other. Can we phrase a thesis sentence? How about "A man should be allowed to mature at his own rate and in his own way"? It misses the charm and persuasiveness of Thoreau's words, but it gives us his kernel of meaning.

Unity and Coherence

Every good paragraph has two qualities: unity and coherence. It has unity in the sense that it is about a single subject, and coherence in the sense that its sentences fit together to make a connected whole. A simple way to test for these qualities is to write in one sentence the thesis of an essay and then do the same for each of its successive paragraphs. Your series of thesis sentences should give you in brief form the basic argument of the essay. If it does not, the essay probably suffers from logical gaps, irrelevancies, or padding. Further scrutiny of the thesis sentences should tell you where the trouble is and what kind of change would make things better.

Length

The following paragraph is from a review of pornographic films by David Denby:

> Going to these theatres produces a heavy depression hard to shrug off: the shabbiness of the material settles on the audience like ash, and prurient fascination struggles against distaste at oneself for not being out in pursuit of the real thing. At ordinary bad movies one can talk back to the screen, create an instant community of wise guys and complainers, and have a good time that way; at dirty movies a muttered complaint would destroy the concentration of a hundred men lost in the pornographic trance, a unique state of being which requires silence, isolation, and passivity. And even if one gives oneself over to the trance, the movies often fail to justify their only excuse for existence: keeping the viewer aroused. In Steven Marcus' excellent study of Victorian pornography, *The Other Victorians*, the author remarks, "Language is for pornography a bothersome necessity; its function is to set going a series of non-verbal images, of fantasies—and if it could dispense with words it would. Which is why, one supposes, the motion-picture film is what the genre was all along waiting for." But actually, words are more effective: they outline a situation, and then release the imagination to fill it out with ideal shapes and acts. Pictures imprison one in the actual; the imperfections of human forms, the clumsiness of the actors, the ugliness of the lighting and shooting—all eliminate the freedom of fantasy and depress desire.

Although this paragraph carries its length with considerable grace, it is a fairly big block of prose and some readers would find it hard going. Can things be made easier for them? Why not begin a new paragraph with the third sentence? The first two sentences are concerned with the audience's reaction to such films; all the rest have to do with whether words or pictures are more erotically stimulating. Since two shorter paragraphs as proposed would each be as unified and coherent as the original long one, nothing would be lost by the change.

How long should a paragraph be? The only general rule is that it should be long enough to convey one more or less complex thought, and not so long as to alienate or stupefy its readers. Very short paragraphs are no better than very long ones. A series of one- and two-sentence paragraphs (a favorite strategy in political speeches and witty newspaper columns) suggests that the author is presenting a series of one-liners designed to evoke bursts of applause or laughter rather than a message to be considered and understood as a whole. An occasional one-sentence paragraph may be useful as a transition to a new line of thought, or for dramatic effect; but short paragraphs as a class should be left to the politicians and journalists, who have their own reasons for using them.

One exception, of course, is in written dialogue: convention decrees that each successive speaker's remarks, however brief, are given a separate paragraph.°

Transitions

What ties the sentences of a paragraph together? Sometimes transitional words and phrases (*moreover, thus, on the other hand, in retrospect,* etc.), sometimes coordinating conjunctions (*and, but, yet,* etc.). Sometimes the repetition of a key word or idea: for example, *trance* in the middle of the Denby paragraph above, or the idea of depression in the first and last sentences. Sometimes a vivid image or analogy that connects things up: for example, Thoreau's *drummer* or Denby's *ash* simile. Sometimes the examples supporting a generalization, or a generalization climaxing a series of examples. Sometimes nothing more than the rhythm of the writer's excitement, or of the reader's interest. Much is made of so-called transitional devices by some teachers, but few writers consciously use such devices as a way of constructing paragraphs. In our view, the idea comes first, the writing follows, and the transitions from sentence to sentence are generated as by-products of the writer's effort to make the reader see exactly what he means.

Indeed, the best writers make sparing use of routine transitional words and phrases in linking their sentences together. Such words and phrases are not bad in themselves, but when used to excess they make a paragraph seem full of hinges, like a trick floor at a carnival; it hangs together but is hard to walk on. If you know what you want to say, your ideas will jump from sentence to sentence like electric sparks, or flow like an underground stream. If your thought makes a coherent unit, transitions will be no problem.

° Another exception is a paragraph like this one, where one sentence exhausts the subject.

Transitions between paragraphs follow the same general rules as transitions within paragraphs. If the ideas of two successive paragraphs are properly related, the transition between them will be clear and obvious. If the transition causes difficulty, the two ideas are no doubt faultily related; perhaps an intervening paragraph, or some different tack altogether, is needed to make the argument work. Some beginning writers give up when this happens and hope the difficulty will not be noticed. Even if it is not, the confusion it causes will be: a reader may not know where he has left the road, but he knows when he is in a swamp. There is no substitute for getting your ideas in a workable sequence before you begin to write, or at the latest before you begin work on your final draft. When transitions between ideas are logical, transitions between paragraphs are no problem.

Variety

Another way of tying a paragraph together is to use different kinds of sentences in composing it. One possibility, illustrated in the paragraph from Thoreau, is to mix interrogative and imperative sentences with declarative ones. Other devices are just as effective. Follow a short sentence with a long one. Vary the subject-predicate-object form; begin some sentences with an introductory phrase or a subordinate clause. Don't have all compound or all complex or all simple sentences; have some of each. These rules, like all rules, are made to be broken by masters—the final arbiter is the taste and judgment of the writer—but it is well to be aware that one can bore as much by the sameness of one's style as by the dullness of one's thoughts.

We had thought to add a word of warning against the paragraph consisting of one monster sentence. But consider this paragraph from Norman Mailer's *Presidential Papers*:

> It is not that Los Angeles is altogether hideous, it is even by degrees pleasant, but for an Easterner there is never any salt in the wind; it is like Mexican cooking without chili, or Chinese egg rolls missing their mustard;[1] as one travels through the endless repetitions of that city which is the capital of suburbia with its milky pinks, its washed-out oranges, its tainted lime-yellows of pastel on one pretty little architectural monstrosity after another, the colors not intense enough, the styles never pure, and never sufficiently impure to collide on the eye, one conceives the people who live here—they have come out to express

themselves,[2] Los Angeles is the home of self-expression, but the artists are middle-class and middling-minded; no passions will calcify here for years in the gloom to be revealed a decade later as the tessellations of a hard and fertile work,[3] no, it is all open, promiscuous, borrowed, half bought, a city without iron, eschewing wood, a kingdom of stucco, the playground for mass men—[4] one has the feeling it was built by television sets giving orders to men.

Here is variety enough, detail enough, rhythm enough, to keep all readers aboard till the end of the ride. But is this *one* sentence? Only in the most technical sense. If periods were put in at 1, 2, 3, and possibly 4, we probably would not notice much difference—perhaps only a slight slowing down in our reading speed. Which punctuation is better? It is a matter of taste. If you can write paragraphs this good, go ahead and punctuate them any way you like.

Emphasis

Emphasis in paragraphs, as in sentences, is achieved less by raising one's voice than by skill in marshaling one's thoughts. An occasional one-line paragraph may be emphatic; three in a row, or even three in a given essay, will be seen as a tedious straining for effect. An occasional exclamatory sentence can shock or excite, but strident or self-congratulatory exclamations like "I went through hell that day!" or "It was a *tremendous* experience!" will irritate the most sympathetic reader. A little shrieking goes a long way, whether the emotion is pain or rapture.

Although the first and last sentences of a paragraph tend to pack the strongest rhetorical wallop, on the whole we think coherence is the key to emphasis. Nothing underscores like clarity; nothing hammers a point home like a compelling reasonableness. Once again we come back to the importance of a coherent overall argument. However lucid and adroitly constructed a paragraph may be, if it does not hang together with the whole essay, it will hang separately.

OPENING AND CLOSING PARAGRAPHS

Opening Paragraphs

The opening paragraph of a story or essay sets the tone of what follows and the level of the reader's expectations. If an essay is to attract and hold readers, its opening paragraph must be inviting; it should make people want to read on, to follow wherever the writer leads. Too many student essays begin with dull paragraphs like the one on pp. 131–132 below, which in promising nothing but further dull paragraphs will lose nine readers out of ten. By contrast, consider this opening paragraph of an essay by Kenneth Burke dealing with the writers Thomas Mann and André Gide:

> When Gustav von Aschenbach, the hero of Thomas Mann's *Death in Venice*, was about thirty-five years of age, he was taken ill in Vienna. During the course of a conversation, one keen observer said of him, "You see, Aschenbach has always lived like this," and the speaker contracted the fingers of his left hand into a fist; "never like this," and he let his hand droop comfortably from the arm of a chair. It is with such opening and closing of the hand that this essay is to deal.

This is an excellent beginning. The image of that opening and closing hand piques our curiosity and makes us eager to see how it is applied to Mann and Gide. Burke has caught our attention; we want to read on. The paragraph has a further virtue: it is short. In writing as in speaking, when you are out to capture an audience it is a good idea not to be long-winded.

Sometimes a writer wants merely to suggest his topic in the opening paragraph, to tease us into attention rather than to declare his theme unambiguously. The first sentence of a 1969 article by Paul Ehrlich makes use of a perennially effective device, the prophecy of future catastrophe expressed as historic fact: "The end of the ocean came late in the summer of 1979, and it came even more rapidly than the biologists had expected." Another classic come-on opener reserves its punch for its final sentence, as in this paragraph by Roy Bongartz:

> They used to teach kids back in the Thirties that Americans were all alike—or at least were supposed to be all alike—and there was this monumental pretense that racial and religious differences did not actually matter. This false game of course made no breach in the walls the Wasps built around themselves, but it did damp down the minorities, who tried to dilute their identities—even dyed their hair or trimmed their noses—so as to look, or feel, a bit more like Doris Day or John Wayne. But that old sham has been blown to bits by Power of various colors, first Black, and then Brown (Mexican-American) and Red (Indian). Now here's another: the Superjew.

The one characteristic all these examples have in common is that they make us ask on our own the very question the writer proposes to answer. How are Gide and Mann like open and closed fists? What happened to the ocean in 1979—or what will happen if our indifference persists? What on earth is a Superjew? After a good first paragraph we can hardly wait to read the second.

Closing Paragraphs

An essay should be a package with a string around it, not a gathering of fragments. In your closing paragraph, do not simply summarize what you have already said. We heard it the first time; what we want to know now is what to make of it, what you think it adds up to. Your closing paragraph should reveal in some fresh light what the essay has been driving at all along, or perhaps open our eyes to something new. It should not clobber our minds with repetition.

A good example is the closing paragraph of the sample research paper presented on pp. 239-247. Another is this paragraph from a student essay on E. M. Forster's "What I Believe":

> The "aristocracy of the sensitive, the considerate, and the plucky" is, then, at the very heart of Forster's thinking. It is an attractive aristocracy in its way: cultured, non-violent, good company. But what a private and limited aristocracy it is! None of its members would be comfortable in industry or politics, or even at a football game. No black leader from the ghetto—however sensitive, considerate, and plucky—would seek to become a member. It is an aristocracy of the leisured and the well-off, a limitation that excludes most of mankind.

The first sentence serves as a transition from what has gone before. The second switches the focus from description to evaluation, and the last four make the writer's point.

KINDS OF PARAGRAPHS

It is the adage of a certain school of modern art that form follows function. That rule applies to good writing as well, especially if we broaden the notion of function to include the intention of the writer. For whenever you collect words and sentences into paragraphs, or paragraphs into whole essays, you are inevitably creating forms, or structures, that are the offspring of those intentions. Although some of those forms defy labeling, others like the following represent ordering processes that nearly all writers know and use.

Description

In describing something, be it an action or a landscape or a person or a thought, a writer always does one basic thing: he chooses a set of particulars, of details, that to his mind add up to a satisfactory picture. A scientist will normally choose the particulars most likely to convey his scientific findings without distortion; his appeal is to the intellect. A writer of fiction, aiming perhaps to evoke an impression or mood, will often emphasize particulars that appeal to our senses, as in this paragraph from Isak Dinesen's *Out of Africa*:

> Here now, as soon as the sun was down the air was full of bats, cruising as noiselessly as cars upon asphalt, the night-hawk swept past too: the bird that sits on the road and in the eyes of which the lights of your car gleam red a moment before he flutters up vertically in front of your wheels. The little spring-hares were out on the roads, moving in their own way, sitting down suddenly and jumping along to a rhythm, like miniature Kangaroos. The Cicada sing an endless song in the long grass, smells run along the earth and falling stars run over the sky, like tears over a cheek. You are the privileged person to whom everything is taken. The Kings of Tarshish shall bring gifts.

This paragraph is unified not only by its images and vivid details, but by its movement: the rhythm of the moving car from which everything is (we feel) observed, and the rhythms of the animals. Even smells "run along the earth."

Another kind of descriptive paragraph, one that can be hilariously funny, is the straight list: of facial expressions in an old photograph, bric-a-brac in a pretentious living room, or whatever. In Thomas Pynchon's novel *Gravity's Rainbow*, we are treated to a picture of Slothrop's desk:

> Tantivy's desk is neat, Slothrop's is a godawful mess. It hasn't been cleaned down to the original wood surface since 1942. Things have fallen roughly into layers, over a base of bureaucratic smegma that sifts steadily to the bottom, made up of millions of tiny red and brown curls of rubber eraser, pencil shavings, dried tea or coffee stains, traces of sugar and Household Milk, much cigarette ash, very fine black debris

picked and flung from typewriter ribbons, decomposing library paste, broken aspirins ground to powder. Then comes a scatter of paperclips, Zippo flints, rubber bands, staples, cigarette butts and crumpled packs, stray matches, pins, nubs of pens, stubs of pencils of all colors including the hard-to-get heliotrope and raw umber, wooden coffee spoons, Thayer's Slippery Elm Throat Lozenges sent by Slothrop's mother, Nalline, all the way from Massachusetts, bits of tape, string, chalk . . . above that a layer of forgotten memoranda, empty buff ration books, phone numbers, unanswered letters, tattered sheets of carbon paper, the scribbled ukulele chords to a dozen songs including "Johnny Doughboy Found a Rose in Ireland," . . . an empty Kreml hair tonic bottle, lost pieces to different jigsaw puzzles. . . .

Not everyone can mount such a dazzling display; and only a brilliant writer, having us on the ropes with "the hard-to-get heliotrope and raw umber," can knock us out of the ring with the totally irrelevant name of Slothrop's mother. But even a writer of modest gifts with a modest subject—your father's poker cronies, your roommate's closet—can use the list to good effect.

Deduction and Induction

When a paragraph (or an essay) begins with a general statement and moves to the particulars supporting it, we call the order of reasoning deductive, from the Latin *deducere*, "to lead out or away." When, on the contrary, a paragraph moves from particular facts or details to a general statement, we call its order inductive. Deductive paragraphs, which begin by asserting a thesis and go on to illustrate or support it, are by far the more common and the easier to write. Here is a good one from Alvin Toffler's *Future Shock*:

> This startling statement [that history is "speeding up"] can be illustrated in a number of ways. It has been observed, for example, that if the past 50,000 years of man's existence were divided into lifetimes of approximately 62 years each, there have been about 800 such lifetimes. Of these 800, fully 650 were spent in caves. Only during the past 70 lifetimes has it been possible to communicate effectively from one lifetime to another—as writing made it possible to do. Only during the past six lifetimes have masses of men ever seen a printed word. Only during the past four has it been possible to measure time with any precision. Only in the past two has anyone anywhere used an electric motor. And the overwhelming majority of all the material goods we use in daily life today have been developed within the present, the 800th lifetime.

Few paragraphs are purely inductive, but our next two examples illustrate the inductive style of movement from the particular to the general. The first is from George Wald's "A Generation in Search of a Future," the second from Dwight Macdonald's *Memoirs of a Revolutionist*. Both begin with a first-person anecdote and end with generalized reflections about the human condition.

How real is the threat of full-scale nuclear war? I have my own very inexpert idea, but realizing how little I know and fearful that I may be a little paranoid on this subject, I take every opportunity to ask reputed experts. I asked that question of a very distinguished professor of government at Harvard about a month ago. I asked him what sort of odds he would lay on the possibility of full-scale nuclear war within the foreseeable future. "Oh," he said comfortably, "I think I can give you a pretty good answer to that question. I estimate the possibility of full-scale nuclear war, provided that the situation remains about as it is now, at 2 percent per year." Anybody can do the simple calculation that shows that 2 percent per year means that the chance of having that full-scale nuclear war by 1990 is about one in three, and by 2000 it is about 50-50.

I remember when Franco's planes bombed Barcelona for the first time what a thrill of unbelieving horror and indignation went through our nerves at the idea of hundreds—yes, *hundreds*—of civilians being killed. It seems impossible that that was less than ten years ago. Franco's air force was a toy compared to the sky-filling bombing fleets deployed in this war, and the hundreds killed in Barcelona have become the thousands killed in Rotterdam and Warsaw, the tens of thousands in Hamburg and Cologne, the hundreds of thousands in Dresden, and the millions in Tokyo. A month ago, the papers reported that over one million Japanese men, women, and children had perished in the fires set by a single B-29 raid on Tokyo. One million. I saw no expression of horror or indignation in any American newspaper or magazine of sizable circulation. We have grown calloused to massacre, and the concept of guilt has spread to include whole populations. Our hearts are hardened, our nerves steady, our imaginations under control as we read the morning paper. King Mithridates is said to have immunized himself against poison by taking small doses which he increased slowly. So the gradually increasing horrors of the last decade have made each of us to some extent a moral Mithridates, immunized against human sympathy.

The deductive paragraph is more natural to the logic of argument. Here is what I think, it says, and here is why I think so. The inductive paragraph is subtler and harder to construct. Its great virtue is that it builds to a climax; it saves its major statement for the end.

Exploration

Some paragraphs are argumentative in an exploratory rather than an assertive sense. They invite the reader to join the writer in examining several sides of a question or thinking something through. Here, for example, is Lillian Hellman pondering the contrast between her fond memory of a girlhood servant and her angry feelings toward her present servant:

> Sophronia was the anchor for a little girl, the beloved of a young woman, but by the time I had met the other, years had brought acid to a nature that hadn't begun that way—or is that a lie?—and in any case, what excuse did that give for irritation with a woman almost twenty years older than I, swollen in the legs and feet, marrow-weary with the struggle to live, bewildered, resentful, sometimes irrational in a changing world where the old, real-pretend love for white people forced her now into open recognition of the hate and contempt she had brought with her from South Carolina.

And here is a Mexican-American student wrestling with the problem of his dual inheritance:

> I was vaguely aware that I was a Mexican-American throughout junior high, because I remember that whenever the terms "meskin" or "spic" or "greaser" were used by my Anglo friends a burst of anger would nearly consume me, but no one ever noticed. I was not angry with my friends, I was angry with the meskins, spics, and greasers because, finally, they were "meskins" and "spics" and "greasers" to me. The constant irritation of their presence drove me to hate them; thus, my assimilation with the Anglos was completed. Why couldn't they be like me, it seemed so simple? They were dirty, and I was clean; they wore shiny black shirts and baggy khaki pants, and I wore light blue, boldly striped, buttoned-down cottons and slim-fitting corduroys; they fought every night with the cowboys, and I played football; they spoke Spanish, and I made A's in English. But their names were Alvarez, and so was mine. I could choose my friends, and my clothes, but I had no choice in my name.

This kind of thinking out loud, of soul-searching, can degenerate into mere confusion. But thoughtful writers find it an excellent way of exploring complicated questions.

Classification

Classification is the breaking down of a subject into its component parts. Here is part of a paragraph from Loren Eiseley's *The Immense Journey*:

> That food came from three sources, all produced by the reproductive system of the flowering plants. There were the tantalizing nectars and pollens intended to draw insects for pollenizing purposes. . . . There were the juicy and enticing fruits to attract larger animals, and in which tough-coated seeds were concealed, as in the tomato, for example. Then, as if this were not enough, there was the food in the actual seed itself, the food intended to nourish the embryo. All over the world, like hot corn in a popper, these incredible elaborations of the flowering plants kept exploding.

This ordering is clearly deductive: the reader is told that there are three items to be discussed, and the items are thereupon discussed. Most readers are grateful to have this sort of road map.

Classification can get you in trouble if you are not careful. Witness the exasperated English railroad porter whose rate-schedule covered only two of three animals presented for ticketing by a traveling family: "Cats is dogs and guinea-pigs is dogs, but this 'ere tortoise is a hinsect!" If you offer a classification, be complete within the limits specified. If like Eiseley you promise three components, deliver three, not two or four.

Comparison and Contrast

Comparison and contrast are among the most effective means of introducing, defining, or clarifying something. If a reader has never seen or heard an English horn but is familiar with the oboe, a comparison of the two instruments may be the best way of telling him what an English horn looks and sounds like. Similarly, in describing a sonata, a writer may find it useful to contrast it with another sonata, or with a concerto by the same composer.

Here Margery Wolf compares Taiwanese mothers and fathers:

> Oddly enough, it is not mother, the most frequent and often the most violent punisher, the children most fear, but father. Ideally, fathers never punish in anger. A child is brought before father as a culprit before a magistrate. An appropriate number of blows is administered—with dis-

approval but without passion. From the looks on the children's faces, these blows are far more painful than mother's in her greatest fury. Mother, of course, encourages this attitude toward father, both as a disciplinary convenience and as a way of strengthening the bonds that unite her uterine family. Father's distance and the fact that *he* can beat mother (and Taiwanese children have witnessed such events) make him appear to be a tremendously powerful being who is known to punish but rarely to pardon. Mother, in contrast, punishes frequently and pardons even more frequently.

Here, in a passage that takes our Alvarez example (p. 71) a step further, Stokely Carmichael contrasts Stokely the unreflecting boy with Stokely the enlightened man, and by implication the black experience of the 1940's with the black experience of the 1960's:

> I remember that when I was a boy, I used to go to see Tarzan movies on Saturday. White Tarzan used to beat up the black natives. I would sit there yelling, "Kill the beasts, kill the savages, kill 'em!" I was saying: Kill *me*. It was as if a Jewish boy watched Nazis taking Jews off to concentration camps and cheered them on. Today, I want the chief to beat the hell out of Tarzan and send him back to Europe.

Definition

Description, classification, comparison and contrast—these and many other ways of ordering are ways of defining as well. Every writer needs to define his terms, to provide working definitions as he develops his theme or argument. What are we talking about? What does it look like? How did it develop? Where is it found? What are its parts? These are just a few of the questions that can lead to paragraphs of definition. Here is such a paragraph by Mark Schorer in an essay on the nature of the novel:

> When we speak of technique, then, we speak of nearly everything. For technique is the means by which the writer's experience, which is his subject matter, compels him to attend to it; technique is the only means he has of discovering, exploring, developing his subject, of conveying its meaning, and, finally, of evaluating it. And surely it follows that certain techniques are sharper tools than others, and will discover more; that the writer capable of the most exacting technical scrutiny of his subject matter will produce works with the most satisfying content, works with thickness and resonance, works which reverberate, works with maximum meaning.

A paragraph of definition need not say everything there is to be said on its subject; if necessary, it can be supplemented or qualified later in the essay. That is what has happened here. Clearly we will need to know a lot more about "technique" before we understand what Schorer means by the term. This paragraph, his second, is only a start; as the essay moves on, other working definitions will finish the job.

There are many other kinds of paragraphs, but the other ordering principles sometimes invoked—exclusion, syllogistic order, cause and effect, and so on—seem to us either matters of common sense or so specialized as to be unhelpful. Indeed, we see ordering principles in general simply as a convenient way of sketching the range of paragraph types, not as a way of consciously constructing paragraphs. Writers do not organize their paragraphs by principle, but by what they have to say. Get your message straight and your paragraphing will take care of itself.

JUDGING A PARAGRAPH

Here is a paragraph from a student paper. Is it a good one?

> Young people have always been rebellious, anxious for change. Presented with a group of problems they are not responsible for, they have a great urge to change things, to make a better world. They have not yet met with the discouraging realities of life and the accompanying loss of idealism. In college one is presented with a unique opportunity to voice views without the fear of recrimination that people with a fixed place in the community have. There is relatively little to lose because no roots have been set down. The college student is not tied to his college as the ordinary citizen is to his community. He has a sense of detachment which may give him the feeling that he can bring about great changes and certainly allows him to attempt this without fear.

The first question to ask is this: Is there a single idea that governs the whole paragraph and makes a unit of it? Can one state it as a thesis sentence? How about "Young people, especially college students, are rebellious because they have less to lose than their more established elders"? Since all seven sentences relate in some way to this idea, it is fair to consider the paragraph a unit. But now comes the second question: Is the paragraph coherent? Here one encounters difficulties. The first three sentences are about young people in general, the last four about college students. Is a connection established between these two worlds? None that can be put in words. The reader is supposed to infer a connection, but can only guess what the writer intended.

This brings us to our third question: Is the reasoning in the paragraph, or the way evidence is presented, sound and convincing? It is not, primarily because the generalizations of the first three sentences are too broad to be defended or, really, understood. Not all young people are rebellious; some are timid, some are indifferent, and some like things just the way they are. And not all rebellious young people are out to make a better world; some are simply neurotic, and some are juvenile delinquents. As for the claim that young people "have not yet met with the discouraging realities of life," what about young people in ghettos or in famine-ridden East Africa? What people are we talking about, anyway? All young people or only some, and if some, which ones?

As the paragraph stands, then, it has a kind of unity, but little coherence. If the writer had begun by saying "Many young Americans are rebellious today" and otherwise qualified his opening remarks, the paragraph would be better, but since its details are nowhere specific and its point is not clear, it would still be boring and vaguely irritating. With all its defects remedied, the paragraph might read like this:

> In America most young people are brought up to believe in change—to believe that next year's model will be better than this year's, that the new math will supplant the old, that because people are growing taller they must be growing better as well. These illusions are reinforced by the behavior of many American adults, who trade in their cars, their jobs, even their wives and husbands, for new models in the recurrent expectation that the new ones will bring happiness. Small wonder that college students are such active seekers of change. Not only are they encouraged by the training and the example of their elders, but they are uninhibited by responsibility to a profession, a family, or a community, and unsobered by the recollection of their own past errors. In theory, at least, they are the perfect revolutionaries.

The revised paragraph has expressed much the same general idea as the original, but its generalizations are rooted in reality, its details are concrete and alive, and its final sentence makes the writer's message clear. And this is the point we have made throughout this chapter: If you have something to say and really want to say it, the chances are that your paragraphs will shape themselves. The person who is full of his subject almost *has* to communicate it clearly and convincingly. That motive in itself tends to be a shaper of good paragraphs.

5

SENTENCES

In this chapter we are concerned with writing good sentences, and in particular with choosing the most effective wording from among two or more equally correct alternatives. This choice is among the most important a writer can make. If you persistently write clumsy or tedious sentences, your readers will weary of your writing and turn elsewhere. If you write good sentences, they will stay with you. Good writers try to hold their audience by the practices set forth in this chapter.

BASIC PREFERENCES

Most good writers agree on five basic preferences:

1. Prefer verbs to nouns.

2. Prefer the active to the passive.

3. Prefer the concrete to the abstract.

4. Prefer the personal to the impersonal.

5. Prefer the shorter version to the longer.

Prefer Verbs to Nouns

New nouns and noun compounds pour into the language daily like so many boulders into a river, until one wonders if they will someday dam the flow forever. From electronics and space technology alone we have thousands of new names for things, ranging from simple compounds like *thermostress* and *countdown,* through contrived acronyms like *sonar* and *laser,* to sodden six- and seven-noun strings like *nozzle gas ejection ship attitude control system.* The effect of these nouns is to displace verbs. We do not begin *to count down* (verb); we begin the *countdown* (noun). We do not have a system by which gas *is ejected* through nozzles *to control* the way an aircraft *orients* itself (three verbs). Instead, we have the monstrosity cited above (seven nouns), from which our only hope of delivery is the equally unacceptable acronym NGESACS.

Indeed, the mere proliferation of new nouns is less alarming than the increasing tendency to overuse all nouns, new and old alike, at the expense of verbs, which give language most of its life and movement. Fifty years ago it would have been natural to write *McCormick also invented a machine for picking corn;* today we incline to write *Another of McCormick's inventions was a mechanical cornpicker.* Fifty years ago, *This book tells you how to promote local sports without spending much money;* today, *The subject of this book is low-budget sports promotion techniques.* The modern versions are heavy and lifeless. Not only have the verbs given way to nouns, but the nouns themselves have lost their color: *corn* is buried in *cornpicker, sports* hangs grayly on a clothesline between abstractions, *money* has disappeared.

One finds writing of this sort everywhere. Scientists and technologists are perhaps the worst offenders, government officials the second worst, but no large class of writers is free of the disease. Here is a sentence from an academic report with its nouns italicized: "There has necessarily been a *tendency* on the *part* of *researchers* to continue *studies* with *equipment* now approaching *obsolescence.*" As rewritten to cut down the nouns: "*Researchers* have necessarily gone on using obsolescent *equipment.*" Here is an Army dispatch: "The enemy has had no *opportunity* to assemble *forces* in sufficient *quantity* to mount an *offensive* against *Danang.*" As rewritten: "The enemy has failed to assemble a big enough *force* to attack *Danang.*"

Nouns are of course indispensable; the problem is to avoid using them at the expense of livelier words. A sentence with too many nouns—and "too many" may usually be defined as one more than is strictly necessary—is slightly harder to read than it need be. Multiply this extra effort by six or eight paragraphs and you have a fatigued reader, which is to say no reader at all.

Prefer the Active to the Passive

The subject of an active verb acts: "Bill *broke* his arm" / "The other child *laughed*." The subject of a passive verb is acted on: "Bill's arm *was broken*" / "The poem *is* highly *regarded* by critics." As the examples indicate, passive verbs always have two components: a form of the verb *be* and a past participle.

Passive verbs tend to yield dull sentences. In each of the following pairs the first sentence is passive, the second active:

> She was not told by anyone.
> No one told her.

> Instincts are explained in strictly molecular terms.
> Luria explains instincts in strictly molecular terms.

> A fair decision was rendered difficult by the judge's evident bias.
> The judge's evident bias made it hard for him to decide fairly.

All three active versions are more forceful and direct. Moreover, there are secondary advantages. In the first example, the active saves two words; in the second, it tells us who is doing the explaining; in the third, it makes for lighter and less formal language. Such advantages are common in switching from passive to active.

Another difficulty of the passive is that it avoids placing responsibility. It presents no subject, no actor, only the action and its object. Typical is the following murky recommendation from a government report: *It is urged that special study be given to the question of how the positive values in migrant life can be exploited in improving the teaching of the migrant child.* Urged, given, exploited by whom? We can only guess. Here are two sentences from student themes:

Frost's work contains much symbolism, symbolism that is strongly felt.

Pathos is aroused at Andrea del Sarto's meek submission to his wife.

By whom, the reader wonders, is Frost's symbolism strongly felt? By Frost? By his readers? By the writer? Whose pathos is aroused in the second example, and by whom or what? The answers to these questions make a difference, but there is no knowing what they are from the agentless passive construction.

To be sure, the passive has its legitimate domain. Sometimes the subject of a verb is irrelevant or too complex to identify: *He will be released from prison tomorrow / Two majors were promoted to lieutenant colonel.* The point is not to avoid the passive altogether, but to use it sparingly. Use the active, with its superior vigor and directness, when you can.

This rule has a corollary: Prefer action verbs to linking verbs, and more forceful action verbs to less forceful ones. Linking verbs are the dozen or so verbs that take nouns or adjective complements as opposed to direct objects; the main ones are *be, become, look, seem, appear, sound,* and *feel.* These pallid verbs, especially *be,* are flourishing as never before in this golden age of nouns. Where once people said *George drives well / George drives a bus,* we now say *George is a good driver / George is a bus driver*; an action verb, *drive,* has dwindled into a noun, leaving the field to the linking verb *is. Is* supplies no motion to a sentence; it is inert, a kind of equals sign between nouns. No writer, of course, can avoid *is* and *are, was* and *were,* but good writers replace them wherever possible with verbs of greater impact. Consider the following alternative versions of a sentence, listed in order of increasing effectiveness:

First verb passive, second verb linking

It *was decided* that changes in the rules *were* necessary.

First verb linking, second verb passive

The decision *was* that the rules *must be changed.*

Action verb and noun

> We *decided* on a *change* in the rules.

Two action verbs

> We *decided* to *change* the rules.

Verbs are the wheels of writing. As they move, so moves the message they carry. If your writing runs heavily to passive verbs and forms of *be*, your wheels will move slowly.

Prefer the Concrete to the Abstract

Concrete nouns stand for things. They are words like *hog, heart, helicopter, Harry*: specific designations for specific entities. Abstract nouns stand for ideas. They range along a spectrum from near-concrete words like *housing* through relatively simple concepts like *sympathy* and *difficulty* to more general terms like *situation* and *socialism*, and on to the formidable abstractions of science and scholarship.

Abstractions are general, intangible, elusive. The human mind works best on particulars: on tangible, finite units. The *poor need better housing* is a simple enough sentence, but no two people can truly agree on its meaning until *better housing* is defined in terms of number of units, size of rooms, rental rates, and so on, and until *the poor* are defined as a particular class of people—for example, families of four or more persons living in New York City with an annual family income of under $5,050. Similarly, *Tom is brave* or *The situation is desperate* makes no sense without particulars. For example, we may know that Tom is brave because he stood up against a bully or saved a child from a fire; the situation may be desperate because enemy tanks are only a mile away or because Dad cannot find a job. In short, to make sense of abstractions we must see them in concrete terms.

Some writers mistakenly feel that abstractions lend tone to writing, that they are more dignified than everyday words like *cat* and *dog*. Others use abstractions to avoid committing themselves to particulars—which means, in effect, to avoid the kind of careful thinking that goes into all good writing. In both cases, the results tend to be vague and irritating, as in these sentences from student themes:

> Other lessons were absorbed through his experiences.

> Attitudes and opinions resulted from these environmental occurrences.

> There is no way to overcome the situation of racial relationships.

The first writer seems to mean simply *He learned other lessons as well,* the second *He got his ideas from what he saw and heard,* the third *There is no way to end racial tensions.* Note that we say "seems to mean"; in none of the three cases can we be sure. It is as if the writer had tried deliberately to keep us guessing.

In general, specific concrete details make for clearer communication; and the more specific, the clearer. Here are our three defective sentences made clear by the addition of details:

> He learned even more from talking with the lumberjacks.

> All he knew about Glasgow was what he could see from his window and what his nurses told him.

> Tensions between whites and blacks are inevitable in a mixed neighborhood.

Whatever the original writers meant, they would have done better to explain their meaning in concrete terms like these. Tell your readers what you mean in words they can understand. If you don't, you will lose their attention.

Prefer the Personal to the Impersonal

Sentences with people in them make more interesting reading than sentences without people. Most sentences have people in them in the nature of things. Others have no people and no room for any: *The water was six feet deep/Transistors have replaced vacuum tubes.* Our concern here is with a third class of sentences, those that can go either way: that is, those whose meaning, though it involves people to some extent, can be expressed clearly and idiomatically either with or without a personal noun or pronoun. Our advice is to put the people in.

The point is illustrated in the following pairs of sentences. In each pair the first is perfectly acceptable but the second is slightly better:

> Basketball requires more stamina than baseball.
>
> Basketball players need more stamina than baseball players.

> What was the casualty count?
>
> How many people were hurt?

It is also a good idea to replace abstractions like *membership*, when used of people, with concrete nouns like *members*, which sounds more human than anything ending in -*ship*. In each of the following pairs, the second sentence is the more effective:

> The leadership was completely replaced last summer.
>
> The leaders were all replaced last summer.

> The medical profession considers the practice unsafe.
>
> Doctors consider the practice unsafe.

The principle extends to more formal writing as well. Here is a passage from a preface to a book of readings:

> Literary criticism as such did not seem useful for the purposes of this book. This is not to denigrate the art of criticism, but only to suggest that literary criticism, to be properly appreciated, must be accompanied by the texts it examines.

Here is the same passage with people in it:

> *We* decided against including literary criticism in this book, not because *we* have anything against it, but because *readers* cannot properly appreciate *a critic's* ideas without first reading the works *he* is writing about.

Putting people in your writing is no different in principle from putting people in a television commercial rather than simply showing a car or a box of cereal and some printed words urging its claims.

People respond to seeing other people doing and saying things. If you want to reach people with what you write, give them people to respond to.

Prefer the Shorter Version to the Longer

Other things being equal, the shorter of two versions is the better. To be sure, other things *must* be equal—that is, the shorter version must convey the same information as the longer, and convey it just as clearly. *The tables were arranged in quincunx fashion* is shorter than *Four tables formed the corners of a square and the fifth was in the middle,* but the longer version will be clearer to most readers. Again, *according to Marcel* is shorter, but may be much less helpful, than *according to the Catholic existentialist philosopher Gabriel Marcel.* Readers for whom *Marcel* would have been enough will not be troubled by the extra words, and other readers will be glad to have them. It is basic good sense (not to mention courtesy) to explain matters that may be unfamiliar to your reader.

The idea of keeping things short is not to reduce all writing to three-word sentences, but to eliminate the redundancies and dead words that so often clog the pipes. Why write *It was Harry who did it* when you can write *Harry did it?* Why write *There is a lot for us to talk about* when you can write *We have a lot to talk about?* What do the extra words add besides deadweight? A few further illustrations may help:

> It was clear to Havlicek on what basis the request for his resignation had been made.
>
> Havlicek knew why they wanted him to resign.
>
> The fact that Susan had made up her mind to leave college was distressing to her parents.
>
> Susan's decision to leave college distressed her parents.
>
> As a result of the labor policies established by Bismarck, the working class in Germany was convinced that revolution was unnecessary for the attainment of its ends.
>
> Bismarck's labor policies convinced most German workers that revolution was unnecessary.

In each of these pairs, the shorter version is only about half the length of the longer. You can often make savings of this order in editing first drafts written at full tilt. But smaller savings than this are also worth making:

There was nothing for Alice to do.

Alice had nothing to do.

Banks in England are more helpful than banks in this country.

English banks are more helpful than ours.

It is predicted in the report that many polluted lakes will be pollution-free by 1985.

The report predicts that many polluted lakes will be pollution-free by 1985.

Of our last eight examples of unnecessarily long sentences, no fewer than five begin with *It is, It was, There is,* and *There was.* No other construction is so alluring to novice writers, perhaps because they mistake its ponderousness for dignity. Sometimes, to be sure, this construction is the best available, as in *It was my fault we lost* or *There was too much to eat.* But more often, as our examples show, *It is* and *There is* commit the writer to an arid sequence of passive or linking verbs and abstract nouns where an active construction would be briefer and more effective. In editing keep an eye out for such sentences. Probably two out of three can be effectively shortened.

Shortening a sentence often improves it in terms of one or more of our other four "basic preferences" as well. The Havlicek revision, for instance, dispenses with three abstract nouns, replaces a linking verb with an action verb, converts a passive construction to active, and adds some people (*they*); these changes, plus a halving of the word count, make a conspicuously better sentence. In the Susan example, and in two of the three shorter examples that follow it, action verbs replace linking verbs. In the Bismarck example, a passive construction becomes active and the nine nouns of the original are reduced to five. Conversely, nearly all the changes recommended under our four earlier headings—that is, changes to make sentences less noun-ridden, more active, less abstract, and more personal—had the additional effect of making the sentence shorter. Clearly the five rules are interrelated, and each reinforces the others.

We conclude this section with a horrendous example of academese from a book on juvenile delinquency:

> Contemporary economic perquisites and differential standards have an important conscious and unconscious effect upon the individual's expectation of what he considers to be his right. If the degree of social permissiveness generally sanctioned for attaining pleasures and status is not adequately available to the less economically or culturally favored, the deprivation begets resentment.

This passage violates every one of our five rules. It is sodden with nouns, all but one of them abstract. Though none of its four verbs is passive, only one, *begets*, has any motion. Its only human component, if human is the word, is a faceless social unit called *the individual*. It is at least a dozen words too long. One can only guess at what it means. Not only does such writing offend the ear and stun the mind; it separates the writer from the specifics that were his original point of departure, in this case the pressure of poverty and powerlessness on flesh-and-blood people.

Our first advice to a beginning stylist is to be honest and unpretentious. Our second advice is to learn the five preferences listed on p. 77 and learn to apply them in practice. They are the very foundation stones of style.

EMPHASIS

Word Order

In writing, as in speech, most sentences follow the natural sequence of ideas in the mind: subject—object—circumstances—afterthoughts. Emphatic sentences, by contrast, are a matter of deliberate artifice. Typically, the chief element to be emphasized is placed at the end; the lesser elements precede it, setting the stage for the main act.

Compare the following versions of the same incident, the first in natural word order, the second with the word order changed to emphasize *sister*:

I started at the noise and looked up guiltily. My sister stood there in the doorway.

I started at the noise and looked up guiltily. There in the doorway stood my sister.

Although, as this example suggests, the word or statement to be emphasized should come at the end of the sentence if possible, you can get the same effect, with somewhat diminished intensity, before a semicolon, a colon, a dash, or even a comma. The emphasis comes from a sort of echo in the moment of silence signaled by the punctuation mark. The stronger the punctuation, the longer the moment; the longer the moment, the more impressive the emphasis. In the emphatic versions of the sentences that follow, the emphasized elements (in italics) come before a period, a semicolon, and a comma, respectively:

Unemphatic

Ellen had her first sight of the sea at 24, after living in Kansas all her life.

Emphatic

At 24, after living in Kansas all her life, *Ellen had her first sight of the sea.*

Unemphatic

He was skinny and weak when I first knew him; today he must weigh 200 pounds.

Emphatic

When I first knew him, *he was skinny and weak*; today he must weigh 200 pounds.

Unemphatic

Lincoln was such a man, it is said.

Emphatic

Lincoln, it is said, was such a man.

Although in these examples the emphatic versions are clearly better at getting the emphasis where it belongs, unemphatic sentences also have their uses. Most are in any case inoffensive, and many are eloquent. Good writers use both kinds of sentence.

Coordination and Subordination

Good writers are careful, however, not to overuse one kind of unemphatic sentence. That is the compound sentence, consisting of two or more clauses joined by coordinating conjunctions, usually *and* or *but*. Sentences of this form have neither the potential elegance and strength of the simple sentence, nor the possibilities of emphasis afforded by the complex sentence. They have an inherently boring symmetry: *John played baseball, and Mary went to the movies.* An occasional sentence of this sort is fine. A sprinkling of them makes for writing that is blander than necessary. A preponderance of them is fatal to good prose.

Lazy writers like the compound sentence because it covers all possibilities without committing itself to any. Does *He was rude and she was angry* mean that his rudeness made her angry, or were their reactions simultaneous, or what? The writer who uses *and* this way saves himself the trouble of deciding and specifying which of these relationships he means, if indeed there is any relationship at all. Here are two typical compound ramblers from student papers:

> I don't think I ever actually talked to him, *but* he was the ultimate symbol of authority, *and* the mere sight of him used to fill me with physical terror.

> The play is very funny *but* it is also sad, *and* one is never allowed to forget the theme.

In the first, there is no *but* or *and* relationship worth the name. Properly reorganized, the sentence becomes two sentences with no conjunctions at all: *He was the ultimate symbol of authority; the mere sight of him used to fill me with physical terror. I don't think I ever actually talked to him.* The second sentence needs subordination of the less important ideas to the more important one: *Funny as the play is, one is never allowed to forget the underlying sadness.* Both writers, by reaching mechanically for their old friends *and* and *but*, have obscured the true relationships between the elements they are relating.

Before you connect two clauses with *and*, stop and think. Is there really any *and* connection at all? Do we need *and* in a sentence like *Steve was a hero-worshiper, and his hero was Terry Bradshaw*, or would a semicolon or a period be enough? Even if there is a legitimate *and* connection, is the *and* construction the best possible, or is one idea in fact subordinate in meaning or importance to the other? Which is better, *Mary went away, and John was unhappy*, or *After Mary went away, John was unhappy*? Most good writers would vote against *and* in both these examples. Write *and* as often as you like in your first draft, but in editing get rid of as many *and*'s as you can.

SOME IRRITATING CONSTRUCTIONS

So far we have been concerned with ways of making writing more lively; in this section we shall consider ways of making it less irritating. Writing can be irritating in many ways: it can be perverse, superficial, dishonest, cryptic, boring, cute. Bad grammar is irritating, so is bad syntax, and so are the various forms of dull writing discussed earlier in this chapter. Our concern here, however, is exclusively with minor irritations produced by clumsy sentence structure in sentences otherwise perfectly acceptable.

We shall consider four irritating constructions: (1) the breaking up of auxiliary verb constructions by obtrusive adverbial phrases; (2) the following of one *but* or *however* with another; (3) the excessive repetition of the same sound or word in a sentence; and (4) false telegraphy, that is, leading the reader to suppose a sentence has one construction when in fact it has another.

Obtrusive Adverbial Phrases

In an auxiliary verb construction like *were doing, have done, has been done*, a simple adverb usually goes between the auxiliary and the verb (We HAVE *always* DONE well) or between the two parts of the auxiliary (It HAS *often* BEEN DONE that way). The same placement works well enough for a short adverbial phrase (We HAVE *at least* DONE our best / It HAS *more often than not* BEEN DONE that way). It does not work at all well, however, for a phrase longer than three or four words, or for a word or phrase of any length that is set off by punctuation. The following examples of obtrusive adverbial phrases progress from least to most irritating:

> The point HAD BEEN *angrily and almost hysterically* MADE.

> The explorers of this terrain HAVE, *as yet,* BEEN few.

> A parallel HAS—*justifiably, I think*—BEEN DRAWN between Ivy Compton-Burnett and Jane Austen.

> I could see that I WAS *one way or the other* GOING to have to spend the evening with Charley.

> The nations of the Third World HAVE, *in the twenty years since the Bandung Conference,* LOOKED in vain for a leader and a program.

The first sentence will pass as it stands but would be improved by joining the verb to its auxiliary: *had been made angrily and almost hysterically.* The word order of the second sentence is fine; we need only delete the commas, which give *as yet* a seemingly pointless and thus irritating emphasis. In the third sentence the emphasis given by the dashes is proper enough, but it comes at the wrong place. Joining the verb to its auxiliary improves things immensely: *has been drawn—justifiably, I think—between.* In the last two sentences the adverbial phrases are too long where they are and should be moved: *I could see that one way or another I was going / In the twenty years since the Bandung Conference, the nations.*

Standard verb-complement constructions may also be disrupted by an obtrusive adverbial phrase, as these examples show:

> The miniskirt is *in the eyes of the fashion industry* a dead issue.

> How many minority group members are *by actual count of the Census Bureau or its state counterparts* on welfare?

> Gambetta's indifference destroyed, *if we can believe Denis Brogan,* what hope there was of a reconciliation.

Each of these italicized intruders—and most adverbial phrases and clauses longer than three or four words—should be put at the beginning of the sentence.

Double But

The double-*but* construction jerks the reader's mind back and forth from *but* to *but* like the eyes of someone watching a tennis game. *However, yet, nevertheless,* and other action-reversing words are as irritating with *but* as another *but* would be. Some examples:

> She wanted to go, *but* her father would not let her, *but* then he changed his mind.

> Earl, *however*, hung back, *but* no one even noticed.

> I was good at translation, *though* my pronunciation was only fair; *however*, I did well on the test.

To repair such a construction, get rid of at least one *but* or *however*. This is sometimes simply a matter of dropping one word of the pair: *Earl hung back, but no one even noticed.* More often, rewriting is necessary:

> At first her father refused to let her go, *but* later he changed his mind.

> Even *though* my pronunciation was only fair, I was good at translation and did well on the test.

The objection to the double-*but* construction applies only when each *but* introduces or governs a complete clause, as in the examples above. In particular, avoid beginning two successive sentences with *but* or the equivalent, as is done in the following passage from a student paper:

> This line of criticism has so far only penetrated the periphery. *But* in the next few years it will undoubtedly be one of the main areas of interest to students of science fiction. *However*, some things stand out at first glance.

Repetition of the Same Sound

Still another kind of doubling irritation comes from the excessive repetition of the same sound within a limited number of words. The repeated sound is typically a suffix or a preposition, as in the following examples:

> For a painter, he works remarka*bly* quic*kly.*

> According to our inform*ation,* accommod*ations* were available only to people with reserv*ations.*

> The thing *to* do was *to* change her strategy *to* adjust *to* the new situation.

> Some *of the* parents *of the* members *of the* club could not be reached.

None of these sentences is impossible, but each can stand improvement. Why not *he is a remarkably quick worker* in the first sentence? In the second, *According to our information* can be changed to *We had heard that,* or *accommodations* to *rooms.* The end of the third can be edited to *was adjust her strategy to the new situation,* the beginning of the fourth to *Some of the club members' parents.*

Of is the most frequent culprit under this heading. When you find yourself writing a sentence with three or more *of*'s, try rewriting it to cut the number down:

> Briffault was one *of* the early popularizers *of* a growing historical awareness *of* the impact *of* Islam on the forging *of* the modern mind.

> Briffault was one *of* the first to popularize historians' growing awareness *of* the large part played by Islam in forging the modern mind.

False Telegraphy

Some sentences confuse the reader by telegraphing one construction and delivering another. Here are a few examples:

> To Germany, France, England, and Russia are natural enemies.

> Reports reached the dean of students arrested for throwing firecrackers at the Governor's limousine.

Mr. Hastings, the vice-chairman, and General Benton were absent.

I said that Tuesday was impossible, not every Tuesday.

In the first sentence, the reader infers a series of four; this does not work, and he has to reread the sentence carefully to discover that it breaks after *Germany*. In the second, the reader mistakenly makes a unit of *dean of students*. In the third, is Mr. Hastings the vice-chairman or are they two different men? In the final sentence, the writer means "I said [that] that [particular] Tuesday was impossible, not [that] every Tuesday [was impossible]." The most adroit reader would have trouble extracting this meaning from the sentence as it was written.

False telegraphy is easy enough to fix; the problem is to spot it. It helps if you can put your paper aside for a while between first draft and final typing. After a day or so, you can approach your own writing as another reader might, critically and with a fresh eye. If you find a sentence baffling at first—however momentarily—so will other readers, and revision is accordingly in order.

HOBSON'S CHOICES

Thomas Hobson was an irascible Englishman of Elizabethan times who rented horses to travelers on the condition that they take the horse he chose for them or none at all. Since his horses were a sorry lot, "Hobson's choice" has come to mean a choice between alternatives all of which have serious drawbacks.

Confronted by a Hobson's choice between a technically correct sentence that sounds awkward and a good-sounding sentence that is technically deficient, many students resignedly opt for one or the other without reflecting whether there may be some third alternative that is neither awkward nor unsound. Consider the following sentences:

Either you or I *(are) (am)* wrong.

There was a furor about the Undersecretary of *(State) (State's)* not being invited.

Willie Mays was as good an *(outfielder)* *(outfielder as)* or better than Joe DiMaggio.

"Th' expense of spirit" is one of the best, if not the best *(sonnet)* *(sonnets)* ever written.

Bohr thought of Einstein as much a friend *(as)* *(as as)* a teacher.

In each of these sentences, the first alternative listed is the more natural or unobtrusive, but is technically defective; the second is better technically, but is rhetorically ugly. A Hobson's choice, then, but with one important difference: Hobson's customer had to choose between the alternatives offered him, and we do not. Why confine ourselves to the possibilities in parentheses? Why not rewrite the sentence to get around the difficulty?

Either you are wrong or I am.

There was a furor when people learned that the Undersecretary of State had not been invited.

Willie Mays was at least as good an outfielder as Joe DiMaggio.

"Th' expense of spirit" is one of the best sonnets ever written, maybe even the best.

Bohr thought of Einstein not only as a teacher, but as a friend.

Don't just give up and allow an awkward sentence to stand. If a sentence is intractable on its own terms, choose other terms. If you find yourself wound up in a construction you cannot handle, choose another construction, one you are more at home with. The language is flexible; it has many ways of saying what you want to say. Why run into a wall when you can walk around it?

6
WORDS

Writers choose words in a context, not in a vacuum. They do not ask whether one word is "better" than another, but which word will make their tone right, their meaning clearer, their sentence leaner and more effective. What they are looking for may be not a word but a phrase, or an image, or even a whole new idea. Yet in the end it comes down to choosing words. In this chapter we shall examine the main principles (other than immediate context) affecting that choice.

To choose words well you need to know a lot of them, to have a vocabulary that offers alternatives. Building a vocabulary is sometimes presented as a matter of learning fancy words like *stipulate* and *indubitable*. We think of it rather as mastering a number of slightly different words for the same general meaning, of not always having to write *quiet* when in some contexts a better word might be *silent*, *tranquil*, or *calm*. The only way to build a good vocabulary is by reading good writing: not comic books or sports pages, but serious writing for adults. Whether your taste runs to Shakespeare, Gloria Steinem, or *Scientific American* does not matter, so long as you read attentively and often.

USING THE DICTIONARY

Any discussion of diction must begin with the dictionary, a book whose formidable appearance needlessly frightens many students. To use a dictionary well, you need only learn the half dozen or so conventions illustrated and discussed in this section. Other, less important, conventions you can learn as needed with the help of the brief explanations at the front of every dictionary.

> ¹de·lay \di-'lā\ *n* **1 a :** the act of delaying : the state of being delayed **b :** an instance of being delayed **2 :** the time during which something is delayed **3 :** a football play in which an offensive back delays momentarily as if to block and then runs his prescribed pattern
> ²**delay** *vb* [ME *delayen*, fr. OF *delaier*, fr. *de-* + *laier* to leave, alter. of *laissier*, fr. L *laxare* to slacken — more at RELAX] *vt* **1 :** to put off : POSTPONE <decided to ~ our vacation until next month> **2 :** to stop, detain, or hinder for a time ~ *vi* **1 :** to move or act slowly **2 :** to pause momentarily — **de·lay·er** *n* — **de·lay·ing** *adj* **syn** DELAY. RETARD. SLOW. SLACKEN. DETAIN *shared meaning element* **:** to cause to be late or behind in movement or progress *ant* expedite, hasten

By permission. From *Webster's New Collegiate Dictionary*, copyright © 1973 by G. & C. Merriam Company, Publishers of the Merriam-Webster Dictionaries.

The entries for the word *delay* shown above appear in *Webster's New Collegiate Dictionary* (1973). The first entry, ¹**de·lay**, is for the noun *(n)*; the second, ²**delay**, is for the verb *(vb)*. The dot between *de* and *lay* in the first entry indicates that *delay* may be divided at this point if it comes at the end of a line. The notation \ di-'lā \ is the standard pronunciation; the exact weight of *i* and *ā* and the meaning of ¹ are explained on the dictionary's endpapers. The information in brackets is the standard derivation of the word: through the Middle English verb *delayen* from the Old French *delaier*, a compound of *de-* and *laier*, "to leave," which in turn derived, through its alternative form *laissier*, from the Latin verb *laxare*, "to slacken." By convention, when there are separate entries for the noun and verb forms (or whatever) of a single word, the word break, pronunciation, and derivation indications are given only once.

The entry ²**delay** has two major divisions, *vt* and *vi*. *Vt* stands for "verb, transitive," the kind of verb that takes a direct object: *He delayed his decision / The soldiers delayed the train.* *Vi* stands for "verb, intransitive," the kind of verb that does not take an object: *Even when urged to hurry, they delayed.* Two derivative forms, the noun *delayer* and the adjective *delaying*, are listed without definitions, since their meaning can be unmistakably inferred from what precedes. Finally, we are given four synonyms *(syn)* and two ant-

onyms *(ant)* of the transitive verb *delay,* the small capitals for the
synonyms being a conventional signal to the user to look up the definitions of these words if he is not sure which of them will best serve
his purpose.

The previous edition of *Webster's New Collegiate* included in the
delay entry itself separate synonymies for the transitive and intransitive forms:

> **syn** DELAY, RETARD, SLOW, SLACKEN, DETAIN, mean to cause to be
> late or behind in movement or progress. DELAY implies a holding
> back, usu. by interference, from completion or arrival; RETARD
> applies chiefly to motion and suggests reduction of speed without
> actual stopping; SLOW and SLACKEN both imply also a reduction of
> speed, SLOW often suggesting deliberate intention, SLACKEN an
> easing up or relaxing of power or effort; DETAIN implies a holding
> back beyond a reasonable or appointed time
> **syn** DELAY, PROCRASTINATE, LAG, LOITER, DAWDLE, DALLY mean to
> move or act slowly so as to fall behind. DELAY usu. implies a putting
> off (as a beginning or departure); PROCRASTINATE implies blame-
> worthy delay esp. through laziness or apathy; LAG implies failure to
> maintain a speed set by others; LOITER and DAWDLE imply delay
> while in progress, esp. in walking, but DAWDLE more clearly suggests
> an aimless wasting of time; DALLY suggests delay through trifling or
> vacillation when promptness is necessary

By permission. From *Webster's Seventh New Collegiate Dictionary,* copyright © 1967 by G. & C. Merriam Company,
Publishers of the Merriam-Webster Dictionaries.

For space reasons the 1973 edition eliminated such synonymies
except for a very few words "believed to present special problems,"
e.g., *gaudy, penitence, relinquish,* and their near-synonyms. If you
need help, as most of us do, in distinguishing between pairs like
illusion and *delusion, financial* and *fiscal,* a good dictionary is *The
American Heritage Dictionary of the English Language* (1969).

The boldface numbers in the *delay* entry indicate the various definitions of a word. In *Webster's New Collegiate* and most other dictionaries, the sequence of definitions is strictly historical. That is, sense 1
of a word is neither necessarily better (in any way) nor necessarily
more often encountered than sense 2; it simply entered the language
earlier than sense 2. Most such decisions are based on historical examples presented in the greatest of all dictionaries, the *New English
Dictionary on Historical Principles* (1884–1928), reissued in thirteen
volumes in 1933 as the *Oxford English Dictionary* and known famil-
iarly as the OED. Approximately one-fifth of the OED entry for
delay and its derivatives is shown on page 98.

College students rarely have occasion to consult the OED, and
many can go for months at a time without consulting its nearest
American equivalent, the 2,662-page, 13-pound, 4-inch-thick *Webster's Third New International Dictionary* (1961), with its 450,000
entries and its controversial hands-off approach to status labels. Your

1. *trans.* To put off to a later time ; to defer, postpone. † *To delay time* : to put off time.

c **1290** S. *Eng. Leg.* I. 87/30 And bide þat he it delaiȝe Ane þreo ȝer. **1297** R. Glouc. (1724) 513 Me nolde nouȝt, that is crouninge leng delaied were. **1393** Gower *Conf.* III. 290 For to make him afered,The kinge his time hath so delaied. **1489** Caxton *Faytes of A.* I. xxii. 68 To delaye the bataylle vnto another day. **1586** B. Young *Guazzo's Civ. Conv.* IV. 181 b, Delaie the sentence no longer. **1594** West *2nd Pt. Symbol.* Chancerie § 140 Who .. with faire promises delaied time, and kept the said C. D. in hope from yeare to yeare. **1611** Bible *Matt.* xxiv. 48 My Lord delayeth his comming. **1737** Pope *Hor. Epist.* I. i. 41 Th' unprofitable moments .. That .. still delay Life's instant business to a future day. **1821** Shelley *Prometh. Unb.* III. iii. 6 Freedom long desired And long delayed. **1847** Grote *Greece* I. xl. (1862) III. 433 He delayed the attack for four days.

b. with *infin.* To defer, put off.

a **1340** Hampole *Psalter* vi. 3 How lange dylayes þou to gif grace. **1611** Bible *Ex.* xxxii. 1 When the people saw that Moses delayed to come downe. **1799** Cowper *Castaway* v, Some succour. .[they] Delayed not to bestow. **1847** Tennyson *Princ.* iv. 88 Delaying as the tender ash delays To clothe herself, when all the woods are green.

† c. With personal object : To put (any one) off, to keep him waiting. *Obs.*

1388 Wyclif *Acts* xxiv. 22 Felix delayede hem. **1512** *Act* 4 *Hen. VIII,* c. 6 § 2 If..the same Collectours .. unreasonably delay or tary the said Marchauntes. **1530** Palsgr. 510/1, I delaye one, or deferre hym, or put hym backe of his purpose. **1639** Du Verger tr. *Camus' Admir. Events* 88 It was not fit shee should delay him with faire wordes. **1768** Blackstone *Comm.* III. 109 Where judges of any court do delay the parties.

2. To impede the progress of, cause to linger or stand still ; to retard, hinder.

1393 Gower *Conf.* III. 261. Her wo to telle thanne assaieth, But tendre shame her word delaieth. **1634** Milton *Comus* 494 Thyrsis ! whose artful strains have oft delayed The huddling brook to hear his madrigal. **1709** Steele *Tatler* No. 39 ⁋ 4 Joy and Grief can hasten and delay Time. **1813** Shelley *Q. Mab* II. 197 The unwilling sojourner, whose steps Chance in that desert has delayed. **1856** Kane *Arct. Expl.* II. xv. 161 To delay the animal until the hunters come up.

3. *intr.* To put off action ; to linger, loiter, tarry.

1509 Hawes *Past. Pleas.* xvi. lxix, A womans guyse is evermore to delaye. **1596** Shaks. 1 *Hen. IV,* III. ii. 180 Aduantage feedes him fat, while men delay. **1667** Milton *P. L.* v. 247 So spake th' Eternal Father .. nor delaid the winged Saint After his charge receivd. **1850** Tennyson *In Mem.* lxxxiii, O sweet new-year delaying long..Delaying long, delay no more.

b. To tarry in a place. (Now only *poetic.*)

1654 H. L'Estrange *Chas. I* (1655) 3 Paris being .. in his way to Spain, he delaid there one day. a **1878** Bryant *Poems, October,* Wind of the sunny south ! oh still delay, In the gay woods and in the golden air.

c. To be tardy in one's progress, to loiter.

1690 Locke *Hum. Und.* II. xiv. § 9 There seem to be certain bounds to the quickness and slowness of the succession of those ideas .. beyond which they can neither delay nor hasten.

own abridged dictionary, whether *Webster's New Collegiate* or another, should be sufficient for most uses.

A dictionary will answer a thousand questions if you will only ask them: on spelling (*indispensible* or *indispensable*?), on pronunciation (*boo-kay* or *bo-kay*?), on word breaks (*plea-sure* or *pleas-ure*?), on definitions (what does *strophe* mean?), on the choice of words (*compulsory* or *obligatory*?), on the choice between different forms of a word (*dwelled* or *dwelt*?), on levels of usage (can I call someone a *hophead* in a term paper?), on any subject having to do with the form, meaning, and status of words.

Or for that matter on their very existence. Students tend to invent words that do not exist, often by false analogy to another word; we have seen in student papers such inventions as *appropriacy* (cf. *intimacy*), *happenstantial* (cf. *substantial*), and *sensical* (cf. *commensensical*). A look at the dictionary would have spared the writers these errors. So also if the student who wrote that President Ford had *received a vendetta to deal with the oil crisis* had looked up *vendetta*, he might have found his way, if not to *mandate*, at least out of trouble.

Modern dictionaries do more than define ordinary lowercase words. They list common abbreviations, offer basic geographical and biographical information, and present other material as well, either in the main alphabetical sequence or in separate sections at the end. The dictionary may not be the liveliest book around, but to the writer—any writer—it is by far the most useful. Keep one on your desk, and use it.

THE CHOICE OF WORDS: MEANING

Connotation

A word's connotations are the associations it evokes. These associations, which may or may not be well enough established at a given time to rate dictionary notice, are of several types. Some are simply echoes of one of the word's other established meanings: this is why the Tenth Commandment's injunction not to covet our neighbor's ass evokes snickers today. Others are historical associations: *escalate*, for example, formerly a neutral word coined to describe the motion of an escalator, took on connotations of planned violence when journalists and others applied it to American policy in Vietnam. Still others are social: thus *square*, in the sense of a person seen as offensively conventional, carries a connotation of rejection by the young.

Still others originate in the marketplace. A faculty committee report criticizing students for seeking "instant poetry, instant psychoanalysis, and instant mysticism" by experimenting with drugs uses *instant* in the sense of instant coffee, instant cake frosting, and other such ersatz products. The idea is that instant poetry and the rest are not only too quickly come by but second-rate.

Thus a new combination of words creates a new idea, a new impression, a new meaning. Human experience and history and literature are always doing this to words. *Collaborator,* from *co-* (with) and *labor* (work), once meant simply one who worked together with someone else; later the word came to be restricted largely to literary work, and still later it acquired the unpatriotic connotation of working willingly with the enemies of one's country. Thanks in part, perhaps, to the Women's Christian Temperance Union, *temperance,* which once meant nothing more than moderation in speech and conduct, has come to connote not only abstinence from liquor but an offensively high-minded moral strictness.

Euphemism

Euphemism—calling things by prettied-up names—is another force for change, especially when it comes to unglamorous or undignified jobs. Thus dogcatchers in some New Jersey towns have rebaptized themselves *animal custodians,* technical writers in the electronics industry are commonly called *publications engineers,* and lifeguards in Long Beach, California, are officially *marine safety officers. Employment* itself, once a euphemism for *job* or *work,* has apparently become a dirty word in California, where the former Department of Employment has been renamed the Department of Human Resources Development.

The essential thing about euphemisms is that they seek to lend dignity to some function or cause. Though most are harmless enough, some bear the taint of an unworthy origin and are best avoided: thus *inoperative* for *untrue, inner city housing* for *slums, air support* for *saturation bombing of civilians,* and the like deserve no place in honest writing. Use euphemisms if you must, but don't let them take you in. Good writing seeks the truth about things, even painful things; euphemisms seek to hide it.

Connotation and the Dictionary

Time and accident corrode words, change them, encrust them with connotations. The dictionary sometimes spells these connotations out, either by adding them as new denotations ("**square** . . . **8:** a person who is overly conventional or conservative in taste or way of life"), or by adding qualifying phrases to existing denotations ("**collaborate 1:** to work jointly with others esp. in an intellectual endeavor"), or by labeling a word slang, substandard, archaic, or what have you.

Often, however, the dictionary is no help. *Webster's New Collegiate*, for example, gives no hint that *switch-hitter* is widely used to mean someone sexually active with both sexes, or that to *stonewall* (*"chiefly Brit:* to engage in obstructive parliamentary debate or delaying tactics") has a connotation of barefaced lying under oath. It has no entry at all for *bottom line*, referring to the net gain or loss that appears at the end of a financial statement, a term frequently used by businessmen to mean hard facts or realities and by their detractors to deride an insensitivity to problems other than financial. When it comes to new words and new combinations and uses of old words, the ponderous process of lexicography is no match for the lightning leaps of the language.

So the dictionary can sometimes help, though the main burden of getting connotations straight falls squarely on the writer's experience and observation. We have no advice to offer here except to keep your eyes and ears open. If you don't know exactly what a word means but think it may give offense, you presumably refrain from using it in a conversation with your friend's mother. Do the same in your writing. Try to use only words whose connotations you feel confident you understand. If you are moved to use other words as well—and of course you will be and should be—see who else is using them and how they are being used, in conversation, in lectures, in what you read. There is no need to use them in writing until you have made them your own.

THE CHOICE OF WORDS: STATUS

Standard and Nonstandard English

One of the most important aspects of connotation is status. A word's status has no necessary connection with its meaning: there are "respectable" words for nonrespectable things, and nonrespectable words for respectable things. For example, in the sentence *I was snowed*, the word *snowed* has the perfectly respectable meaning "overwhelmed," perhaps by someone's good looks or suave approach. And yet the connotations of *snowed* make it less than perfectly respectable; it is a teenage word, suitable for casual teenage conversation or a letter to a friend but too colloquial for formal writing. *Overwhelmed* has the opposite connotation; one rarely hears the word spoken, but it is acceptable in formal use as *snowed* is not. One word is acceptable spoken English, at least for teenagers; the other is acceptable written English.

How do such distinctions come about, and what are we to make of them? They come about naturally rather than artificially. New words are introduced into the language to denote new things, new ideas, new shades of meaning; and immediately people face a choice between the new word and whatever word or phrase was used to express roughly the same idea before. Some new words are accepted immediately: *television* is an example. Others are accepted after a brief struggle with an existing equivalent (*radio* versus *wireless*) or with an alternative new word or form (*automation* versus *automatization*). Still others spend years in colloquial status before they win formal acceptance: the word *swamped*, in the sense "overwhelmed with work," ran this course many decades ago. Finally, some words—for example, the names of such ephemeral dances as the *frug* and the *watusi*—never rise beyond colloquial status and ultimately drop from the language altogether.

At any given time, then, the language consists broadly of two kinds of words, those acceptable for formal use and those acceptable for informal use only, plus a borderland of words on probation. By formal use we mean primarily serious expository writing, though the term extends to public speaking, business letters, and so on. Whether a word is acceptable or unacceptable for formal use is determined by a consensus of educated persons, as evidenced in what they write and read. Formerly, dictionaries signaled this consensus by status labels. Standard English was unmarked; nonstandard English was marked *colloq.*, *slang*, or the like, or left out of the dictionary as trivial, ephemeral, or vulgar. *Webster's Third* startled everyone by omitting these labels as too crude to capture the complexities of usage and too vulnerable to unpredictable changes in our language habits. But people wanted status labels despite these irrefutable arguments against them, and more recent dictionaries, notably the *American Heritage Dictionary*, have not followed Webster's lead.

Nonstandard English as subdivided by *American Heritage* embraces four main status categories: NONSTANDARD, chiefly well-established errors like *disinterested* for *uninterested* and rusticisms like *anyways* and *ain't*; INFORMAL, words used in "the speech of educated persons when they are more interested in what they are saying than how they are saying it," e.g. *mad* for angry, *gripe* for complain; SLANG, words designed "to produce rhetorical effect, such as incongruity, irreverence, or exaggeration," e.g. *junkie* for heroin addict, *broad* for woman; and VULGAR, words like *shit* and *fuck*. All words in the first category, nonstandard, can be dismissed as unacceptable in writing, except of course in dialogue, with which we are not concerned here. The other three categories are discussed at greater length in the following pages.

Contractions

Contractions like *don't* and *can't* are now used freely in all but the most formal writing: *They don't make cars the way they used to / Sometimes you just can't win / Let's face it.* No one with an ear for idiomatic English would write *Sometimes you just cannot win* or *Let us face it.* Yet only in dialogue, if there, would a good writer write *Dr. Blake's an eye specialist* or *That'd be a foolish thing to do.* Why?

We're not sure. What is clear is that contractions have risen in status with the present trend toward a more informal written English. If the trend continues, *Dr. Blake's an eye specialist* may someday seem as standard as *It's better that way* or *What's the difference?* Until then follow your ear. If something sounds right either way, we prefer the spelled-out form.

Abbreviations

The abbreviations *Mr.*, *Mrs.*, *Dr.*, and *Ms.* are standard in front of a name; do not spell out *Doctor*. You may use abbreviations and acronyms *(IBM, GHQ, UNESCO)* in formal writing if you observe three conditions. First, make sure your readers know what they stand for, since abbreviations familiar to you may be Greek to others. When in doubt, spell things out the first time: *gross national product (GNP)*. Second, keep the incidence of abbreviations as low as you can, since pages bespattered with clusters of capital letters are uninviting. Write *United States* or *American* rather than *U.S.*, and *Soviet Union* rather than *U.S.S.R.* Write *electrocardiogram* rather than *EKG*; and before using *ICBM* for a second time, see whether plain *missile* will serve. Third, avoid headlinese. *LBJ* for *Lyndon B. Johnson*, *GOP* (Grand Old Party) for *Republican*, and *GM* for *General Motors*, however indispensable to headline writers, have no place in formal expository writing. The same goes for common-noun abbreviations like *P.O.* for *post office* and *TV* for *television*.

Shortenings and Simplified Spellings

"Shortenings" is the term used in Wilson Follett's *Modern American Usage* for words like *quote* (for *quotation*), *recap* (for *recapitulate* or *recapitulation*), *photo, exam, psycho, grad, lab,* and *prof,* all of which Follett properly considers unsuitable for formal writing. Some shortenings have become standard; we no longer think of *bus* as short for *omnibus, coonskin* for *raccoon skin,* or *taxicab* for *taximeter cabriolet.* Those that have not become standard should be avoided.

Another form of shortening is simplified spelling. Spelling reformers from the time of George Bernard Shaw and Theodore Roosevelt to the present day have affected such simplified spellings as *tho* and *thru*; advertisers have offered us *lo-cal* and *lo-fat* food and *U-Haul* trailers; restaurants serve *donuts, ham 'n' eggs,* and *leg o' lamb*; high schoolers fill their letters and diaries with *'cause, alrite,* and *tonite.* What slight appeal these forms may have soon wears thin; only a few, e.g. *rock 'n' roll* and *hi-fi,* have become standard.

Clichés and Vogue Words

Clichés are commonly stale metaphors (see p. 122), expressions like *bite the bullet, can of worms,* and *eyeball to eyeball,* words like *crucial* and *thrust.* Vogue words and phrases tend also to be metaphorical but have the additional characteristic of having achieved prominence from their conspicuous use in some area of public interest or concern. Thus in the 1960's we had the computer people's *input* and *interface* and President Kennedy's *missile gap,* which gave rise to *generation gap, credibility gap,* and other gaps; the early 1970's brought us crisis phrases like *population explosion, green revolution,* and *double-digit inflation.* Both clichés and vogue words are typically standard in denotation; their connotations are what make their status questionable.

Some clichés and vogue words go on to become permanent parts of the language in their vogue sense, but most soon lose their original aptness and linger on as favorites of the insensitive and the uninformed. Everyone uses some vogue words, but good writers keep the number small by scrutinizing their words for wrong connotations or shades of meaning, or for excessive vagueness. Must this unpleasant experience, they ask, be called *a bad scene,* this enjoyable opera or picnic be described as *out of sight,* these new circumstances summed up as *a whole new ball game?* Hasn't the time come to give up *for real* (as in *Is he for real?*) and go back to *real,* to forget about *put it all together* and use standard English for whatever it means? That is the good thing about standard English: it can say what you mean if you let it, rather than what somebody else once said about something else. And that is why good writers are wary of vogue words.

There are vogue suffixes as well as vogue words, notably in recent years *-ize, -type,* and *-wise.* Some words in *-ize* are clearly here to stay: *winterize, Americanize, tranquilize.* Others—among them *concertize, accessorize,* and *slenderize*—have been accepted by Webster but are not used in formal writing by most educated people. A good rule is to use only such words with this suffix as have no ready equivalent, and to coin no new ones.

As for *-type,* in such expressions as *hose-type apparatus* and *California-type sunglasses,* it should be restricted to supply sergeants and commercial travelers. Good writers shun the construction as vulgar; bad ones embrace it as a way of sounding authoritative without the labor of fully articulating their meaning. The reckless addition of *-wise* to nouns to form adverbs (*saleswise, percentagewise, footballwise*) is in the same class.

Slang and Vulgar Words

Some student writers pepper their themes with current slang like *uptight* for antagonistic or conservative, *rip off* for steal or cheat, and *gross* for offensive, unpleasant, or unattractive. The effect is not so much vigorous as noisy and shallow. These are vogue words as surely as the kind just discussed—as ephemeral in their power to differentiate, as sure a sign of a stereotyped world view. Just as a word like *finalize* signals the routine-bound bureaucrat or Army officer, so a word like *dig* for comprehend or enjoy signals the perennial sixteen-year-old.

An occasional well-chosen slang expression is all right, especially if no standard equivalent comes to mind; but a lot of slang, like a lot of any other kind of cliché, shows us that the writer's mind is not on his work. Use slang in speaking with your friends; everyone does. Use it if you like in your notes to yourself, as the writer of the research paper discussed in Chapters 13 and 14 used *pot* for *marijuana* on his note cards. But when you are performing for a serious audience, put away your tin piano and use the Steinway.

Vulgar words do not shock; they bore. Used well in dialogue, as in certain modern movies, they are helpful in evoking character, and we may all rejoice that the former ban on their use no longer exists. But they have no place in expository prose, being at once overemphatic and maddeningly vague. What is meant by *The Chancellor's so-called "program" is a lot of liberal bullshit*? The writer clearly disapproves of the program, but we have not the foggiest notion why; what is worse, his words suggest that he himself cannot explain why and is raising his voice to hide his confusion.

Terms designedly offensive to a given race, sex, occupation, or other large class of people should also be avoided. No college student today would refer to a black as a *nigger* or an Italian as a *wop*, but some see nothing wrong with writing *queer* for *homosexual* or *pig* for *policeman*. *A visible tension built up between the pigs and the demonstrators,* writes a Japanese-American girl who sympathized with the demonstrators. But are policemen any more *pigs* than she is a *broad* or a *gook*? Disparaging terms like *pig* not only assert a doubtful claim to ethical superiority but implausibly impute evil characteristics to a whole class of which the writer can know at most a few members. Readers respond not by endorsing the writer's values but by writing him off as a bigot.

Status and the Dictionary

Dictionaries like *Webster's Third International* and *Webster's New Collegiate,* which keep status labels to a minimum, offer a writer little help in distinguishing standard from nonstandard. They omit vulgar words and label blatant slang, but offer no clue that a sentence like *Bob's yapping about commies drives me nuts*, which no English teacher in the United States would accept, is other than impeccable English.

Dictionaries with status labels are more helpful on this point. To take the sentence just cited, for example, the *American Heritage Dictionary* labels *yap* and *nuts* slang and *commie* "informal." Yet the use of such labels raises almost as many questions as it answers. How, for example, did *American Heritage* decide that *booze* was informal and *hooch* slang? *Dad* informal and *pop* standard? *Bite the dust* standard and *kick the bucket* slang? Sentences every bit as bad as our Webster example would be accepted as standard by *American Heritage* definitions: for example, *The Indians laughed when that schnook Custer bit the dust* and *The D.A. put the screws to the chintzy bugger*.

Some of the *American Heritage's* pronouncements may be idiosyncratic to its publisher's region (New England) or to its editors' social class or other characteristics. But the main problem with status labels is that words' statuses keep changing. Yesterday's illiteracy *(presently* for *now)*, yesterday's genteelism *(perspire* for *sweat)*, yesterday's new word *(smog, polyester)*, yesterday's slang *(joyride, hippie)*, are today's standard English. Not only that, but yesterday's standard English, in a new meaning, may be today's slang: thus *split*, to leave in a hurry; *freak*, an enthusiast; *swinging*, lively and up-to-date. A dictionary cannot encompass this ceaseless flux. It is like a photograph of a stream; by the time the film is developed, the water and some of the pebbles have moved.

Whatever the dictionary may say, then, in the end the writer must choose. He should write standard English when he can, if only because the other kinds are more likely to irritate and puzzle some of his readers. Yet the distinction between standard and nonstandard, important as it is, should not be made too much of. If slangy writing has its faults, so has the other extreme: *I freaked out* may offend, but *My reaction was intense* will as certainly bore. Vigorous writing has the accents and rhythms of speech; so far as possible, it should have the words natural to speech.

This is not to say that you should simply define as standard whatever words you feel comfortable with. If you feel that a certain nonstandard word ought to be standard, that only stuffy people are against it, you may be right, and ultimately your opinion may help to form the subtle consensus that changes a word's status. But until that time proceed with caution. A distinction between words is like a legal distinction: it may be unjust or obsolete, its repeal may be imminent, but while it is on the books a prudent person will observe it.

THE CHOICE OF WORDS: IDIOM

Idiomatic and Unidiomatic English

Idiomatic English is English as reasonably well-educated native speakers speak it. Native speakers have far less trouble writing idiomatically than foreigners who learn English as a second language. We do not have to learn, for example, when to say *the* and when to omit it in everyday expressions: we learn as children that people go *to the* movies but go *to* church, that people watch television but listen to *the* radio. There is no rational basis for these distinctions, just as there is no reason why an expression like *the heat of the battle* should have vanquished *the ardor of the combat* or *the passion of the struggle*. The language has simply come in the course of time to favor one form over another. The efficiency of this process is its own excuse. By learning the idiomatic forms of the more common expressions as children, we clear our minds of the many thousands of rejected alternatives with which the uncertain foreigner must grapple.

The difficulty comes with the less common expressions. Everyone knows that we say *bad weather* rather than *ill weather*, but should we say *bad omen* or *ill omen*, *bad tidings* or *ill tidings*, *bad health* or *ill health*? Should we describe Grandma as *kind*, *kindhearted*, or *kindly*? Does one *make*, *take*, or *reach* a decision? Does one differ *with* or *from* someone, and is one's view then different *from* or *than* his? More than one of these alternatives may be acceptable. What is important is not so much to find "correct" answers to questions of this sort as to ask the questions in the first place—that is, to have some sense of the alternatives and not settle for a lazy first stab.

The following sentences illustrate only a few of the many possible kinds of errors in idiom (corrections in parentheses):

Rousseau's argument was the opposite to Hobbes's. (*of*)

The need of action should have been apparent (*need for*; or *necessity of*).

When we finished sweeping the sidewalk, we considered the job as done. (*considered the job done*; or *regarded the job as done*)

Most importantly of all, the Giants' shortstop was ill. (*important*)

She confessed to have seen neither accident. (*to having seen*)

The Tonkin Gulf Resolution made a mountain of a molehill. (*out of*)

Trivial as such errors are, they are irritating, and they are also hard to avoid. The only defense against them is attention. Read a sentence over. If it sounds wrong, even though you cannot say exactly how, switch to a more manageable construction. For example, if you are uneasy with both *opposite to* and *opposite of* in the first sentence, try *Rousseau and Hobbes presented opposite arguments*; if you are not sure what is wrong with *confessed to have seen,* try *confessed that she had seen.* No one alive has a complete mastery of English idiom at the *opposite to / of / from* level. It is plain common sense to stick as much as possible to constructions that you know are idiomatic.

Clichés are another form of idiom. If you use one, you must get it right. *Skating on thin ice* is merely boring; *treading on thin water* is embarrassing. Errors of this sort often come from merging two expressions of roughly the same meaning. Two examples collected by Theodore Bernstein are *left out in the lurch* (merging *left in the lurch* and *out in the cold*) and, incredibly, *Senator Long lowered the whistle on McCarthy* (merging *lowered the boom* and *blew the whistle*). Use *hammer and tongs* if you must, or even *hook, line, and sinker,* but be more careful with your clichés than Senator Hubert Humphrey was when he told supporters that he believed in going at politics *hook and tong.*

For more subtle questions of word choice—for example, between *kind* and *kindly,* between *informer* and *informant,* between *evoke, extract,* and *elicit*—the synonymies in a dictionary are often helpful. So are the dictionaries of English and American usage discussed on p. 259. Still another useful book is a thesaurus, which gives synonyms and near-synonyms for all the most common nouns, verbs, adjectives, and adverbs. If you cannot think of precisely the right word but can think of a word meaning roughly the same thing, a thesaurus will probably lead you to the word you want.

Standard and Nonstandard Idiom

So far we have considered only the idiom of standard English. There are many other idioms—among them black English, Appalachian English, show biz English, sports page English—and language egalitarians have argued that none of them, including standard, is any better than the others. If a black student writes *My mother she live in Detroit now,* or a sportswriter *Csonka got popped good,* don't we know what he means? And if we know what he means, why shouldn't he write whatever he likes?

Why indeed? Nonstandard idioms are often strong in ways standard English is weak. Harlem's speech is looser and more vigorous than Wall Street's, Ozarks language more down to earth than Berkshires language. Nonstandard can be fun: fun to speak and fun to write. And it can get effects beyond the reach of standard, as in this choice example from Edwin Newman:

> As a veteran I was in an army hospital in 1947, and a fellow patient asked me what another patient did for a living. I said he was a teacher. "Oh," was the reply, "them is my chief dread." A lifetime was summed up in those six syllables. There is no way to improve on that.

But equality is another matter. A kind of equality is at work in the case of our sportswriter, who may well have deliberately chosen nonstandard English over standard (*Csonka was hit hard*) to score points with his audience and who can easily switch to standard when he writes for a different audience. But what of our black student, who may not have that option? To our mind, telling him to be satisfied with writing what amounts to a dialect is to deliver bad advice. Of course he has a "right" to his own language, but to combine that right with a refusal to learn the language of the culture, however oppressive, is in our opinion self-defeating.

The writer of a nonstandard idiom gets in trouble when he gets beyond his own limited circle. Though others may understand what he writes reasonably well sentence for sentence, any major departures from their own idiom, or minor departures in large numbers, will ultimately set up that buzzing in the ears that is fatal to communication. What at first may have struck readers as fresh and colorful in the end seems wearisome, if not downright alienating.

Indeed, alienation may be part of the writer's intention, since shutting out outsiders is one of the big attractions of nonstandard idioms. As Edwin Newman puts it, "To choose a lower order of speech is, I suppose, antiestablishment in motive and carries a certain scorn for organized, grammatical, and precise expression. Object to it and you are likely to be told that you are a pendant, a crank, an elitist, and behind the times." Jews use Yiddish terms, blacks use black English, teenagers use pop-culture slang, partly as a way of saying We are different, we are better.

All this can be good fun. It also has its serious side, especially for people who need to define who they are and what they stand for: thus a black minister speaking to his congregation or an editorial writer for *Muhammed Speaks* might reasonably use black English.

But simply to equate nonstandard with standard as a means of communication is a serious mistake. Standard idiomatic American English is the language of opportunity in the United States: the language of congressmen and actors, novelists and newspapermen, engineers and teachers and businessmen—of all but a handful of people who have done anything important or stand a chance of getting anything important done. The problem is not political or linguistic but personal, a problem of self-fulfillment. Ghetto kids, rednecks, foreign-born Americans, and others who can handle standard English have options they would not have without this skill.

Whether these options are important is a matter of opinion, but to us they seem all-important. That is why we think standard idiomatic English should be taught and nonstandard idioms discouraged in the classroom. The charms of nonstandard English—and they are many—remain available for informal speech or writing, and its most appealing words and devices, as suggested earlier, have a way of becoming standard. If standard English were as hard as Latin, and the rewards for learning it as uncertain, the egalitarians might have a point. As it is, we recommend sticking with the system.

THE CHOICE OF WORDS: PRECISION

The Complete Plain Words (1973) gives the three basic rules of good writing as follows:

> Use no more words than are necessary to express your meaning, for if you use more you are likely to obscure it and to tire your reader. In

particular do not use superfluous adjectives and adverbs and do not use roundabout phrases where single words would serve.

Use familiar words rather than the far-fetched, if they express your meaning equally well; for the familiar are more likely to be readily understood.

Use words with a precise meaning rather than those that are vague, for they will obviously serve better to make your meaning clear; and in particular prefer concrete words to abstract, for they are more likely to have a precise meaning.

The first rule, which has little to do with the choice of words as such, we discuss elsewhere (pp. 84-86 and 131-133). The second is illustrated by two examples of writing about computers cited in *The Complete Plain Words*:

> Using the indexed sequential method on an exchangeable disc, the time involved in accessing a record by searching several levels of index and seeking index, data, and overflow areas can amount to well over 200 msec. It is possible to improve upon these timings by systems optimization.

> Further, if the atmosphere is too dry, paper tape may become brittle and cards may shrink and curl; when the air is too damp, cards may expand and jam the reading devices.

A computer itself would be daunted by the first of these examples. The second, which does its work with familiar words like *shrink, curl, damp,* and *jam,* puts the novice at his ease without offending the professional. Bringing your reader into the picture by using words he knows can be an important part of making your meaning clear.

The third rule, "Use words with a precise meaning," is violated in the following sentences:

> The authorities took favorable action on the proposal.

> Our whole program will be affected if any further difficulties develop.

> The situation required Engel to seek financial help.

What have we been told? Vague, abstract words like *authorities, affected, develop,* and *situation* do not clarify meaning but obscure it. To some writers—notably those who are trying to deceive us, sell us something, or allay our anger—obscurity may have its uses. But to the honest writer there is no substitute for the precise word and the necessary detail. If *the situation* can be described, describe it. If *difficulties* means a cement workers' strike, or the likelihood of a riot, or too little money, say so. People conventionally observe a certain decorum in sex and bathroom matters; but these aside, your job as a writer is to say as well as you can exactly what you mean.

The three rules come down to a simple piece of advice: Think about your words. Be on the lookout especially for the colorless but insidious three- or four-word phrase that has elbowed out a perfectly good single word or shorter phrase of the same meaning: *climate of opinion* for *opinion*; *put within the framework of* for *relate to*; *in this day and age* for *today*. George Orwell, in his splendid essay "Politics and the English Language," is succinct on this point: "Prose consists less and less of *words* chosen for the sake of their meaning, and more and more of *phrases* tacked together like the sections of a prefabricated hen-house." He goes on:

> A scrupulous writer, in every sentence that he writes, will ask himself . . . Could I put it more shortly? Have I said anything that is avoidably ugly? But you are not obliged to go to all this trouble. You can shirk it by simply throwing your mind open and letting the ready-made phrases come crowding in. They will construct your sentences for you—even think your thoughts for you, to a certain extent—and at need they will perform the important service of concealing your meaning even from yourself.

Orwell's concern was with English politics of the 1940's; he feared that corrupt language would lead to corrupt government. Newman makes much the same point about the United States of the 1970's:

> Something drastic is needed, for while language—the poor state of language in the United States—may not be at the heart of our problems, it isn't divorced from them either. It is at least conceivable that our politics would be improved if our English were, and so would other parts of our national life. If we were more careful about what we say, and how, we might be more critical and less gullible. Those for whom words have lost their value are likely to find that ideas have also lost their value. Maybe some people discipline themselves in one and not the other, but they must be rare.

This is not professor talk: Orwell was a radical writer, Newman is a television reporter. What they are saying is that if you are sensitive to the meaning of words, whether your own or others', you will make better political choices—elect, if you will, fewer Nixons and more Lincolns. We think they are right.

In the last three sections we have discussed the three main considerations other than meaning affecting the choice of words: status, idiom, and precision. A word like *hangup* may be precise and idiomatic in context, but is unacceptable on status grounds. A word like *badly* is standard and may be precise enough, but is unidiomatic after *feel*. A word like *modernization* is standard and idiomatic, but may be insufficiently precise. Of the three qualities, the most important is precision. Making your meaning clear comes before writing idiomatically and using words of irreproachable status—provided, of course, you are not so unidiomatic or slangy that your meaning never gets through. If you have built your hen-house right, people will not worry much about an occasional flaw in the paint job.

7

IMAGERY

The comedian Shelly Berman once described a hangover in these terms: "My left eyeball has a headache, my tongue's asleep, and my teeth itch." The effect of this sentence depends upon images, in this case bizarre images. By attributing familiar sensations to unlikely parts of the body, Berman obtains some surprising effects. He not only makes us laugh, he gives us a new sensory experience (or the memory of an old one). We are not just told about the hangover, we feel it. Our response to this image is not the same as the actual physical experience, any more than grief felt in reading a story is the same as real grief, but it is a good approximation of reality. In imagination, we have had a hangover.

Images can do such things. They invite us into experience; they do not keep us at a distance, as mere definitions or explanations often do. They communicate the sounds, tastes, smells, sights, colors, and tactile feelings of life. Images are not just figures of speech, though they usually appear in this form; they are all those means whereby sensory experience is conveyed in language. Our senses do not report to us on "justice" or "beauty" or "the gross national product"; these abstract concepts are derived from thought, from ratiocination, rather than from direct experience. Images tell us about the smell of a flower, the beauty of the sound of music, the fear of death. They refer to that immediacy of experience where we live and move and have our being.

This is not to say that imagery is unconnected with abstract thought; on the contrary, it is often the best possible way to make difficult abstractions clear, especially to a lay audience. Thus an atomic physicist will say: "Just as a coal fire needs oxygen to keep it going, a nuclear fire needs the neutrons to maintain it." A biologist explaining spectroscopy to lay readers: "Just as in a crystal chandelier the sunlight is shattered to a rainbow, so in the spectroscope light is spread out in colored bands." A political analyst: "It is as sensible to combat communism by military means as to combat malaria by swatting mosquitoes." A great poet and moralist: "No man is an island entire of itself; every man is a piece of the continent, a part of the main."

The greatest of all English poets, seeking to convey the patriotism of the venerable John of Gaunt in *Richard II*, does so almost entirely in images. Gaunt, near death, speaks of the country he loves:

> This royal throne of kings, this scepter'd isle,
> This earth of majesty, this seat of Mars,
> This other Eden, demi-Paradise;
> This fortress built by Nature for herself
> Against infection and the hand of war;
> This happy breed of men, this little world;
> This precious stone set in the silver sea,
> Which serves it in the office of a wall,
> Or as a moat defensive to a house,
> Against the envy of less happier lands;
> This blessed plot, this earth, this realm, this England.

COMPARISON AND ANALOGY

Definition and Examples

Imagery evokes comparisons, implied or explicit. "He wormed his way into her good graces" sets up an implicit comparison between a man's insinuating tactics and the movement of a worm. "The batter fanned" compares the batter's futile swing to the motion of a fan, which touches only air. And so it is with the data that are *fed in* to a computer, the ship that *plows* the sea, the market that *nosedives*, the teacher who is *snowed under*, the business that stays *above water*, the effort that gets *sandbagged*, the man who is *cowed*, the driver who *rides* the clutch. All evoke comparisons with familiar acts or things.

It is useful here to distinguish between analogy and true comparison. "That man is a rat" is an analogy; "Hitler was a greater tyrant than Mussolini" is a comparison. In the first, two dissimilar things, a man and an animal, are being compared; in the second, two men are being compared. Analogies ask our emotional assent to similarities between two wholes: a man and a rat, war and hell, property and theft. Comparisons ask our intellectual attention to literal and particular similarities or differences. If I compare John F. Kennedy and Richard Nixon as statesmen, I will compare specific and parallel aspects of their statesmanship, such as their success in handling international affairs or in protecting civil liberties. But when Shakespeare asks in a sonnet "Shall I compare thee to a summer's day?" he has no literal or intellectual comparison in mind: to compliment his lady he invites us to see her as possessing, indeed surpassing, the beauty, warmth, and luxuriance of summer.

Analogies that are just and fresh not only delight but clarify, emphasize, instruct—even win arguments. The best are unanswerable. Mrs. Thrale once remarked to Samuel Johnson that a certain young woman would be terribly unhappy to hear of a friend's losing an estate she had long expected to receive. "She will suffer as much, perhaps," replied Dr. Johnson, "as your horse did when your cow miscarried."

Misuses of Analogy

Analogy can be tricky. The Vietnam War, for example, was at one time widely justified by the so-called domino theory, which held that unless Chinese expansionism were stopped in Vietnam, the other countries of Southeast Asia would fall to the Communists like a row of standing dominoes when the first one is knocked into the second. "Domino theory" is a striking phrase, simple and visual; it reduces a most complex issue to terms a child can understand. But is the anal-

ogy true? Are nations really comparable to dominoes? Will they fall
in the same mechanical way when pushed? Why didn't England fall
like a domino before German pressure in 1940? If the analogy is false,
the argument is false.

Does this matter? It depends on how the analogy is used. Literal
truth is not always an issue. Shakespeare's sonnet is no less effective
for the omission of mosquitoes, Dr. Johnson's remark no less compelling for his ignorance of the lady's true thoughts. A lawyer can be an
"ambulance chaser" —that is, someone who makes capital of other
people's disasters—without having ever chased an ambulance. And
who cares if the person who defined a camel as "a horse designed by
a committee" was harder on committees than they deserve?

The trouble comes when an analogy is presented as part of a logical argument, as the domino theory often was in the 1960's. If you use
an analogy this way, as a building stone in a larger argument, you
forgo the poet's right to indulgence. The analogy must be demonstrably sound on all relevant points, the stone able to bear the weight you
put on it. Many faulty analogies pass for true, usually by suggesting
that their two elements are literally comparable when they are not.
Uncle Harry may be a rat, but it does not follow that he can live on
an ounce of cheese a day. The only defense against this sort of thinking is the kind of dogged scrutiny illustrated in the following passage,
in which Julian Huxley examines an analogy supporting the assertion
that God rules the universe:

> I believe this fundamental postulate to be nothing more than the result
> of asking a wrong question: "Who or what rules the universe?" So far as
> we can see, it rules itself, and indeed the whole analogy with a country
> and its ruler is false. Even if a god does exist behind or above the
> universe as we experience it, we can have no knowledge of such a
> power; the actual gods of historical religions are only the personifica-
> tions of impersonal facts of nature and of facts of our inner mental life.

SIMILE AND METAPHOR

Simile

Most figures of speech, and most of the examples given so far in
this chapter, are either similes or metaphors. On a superficial level it
is easy to distinguish between the two. A simile is an explicit compari-

son or analogy using *like, as, compared with,* or the equivalent. Here are some examples:

> The gray chill seeped into him like water into sand.
>
> WILLIAM FAULKNER

> Almost without exception, the men with whom I worked on the assembly line . . . felt like trapped animals.
>
> HARVEY SWADOS

> The female body, even at its best, is very defective in form; it has harsh curves and very clumsily distributed masses; compared to it the average milk-jug, or even cuspidor, is a thing of intelligent and gratifying design.
>
> H. L. MENCKEN

These similes serve in various ways to clarify, to satirize, to dramatize, to support arguments. Faulkner's visual image makes us feel the penetration of the chill; one sensory impression is used to emphasize another. Swados uses his simile to back up an argument; Mencken uses his to start one. All these similes, and 99 percent of all successful similes, are short, simple, and clear. They make their point without straining (whether you agree with them or not), and are free from self-contradiction.

Student writers sometimes have trouble on this last point, as the following examples illustrate:

> Macbeth struggled like a man in a whirlpool formed partly by nature, partly by the witches, and partly by his wife.

> The radio quiz show is like a vast technical jungle that is intent on making itself a pleasant form of gambling.

> The film *Cinderella Liberty* lacks credibility and becomes analogous to an attempt at squeezing emotions from the only dry towel left in a sinking ship.

In all three examples the idea is lost in the strained and overcomplex image. No whirlpool was ever so formed, no jungle so inclined, no towel the object of so ludicrous an endeavor. However clear and just these images may have seemed in the writers' minds, they appeared out of focus on the written page.

Metaphor

In metaphor, *like* and *as* are omitted and the comparison is asserted as an identity; the gap between the things compared is virtually closed. Instead of saying "He's like a jackass," we say "He's a jackass." Instead of saying "The raindrops are coming down *like* pitchforks," we say "It's raining pitchforks." George Orwell, in reviewing Salvador Dali's *Life*, writes: "Dali is even by his own diagnosis narcissistic, and his autobiography is simply a strip tease act conducted in pink limelight." "*Like* a strip-tease act" would have been far less forceful.

A remark of James Baldwin, "I have discovered the weight of white people in the world," is a more complicated metaphor, one that works partly as a literal statement and partly as a play on words. White people, the oppressors, are *like* a weight on the backs of black people; but Baldwin is also using *weight* in the sense of weighty people who make weighty decisions, people with the power to push other people around. When the poet Theodore Roethke, in the course of recovering from an illness that was both physical and mental, wrote "I'm sweating out the will to die," he condensed to one sentence a complex experience: he is saying that the physical "sweating" of his fever is like the figurative "sweating out" of his psychological crisis. When Jesus spoke to the crowd in the Sermon on the Mount, he spoke almost entirely in metaphors, drawing upon their enormous dramatic power to drive home his meaning:

> Ye are the salt of the earth: but if the salt have lost his savour, wherewith shall it be salted? . . . Ye are the light of the world. A city that is set on an hill cannot be hid,

The "bandwagon approach" in advertising, the Iron Curtain in contemporary history, the Oedipus complex in psychology—all these terms are metaphors used as shorthand for more or less complex ideas. Terms like these lighten both the writer's burden of explanation and the reader's burden of understanding by calling on familiar associations already in the reader's mind. More sustained metaphors can yield even greater gains in conciseness, as these examples show:

> The government [is] like an immense, somnolent animal that cannot twitch its toe unless it first moves twenty other parts of its body. And before it can do that, it has to undertake a laborious task of self-inspection. It must notice that its tail is tangled in its rear legs and unwind it; it must cure its right front foreleg of that tendency to move backward whenever the left foreleg moves forward; and, at the end, it must probably take one extra foot, whose existence it had forgotten, out of its mouth. By the time it has finished this process, the animal is often too tired to twitch its toe—if it can even remember that this was its original intention.
>
> CHARLES FRANKEL

> The economic system of orthodox economics had been a machine built by the "divine watchmaker," hence without friction and in perpetual motion and perpetual equilibrium. Keynes's system was a clock, a very good and artful clock, but still one built by a human watchmaker, and thus subject to friction. But the only actions required of the watchmaker were to wind, to oil, and, where necessary, to regulate the clock. He was not to run it; he was only to make it fit to run itself; and it was to run according to mechanical laws, not according to political decisions.
>
> PETER F. DRUCKER

Student writers who attempt such metaphors sometimes end up hanging by one leg from a dry towel in a sinking ship. Like any other skill worth mastering, using metaphors well takes practice; and timid or incurious writers may prefer to stick to safer ground. But the serious writer, aspiring as serious writers do to find unity or truth in a universe of bits and pieces, knows better. "Like and like and like— but what is the thing that lies beneath the semblance of things?" asked Virginia Woolf. There are some truths that only metaphor can reach; whatever that ineffable "thing" may be, it will be expressed (if it is expressible at all) as a metaphor.

MISUSES OF METAPHOR

When metaphors are used well, they call attention less to themselves than to the meaning they carry. When they are misused, they are conspicuous and often absurd. Three errors in particular should be avoided: stale metaphor, mixed metaphor, and inappropriate metaphor. By stale metaphor we mean tired or dead images; by mixed metaphor, combinations of incompatible images; by inappropriate metaphor, images that are likely to make readers uncomfortable.

Stale Metaphor

Imagery, as we have seen, should evoke comparisons in which one element helps to clarify the meaning of the other. Some images, however, no longer have this power. "The field of medicine," for example, no longer calls to mind a piece of land. What was once a living image is now moribund, a cliché without grace or force. Yet such images hang on, and in the hands of thoughtless writers yield sentences like this: "Graphic arts first attracted his attention, but he was soon seduced by a more lucrative field." This writer has lost sight not only of what a field is but of what seduction is. Our language is full of such stock comparisons: "His mind is like a steel trap," "We got down to brass tacks," "Moving to Florida gave them a new lease on life." Images of this sort are all more dead than quick. Writers who habitually rely on such hoary phrases are letting dead people do their thinking for them.

Even worse are those weary old saws that many people confuse with wisdom. Take, for example, the old standby "Where there's smoke, there's fire." When Senator Joseph McCarthy claimed in 1950 that there were 205 Communists in the State Department, many people swore that there was truth in his assertion because—naturally—"Where there's smoke, there's fire." Yet in this instance it would have been truer to say "Where there's smoke, there's a smoke screen."

Mixed Metaphor

A mixed metaphor, says Peter Elbow, is "never bad because it's mixed, only because it's badly mixed," and on early drafts he encourages writers to mix away. He's right; metaphors are evidence that the imagination is at work, and should be encouraged. But when it comes to revision, writers should be critical.

A metaphor is said to be mixed when its components do not add up to a consistent and plausible whole, but instead clash with each other, often ludicrously. Sometimes the literal meaning of a stale metaphor conflicts with its new context. Thus we find "Gubser, with his profitable garlic farm, is in clover," or even "I'd give my right arm to be ambidextrous."

People who write like this are using metaphors without remembering the pictures they were created to evoke. "The sole aim of a metaphor," writes George Orwell, "is to call up a visual image." Orwell was wrong to exclude the other senses, but right to insist on the importance of the visual. The man who wrote "The house system must be geared into the whole teaching arm of the university" was not seeing straight, and thus not thinking straight. Gears do not mesh into arms. And we find such blindness in the highest places. Here is the superintendent of the Chicago public schools: "With limited resources at his command, each youth must meet and conquer his own Achilles' heel." Here is the former Lieutenant Governor of California: "Because of energy shortages, the Arab nations have the upper hand and are using oil to line their pockets." And here is Richard Nixon at a press conference of May 1971: "We have some cards to play and we intend to play them to the hilt." Such errors have a close family likeness to Theodore Bernstein's mixed clichés (see p. 109).

Collecting mixed metaphors is a mean-spirited indoor sport of editors and English teachers, and should probably be discouraged. Still, who could resist the following howlers collected from student essays and exams?

I have come to the point where I must cease casting anxious eyes about, wondering which path in life will be presented to me on a silver platter.

Since Kafka was imbedded in the ice of many frustrations, he naturally formulated ideas for dynamiting the ice.

But as soon as we draw back to define our own conclusions about these novels, a gnawing dissatisfaction, a vague worm of discontent, peeks its head above the back of the tapestry.

Had Jude become a curate, he would have been able to ensconce himself in the pillows of thought, locating himself in an environment designed to cultivate and mature the intellectual seeds which Jude himself planted in his own mind.

What is a young man of this day and age to do, with the octopus of Communism spreading its testicles all over the face of the earth?

The desire is monomaniacal, reaping, if not suicide, at least the stagnant, self-polluting backwaters of nihilism.

By no means all mixed metaphors are as funny as these. Indeed the typical mixed metaphor is not funny at all, just slightly wrong, like these two from essays on Claude Brown's *Manchild in the Promised Land*:

Our social taboos frown on the free give-and-take as Mr. Brown describes it in Harlem.

Many foundations of today's need for racial justice in America are echoed in Claude Brown's book.

Taboos do not frown, and foundations are not echoed. The meaning of these sentences is reasonably clear, but their effectiveness is diminished by the use of metaphors that set off a buzzing in the reader's brain.

Sometimes, of course, metaphors can be deliberately mixed for humorous or other purposes. The student who wrote "Jane Austen is intent on carving her little piece of ivory until the blood runs" mixed a metaphor with happy results, as did a harassed administrator when he remarked, "The sky is dark with chickens coming home to roost." And Sir Walter Scott, in *The Heart of Midlothian*, has Reuben Butler, a dour old puritan, mix a metaphor with spectacular effect. Butler is referring to his son's fitness for the ministry:

I will make it my business to procure a license when he is fit for the same, trusting he will be a shaft cleanly polished, and meet to be used in the body of the kirk; and that he shall not turn again, like the sow, to wallow in the mire of heretical extremes and defections, but shall have the wings of a dove, though he hath lain among the pots.

Wyndham Lewis in *The Apes of God* got a suitably ironic effect by describing a character as possessing "foundations of energy, of the sort that do not grow on every tree." And we are indebted to a newscaster (who may not have been trying to be funny) for "The United Steelworkers will get down to brass tacks today."

Sometimes, too, well-known metaphors can be turned inside out to good effect. It has been said of Henry James, for example, that in writing at great length about small matters "he chewed more than he bit off." And Oscar Wilde once threw new light on the old biblical injunction by saying, "If a man smite thee, turn the other face."

Inappropriate Metaphor

Finally, there is the question of taste. As Keats once said, we hate writing that seems to have a "palpable design" upon us. We turn away from writing marked by excess; we are annoyed, or provoked to laughter, by signs that the writer is working too hard. The excessive or tasteless use of metaphor can give this effect. Take this sentence: "The conscience of man takes precedence in the logistics of American action; it is the silk thread shining through the hair-shirt of our native literary search." Military images and images of sin vie for our attention; the metaphor is not exactly mixed, but it is too rich to swallow. In rejecting a metaphor of this kind, of course, a reader rejects the message as well.

Another kind of error in taste may be illustrated by a prayer, wholly in metaphor, offered by an Oregon minister at a meeting called to promote a golf tournament. The following excerpt is representative:

> Thank you, O God, for Jesus Christ our pro, who shows us how to get the right grip on life, to slow down in our back swing, to correct our crazy hooks and slices, to keep our head down in humility and to follow through in self-control.
>
> May He teach us also to be good sports who will accept the rub of the green, the penalty for being out-of-bounds, the reality of lost balls, the relevancy of par, the dangers of the 19th hole and the authority of our special rule book, the Bible.
>
> And Lord, when the last putt has dropped into the cup; the light of our last day has faded into the darkness of death; though our trophies be few, our handicap still too low and that hole-in-one still only a dream; may we be able to turn in to You, our tournament director, at the great clubhouse, an honest scorecard.
>
> Through Jesus Christ we pray, Amen.

No student would be guilty of such an effort. Yet it is not entirely unlike what many beginning writers try to do—or find themselves doing. It is easy, once a metaphor gets started, to keep it rolling; what is hard is to keep it from rolling off the tracks. Taste in these matters cannot be dictated; it must be felt. But when in doubt, remember Jesus Christ our pro and keep your metaphors short.

8
EDITING

Learning to write is essentially a process of modifying the spoken language, with its natural redundancies and imprecisions, to meet the requirements of another medium. Our first drafts usually yield a kind of written talk. They need to be reconsidered, revised, perhaps condensed or expanded, if their full meaning is to come through. If the revising is left undone, or done badly, the result is at best ineffectual and at worst embarrassing—in a colleague's phrase "the puerile glop that bubbles off the top of your consciousness." Good writing makes people feel or think what the writer wants them to think. First-draft writing, whether puerile or just wordy or dull, usually makes people yawn.

The process of making writing more effective is called editing. All book and magazine publishers assign editors to manuscripts, and newspapers have editors to edit the raw writing of reporters for clarity and consistency of style. College students, having no such help available, must be both author and editor, both writer and rewrite man.

Editing has two functions: to correct and to improve. Correcting has to do with errors of grammar, syntax, punctuation, and so on, and with basic clarity at the sentence level and below. These matters are discussed at length in Part 3 and concern us only incidentally in this chapter. Our concern here is with ways of improving writing, of giving it grace and impact. Dull writing or first-draft writing may be errorless and clear. What it usually is not, and what editing seeks to make it, is readable.

Editing, in our sense of the word, is the last stage of writing. It begins after you have done the hard work of thinking your argument through and getting its elements down on paper in a sequence you think makes sense. It may well take you two drafts just to get some sort of focus to your paper, and a third to work out a sequence you are happy with.° However many drafts it takes, only at this point are you ready to begin editing.

THE NATURE OF EDITING

In deciding what to write about, what to say about it, and what material to present in what order, you have no audience but yourself. This private communion ends when you have a draft ready for editing. Now the time has come to consider how readers will respond to your words.

To edit your writing effectively you need perspective. One good idea is to do something else for a while, so that you can come back to your paper more or less as a reader will come to it: fresh, unbiased for or against, ready to listen. Ideally you should put a piece of writing aside for at least several days—the Roman poet Horace recommended nine years. If your schedule allows no time for such luxuries, shorten the interval, but try not to eliminate it. If you can separate writing and editing by as little as a night's sleep, or even a meal or a game of tennis, you will do a better job of editing than you would after no interval at all.

An even better way is to read your paper aloud, preferably to a roommate or a friend. In matters of rhythm, or even in matters only tenuously connected with rhythm, the ear can sometimes hear what the eye cannot see—that a sentence is too complicated for a reader to take in, or too feebly related to another sentence, or ugly or pompous-sounding or just plain silly.

° An excellent account of this difficult process will be found in Peter Elbow, *Writing Without Teachers* (New York, 1973), especially Chap. 2.

Reading aloud works best with a listener or two, since most of us are sensitive to criticism from others, including unspoken criticism, and since such criticism is likely to tell us more than our own biased promptings. A listener may have an unexpected suggestion: "I wish you had put in more about your crazy aunt." Or a question about something you thought you had made clear: "What did he do with the other boat?" Sometimes a listener's comment will lead to a discussion that ends up clarifying in your own mind what you want to say. But even the most superficial remarks from a listener you respect are valuable assets when you sit down to begin editing.

Alternatively, of course, you can read your paper aloud to yourself, or tape-record it and play back the tape, or read it silently but try to sound the words in your mind. Whatever you do, if something sounds wrong—even if you don't know why—throw it out or find some other way of putting it. Conversely, what your ear tells you is good probably *is* good. If something sounds exactly right when you say it, it will usually pass muster on paper.

Over and above any time you spend getting perspective, you must leave yourself time to do the editing itself. You cannot edit a five-page paper in half an hour; if you try, you will skimp on something important. Nor can you edit under pressure, or while trying to use part of your mind for something else. Maybe you can bat out first-draft material with the radio on, or even do a final typing in a room full of people talking, but editing needs your undivided attention. In editing you have to ask yourself how well a sentence or a paragraph is likely to work for the reader, whether its meaning will be clear, whether it can be made clearer or stronger, what kinds of change might help. If you are pressed for time or distracted, you will be tempted to get the job done by leaving passages intact that you would have done better to rewrite or throw out.

Throw out: there is the heart of it. Nothing is more important to good editing than ruthlessness in eliminating the unnecessary. If your draft makes five pages and your editing cuts it to four, you are doing fine. Some students find this hard to believe. Because it takes more time and labor to write five pages than to write four, they figure the extra labor should earn them extra credit. But writing doesn't work that way. One paragraph that will interest readers deserves far more praise than five that won't—or twenty, or a thousand. Quantity is nothing in writing. Quality is everything.

THREE EXAMPLES

We give an example of editing in Chapter 4, pp. 74-76. In this section we give three more, in each instance following a defective original with an edited version. These originals are all drafts, the first two ready for editing, the third in need of further work before the editing stage. Each edited version is prose—not the prose of a Hemingway or a Churchill, but a kind of writing that is within the reach of any student willing to take the trouble. Our first example is noisy: like a child, the writer tries to get our attention by yelling rather than by talking sense. Our second example is the opposite: lifeless, drowned in a tub of words. Our third example is perhaps the most typical of student writing: interesting material that has not yet jelled.

Example 1

Here is a paragraph from a freshman theme about an essay by George Orwell:

> The descriptions in this essay are incredibly graphic. I was carried along from one beautifully written paragraph to the next, and I was horrified by some, disgusted by others, but I was always amazed by how close the writer's experience had been to mine. After I had finished reading this essay, though, I was in an exceedingly dismal state of mind, recalling how bleak my own childhood had been and realizing that others were the same.

This paragraph is irritating. Its adverbs are too frequent and intense, its two long sentences are poorly constructed, it lacks detail, and its messages conflict. The writer seems simultaneously impressed with Orwell's writing ability, disgusted and horrified by the incidents Orwell describes, amazed at the parallel with his own experience, and plunged into gloom by recalling that experience. Nonsense, says the reader: the mind is no such four-ring circus. One of these emotions we might have believed, or two in sequence; but not all four at once.

Let's get rid of these difficulties and see what happens. Let's bring on the circus acts one at a time, and leave the main act on longest. Let's cut down on the adverbs, tighten up the rambling sentences, and replace empty general words like *descriptions* and *experience* with specifics. With these changes made, our paragraph might look like this:

> Orwell's essay helped me to see my own boarding-school days in perspective. Crossgates and my school were very similar: the snobbery, the concern with money, the sexual anxiety, the obsession with sports. Perhaps all boarding schools are like that; at all events, Orwell helped me to see for the first time that I had been one of many victims. Others were just as timid, just as withdrawn. Dozens of my schoolmates must have suffered as I did, and for as little reason.

This paragraph is not perfect prose, but it has risen above mere writing. It has authority: the writer has understood Orwell's experience and related it to his own. It is spare: there are no gratuitous intensifiers like *incredibly* and *always*, no functionless words like *reading*, no ambiguous words like *others*. It offers details: not "the writer's experience," but snobbery, money, sexual anxiety, sports; not mere bleakness, but persecution for being timid and withdrawn. Finally, it has a rhythm or pace that puts the rambling original to shame.

Reading aloud would almost surely have helped this writer, even if no one else was around. If he had listened to himself as he read, he might have rewritten his long, shapeless second sentence into something more easily grasped; and he might have toned down such over-intense words as *disgusted* and *amazed*.

Example 2

Here is another paragraph in need of improvement:

> There is not very much to be said in favor of the argument that the right to vote in elections should be dependent on residence in a community for a period of at least six months. The living patterns of the American people at the present time are not the same as those of fifty or a hundred years ago, at the time of the passage of the laws that established the six-month residence requirement. There is much more changing of residence

today from one community to another; for example, some men are transferred from one city to another by the companies they work for, and many old people move to California or Florida when they reach retirement age. It does not seem fair that people who move to new communities should have their right to vote taken away from them, and especially that they should be deprived of the right to vote in national elections.

In editing dull writing like this, the first thing to look for is what some professional editors call "fat": long phrases that can be cut or replaced by a shorter phrase with no loss of meaning. Consider the first sentence. Its first thirteen words can be replaced by the shorter and more direct *It seems unjust,* and two later phrases—*in elections* and *a period of at least*—can be simply deleted. The second sentence is just as overweight. *The living patterns of the American people* can be cut down to *American living patterns*; since the time is clear from the context, *at the present time* can be deleted altogether; and the sixteen-word final phrase can be cut to *when the residence requirement was established.* Changes like this give us a much leaner paragraph:

It seems unjust that the right to vote should depend on residence in a community for six months. American living patterns have altered in the hundred years since the residence requirement was first established. People change residence more frequently today: for example, executives are transferred and old people move to California and Florida. It seems especially unfair that people who move should lose the right to vote in national elections.

This is better, but still rather flat. Some further changes, to bolster the argument and introduce variety into the sentence pattern, make it better still:

Why should the right to vote depend on six months' residence in a community? Things have changed since 1900: the nation counts for more, the community for less. Every year thousands of executives are transferred, thousands of old people move to

Florida, thousands of teachers and graduate students move to new universities. Why penalize these people? At least we should let them vote in national elections.

We started with 157 words, which we cut first to 70 and finally to 66. The editing has lost nothing worth keeping; indeed, as sometimes happens, new material has actually been added, with the result that the final version says more in 66 words than the original said in 157. Moreover, with the static suppressed, the message comes through more clearly. Our editing has cut away the fat and kept the meat.

Note also the changes in sentence structure. The four sentences of the original were all declarative; in the final version two sentences are interrogative. These changes help make the argument more direct and immediate, and for the first time give something of that sense of the writer's personality (rather a strident one, in this case) which is indispensable to style.

Example 3

The writers of the previous examples had solved the basic problem of giving their writing shape; it remained only to strengthen their arguments and improve their language. Though editing as we define it is essentially concerned with such last-stage improvements, it is worth remembering that the processes of writing, rethinking, and editing are in fact not easily separated, as our next example shows.

This closing paragraph of a four-page essay ran to a page and a half in typescript:

When we discovered that she had cancer, I could hardly believe it, for disease had no right to hit my grandma. Of all persons I have ever met or read about, she is my idol. Though most people would choose someone famous, if I could be anyone else in the world, I would choose to be like my grandma. She was one of those ageless people, by which I mean, that where communication gaps exist, it was different with her. Although she may have been old-fashioned in certain respects, I never failed to see her adjust to something new, or at least try to accept it, whether it be today's fashions or morals. As she was brought up in a different age, the subject of premarital sex shocked her at first, but I was surprised to hear her admit that it existed in her day also; the only difference was that it was hushed up then and openly discussed today. I could tell her things and discuss matters with her that I would feel uncomfortable talking over with my parents; she was never quick to make a reply before she thought about what I had said. My mom, on the other hand, would frequently come back with an instantaneous reply which would oftentimes be prejudiced and unfair. Grandma could always listen and come back with advice that was reasonable, even if she was in disagreement. Many of the discussions that we had would have upset most older people, but not my grandma; we talked about so much: boyfriends, sex, language, racial prejudices and politics. Many of the subjects in themselves were not shocking, but the opinions she held could be called revolutionary for her time. The interesting thing was that she didn't go to college and most of today's adults have, my father and mother for instance. Yet, she understood, and was so quick in the mind that very little slipped by her. How of all people she should become sick with cancer and die is beyond my comprehension. She was so vital and energetic; I'll never forget those shopping trips we made when I would drag her around in my excitement, but she would always keep up. I saw her go from my 5'2'' chubby grandma, to a skinny emaciated woman. Yet even though I saw her in such contrasting states, I'll remember her only as she was at her best.

Last-stage editing could cut a hundred words or so here, and that would be a big improvement. But the fact is, this draft isn't ready yet for that kind of editing. The writer needs to get rid of the trite posturings of the first few sentences and the unqualified pontifications about older people's experiences and opinions (tell them in India that "most of today's adults" have gone to college!). She needs to throw out the digressions on premarital sex and mom's argument style, which are not grandma's concerns but her own. Above all, she needs to find a focus. This means deciding which of three present aspects of her message—grandma as a model person, grandma as a wise confidant, grandma's unwelcome death—is to be her point.

Since the paragraph is too long by any standard, a good way to go about a second draft might be to write up the material bearing on these three aspects as three separate paragraphs. Her thoughts on her grandmother's death, for example, are now scattered in the first sentence, the next-to-last, and the one beginning *How of all people.* Why not bring them together? However things end up, it usually helps to put apples with apples and oranges with oranges. When the apples and oranges are words, at least two good things happen: you get a clearer idea of what you are trying to say, and you discover and eliminate unnecessary repetition.

A second draft, then, might have three paragraphs, of which the longest and most detailed will be about the writer's talks with her grandmother. Dropping the *could hardly believe* stuff, the digressions, and the more obvious redundancies should make this draft much shorter than the first, and with any luck it will be ready for editing. For space reasons we will not show this second draft, but in its final, edited form the passage might look like this:

> Her health and energy were seemingly boundless. I remember particularly our shopping trips together, when I would almost run through stores in my excitement. She was always right behind me, just as excited and never even out of breath.
>
> Although she was old-fashioned in some respects, I could talk with her about things I would have felt uncomfortable discussing with my parents: boyfriends, premarital sex, language, racial prejudices, politics. Nothing upset her. She did not have a college education, but her mind was quick and her views on manners and morals were almost revolutionary for a person of her generation. She was a good listener, and when she offered advice or a comment on something I had said, she was always reasonable.
>
> She died last month of cancer. I saw her go from my chubby grandma to a haggard, emaciated stranger, but I will remember her as she was at her best. I mean to do more than remember her. I mean to be as much like her as I can.

This final version, like the unshown second draft, has three paragraphs, but only the middle one is unchanged in substance. The new last paragraph combines the ideas of grandma's death and grandma as a model: the writer found that she could not separate these ideas in her mind, that both were a part of her message. The new first paragraph is also a departure from her first revision scheme. It makes a point that she had made clumsily in her first draft, could not easily accommodate in her second, but in the end found essential to what she was saying.

Language editing has done the rest. The unsettling image of grandma being dragged along at top speed on shopping sprees is gone. *Sex* has become *premarital sex* to supply the sense of the eliminated digression and to make it clear that grandma isn't getting by with easy praise of the joys of the marriage bed. The unnecessarily precise 5'2" has been dropped; the idea of short is contained in *chubby*, a word never used of tall people, and anything more exact is out of place in this context. Other changes have been made, but not many. As often happens, little editing is needed once a writer has his basic argument straight.

By using paragraph-length examples we do not mean to suggest that editing is purely a matter of fixing paragraphs. Sometimes what your draft needs is completely new material: a transition to tell the reader how Jack and Jill got from the hill to the hospital, an example to make some general statement clear, a metaphor to liven things up or drive a point home.

More often what you need to do is throw out a paragraph, or even two or three. Writing evolves from draft to draft; what you thought you would need when you started you may no longer need now that your focus is different. If your superfluous paragraph is good in its own right—well-written, say, or witty—you will hate to see it go. But if it is not central to what you now see as your message, go it must for your reader's sake. To understand what a writer means is hard work in the best circumstances; the presence of superfluous passages makes it all but impossible. Good writers know this and are ruthless editors of their own writing.

THE ESSENTIALS OF GOOD WRITING

In this chapter we have seen three examples of clumsy writing transformed by editing into workmanlike prose. What makes the difference? What is it that makes the edited versions better, that makes good writing good?

In the first place, *authority*: the authority that comes from knowing one's subject and one's mind. A good writer knows what he wants to say, often not at first, sometimes not until he is deep into his final draft, but always by the time he is through.

In the second place, *detail*. That grandma *would always keep up* tells us little about grandma; that she *was always right behind me, just as excited and never even out of breath* tells us that wise old grandma had her adolescent side as well. Detail is a tricky quality, to be sure. Too many details make for tiresome reading, and a wrong or obtrusive detail may be worse than no detail at all. But the impulse to precision is central to good prose. The telling detail is the essence of descriptive writing.

In the third place, *economy*. A good writer pares away unnecessary blubber: abstract nouns like *situation* and *circumstances*, mechanical intensifiers like *very* and *really*, flabby phrases like *in such a way as to* and *in view of the fact that*, unnecessary connections and elaborations. *Grandma could always listen and come back with advice that was reasonable, even if she was in disagreement* says no more than *Grandma was always reasonable, even when we disagreed*. The extra words are unnecessary, hence burdensome, all weight and no substance. Good writing is the right length for its content. What can be said in eighty words is said in eighty words, not a hundred.

Finally, *variety*, in the rhythmic sense. There is something in a human mind—in the reader's inner ear—that calls for a short sentence after several long ones, or a longer one after several short ones. Too many simple sentences set us to wishing for a complex sentence, and vice versa. The rhythms of prose are not the rhythms of popular music; steady repetition of the same beat after a point is not pleasing but irritating, and in the end stupefying.

That is all very well, you may say, but how does it translate into advice to the novice writer? Am I really expected to write like Norman Mailer or Jack Anderson—me, Joe Smith, with no particular gifts as a writer and nothing much to write about? Maybe not like Mailer, who is one of a kind. But surely the style of a good newspaper columnist, the style of the final versions of our three examples, is within your reach. Lots of college students write as well as Jack Anderson, and some write better.

If it takes you a while, you aren't the first. Writing is like playing tennis or playing the piano: doing it badly is the necessary first step to doing it well. The big thing to strive for is not virtuosity but competence: not to soar in one great bound to professional heights, but to climb out of the swamp of first-draft writing onto the solid ground of third-draft prose. If you can do that, you will have done all this book asks of you and all anyone could ask.

PART 3
MECHANICS

9
GRAMMAR

In Part 2 we were concerned with the art of writing effectively, with choosing which of various alternatives is *best*. In Part 3 our concern will be with the mechanics of writing correctly, with choosing which of various alternatives is *right*. The rejected alternatives of Part 2 were clumsy or irritating or confusing or substandard. Those of Part 3, though in many cases clear and straightforward enough, have been pronounced unacceptable—or permanently second-best—by the consensus of educated people. Part 2 dealt with choices; Part 3 deals with rules.

Rules in this sense should be seen not as a constraint on the writer but as a convention between the writer and the reader, a mutual agreement on details that clears the way for more important matters. A good writer depends on the rules of grammar, syntax, orthography, and punctuation the way a good general depends on the fundamentals of military strategy: he may violate them for good reason in occasional unexpected circumstances, but they remain the standard to which he refers his decisions. A writer of expository prose who repeatedly violates these rules by ignorance or design builds his house on quicksand. Whatever secondary effects he may achieve, he will fail in his primary duty of making his meaning clear.

Since grammar and syntax are variously defined and understood, let us begin by defining the two terms as we use them. A problem in *grammar*, by our lights, involves a choice between alternatives differing in number, gender, case, or tense. A problem in *syntax* involves a choice between different ways of relating two or more parts of a sentence to each other. Our concern in this chapter is with grammar.

AGREEMENT PROBLEMS

People (is) (are) my business

Everyone knows that singular subjects take singular verbs and plural subjects plural verbs, but it is sometimes hard to tell when a subject is singular and when plural, or which of several words or phrases is in fact the subject. The present section discusses the main kinds of confusion.

When the subject is singular but a predicate noun is plural, stick strictly to the rule. All the following sentences are correct:

My only *source* of support *is* my parents.

My *parents are* my only source of support.

The only *thing* the Allies lacked *was* troopships.

Troopships were the only thing the Allies lacked.

With a subject made up of two or more nouns linked by *and,* use a plural verb: *Wine, women, and song were Bao Dai's downfall.* There are exceptions—for example, *A year and six months was all they needed / Peanut butter and jelly always makes a hit*—where the compound subject, being essentially singular in meaning, takes a singular verb; but these exceptions are few. When in doubt, use the plural: *Rain and sleet were forecast for the week of the convention.*

With a subject made up of two or more singular nouns linked by *or* or *nor,* use a singular verb if the components are singular, a plural verb if they are plural:

Either Egypt or Israel *has* to back down.

The investigation did not reveal whether the pilot, the navigator, or the bombardier *was* responsible.

Neither the ranchers nor the miners *want* a fight.

If some components are singular and some plural, you face a difficult choice:

Usually the coaches or the manager (*gives*) (*give*) the signals.

When money is short, either the farmhouse or the crops (*have*) (*has*) to be mortgaged.

Neither the governor nor the Teamsters Union officials (*were*) (*was*) sympathetic.

Since each of the alternatives in parentheses has its drawbacks, the best thing to do is reword the sentence to avoid the problem. This is often easy enough: *The signals are usually given by the coaches or the manager / When money is short, either the farmhouse or the crops must be mortgaged / Both the governor and the Teamsters Union were unsympathetic.* If you cannot think of a good alternative wording, make the verb agree with the nearest noun or pronoun component of the subject:

Either the Joint Chiefs or *one* of the field commanders *was* lying.

Has Socrates' *question,* or Hobbes's and Rousseau's questions, ever been satisfactorily answered?

Who takes (his) (our) (their) turn next?

Agreement difficulties may involve not only verbs but pronouns and nouns:

The diary never said whether it was Sir Robert or his sister that hanged (*himself*) (*herself*) (*themselves*).

The plan was for me or Ken to take (*my*) (*his*) (*our*) car.

Either the linebackers or the free safety missed (*his cue*) (*their cue*) (*their cues*).

Sometimes you can solve this problem by spelling things out: *The plan was for me to take my car or Ken to take his / Either the linebackers missed their cue or the free safety missed his.* Sometimes you can solve it by rewording: *Either the linebackers or the free safety missed a cue.* If no better solution comes to mind, make the pronoun agree in number and gender with the nearest component of the subject, making this component plural if possible and masculine if there is a choice of genders:

> Either Paul or the *twins* left *their* baggage.

> One would never expect a nurse or a *doctor* to injure *himself* that way.

They each (have) (has) children of (their) (his) (his or her) own

Each as a subject takes a singular verb; so do nouns modified by *each* and *every* and the nouns *anyone, anybody, no one, nobody, everyone, everybody, someone,* and *somebody.* These words cause few problems with verbs; the trouble comes in determining the number and gender of any following nouns and pronouns. Most writers, faced by a choice among *Anybody can try this experiment for himself, Anybody can try this experiment for himself or herself,* and *Anybody can try this experiment for themselves,* choose the first. The convention here, according to H. W. Fowler, is that "where the matter of sex is not conspicuous or important the masculine form shall be allowed to represent a person instead of a man."

In recent years feminists have attacked this long-established practice on the ground that such unchallenged conventions, in the language as in society, help perpetuate the sort of male-centered thinking that enlightened women deplore. Thus, for example, in *Who wouldn't defend (his) (his or her) (their) little sister from attack?* an ardent feminist might insist on *his or her* to give each sex its due. Though grammatically sound, the resulting sentence is graceless; whatever the two extra words may achieve in feminist terms would be more than offset for most readers by their distracting effect. To all but the most impassioned feminists, then, we recommend the conventional *his.* The plural *their,* though neither distracting nor sex-biased and thus in some contexts an attractive solution, does not agree here with the singular *Who* and is thus not recommended.

To the general preference for the singular with words like *each* two exceptions may be noted. First, when *each* modifies a plural noun or pronoun, it takes the plural: thus, whereas the singular is correct in *Each man here has a dollar* and *Each of us has a dollar*, the plural is correct in *We each have a dollar* and *We have a dollar each*. Second, *none*, unlike *no one* and *nobody*, can take either the singular or the plural. If your emphasis is on the individual components of the class of things that *none* refers to, use the singular: *None of these three books is worth reading*. If the components are more sensibly thought of in groups or batches, use the plural: *No letters have been received, and none are expected*. In borderline cases, most good writers use the singular.

One should mind (one's) (his) (their) own business

The pronoun *one* has two uses, the numeral (*One of the boys was named Michael*) and the impersonal (*One cannot please everybody*). In the numeral use, *one* is followed by a form of *he, she,* or *it*: thus *One had her dog with her; another had a parrot*. In the impersonal use, *one* is followed by *one, one's,* or *oneself*: thus *One should not take one's dog into a restaurant*. In the heading above, the correct choice is *one's*. Alternatively, *A person should mind his own business*.

If you begin with *one*, stay with it. Don't dart back and forth between pronouns like this writer:

> The particulars are not even given so that *one* may know how to apply *their* own interpretation of right and wrong. *You* are never even told what "evil" is.

One's for *their* and *One is* for *You are* would make this passage correct, but perhaps a bit dull. In general, rather than pile up *one* after *one* we recommend starting with a noun (e.g. *the reader*) or a different pronoun (e.g. *we*).

The nurses made their own (decision) (decisions)

Whether to use the singular or the plural with the plural possessives *their, our,* and *your* is not always easy to decide. Do we say *The prisoners went to their death bravely* or *went to their deaths bravely*? *We changed our mind* or *changed our minds*? English has no clear rules or patterns on this point, and in borderline cases either form will serve. A rough rule of thumb might be as follows. When the noun is concrete or tangible, use the plural. When it is highly abstract, or when a fixed idiom is involved, use the singular. In between these extremes, take your choice. Thus:

The two girls changed their dresses. *(Concrete.)*

The two girls changed their mind [*or* minds]. *(In between.)*

The two girls changed their religion. *(Abstract.)*

The two girls changed their tune. *(Idiom.)*

Of course, when there is only a single item in question, the singular is used: *We love our country.*

The jury (was) (were) served coffee

With collective nouns—words like *crowd, committee,* and *majority,* which are singular in form but plural in connotation—either singular or plural verbs may be used, depending on context. When in doubt, use the singular: *The crowd was dispersed by the police / The committee is unable to reach an agreement.* If you are not happy with either the singular or the plural, and there are times when you won't be, try a different wording that gets around the problem: *The onlookers were dispersed by the police / The committee cannot reach an agreement.*

Where the *majority* simply means *most,* use the plural: *Some agreed, but the majority were undecided.* Use the plural also with such ostensibly singular expressions as *a number of* and *a handful of* when they mean *some* or *many,* as they usually do: *A small number of people were present / A high proportion of Americans go to college.*

A word cannot be simultaneously singular and plural, as in the following defective sentences:

The Mafia *has* no patience with legal restrictions; *their* law is action.

Two days *was* a long time, and what would happen when *they were* over?

Everyone from the Chinese restaurant *was* there, wearing *tuxedos* and evening *dresses*.

The first two sentences can be made consistently singular by changing *their* to *its* and *they were* to *it was*. In the third sentence, the plural is better: *All the people from the Chinese restaurant were there*.

Mathematics (are) (is) difficult

Some words are plural in form but singular in meaning. For most such words *(scissors, glasses, pants)* the plural is idiomatic. The chief exceptions are *news*, the names of certain diseases *(measles, mumps, shingles)*, and words ending in *-ics* when used to designate a more or less formal body of knowledge or course of study: *Politics is the art of the possible / Ethics attracts modern philosophers more than logic*. In less formal uses the plural is more common: *His politics were dirty / Their ethics are questionable*. The Latin plural *data*, being singular in appearance and to some extent in connotation, often takes the singular in modern usage and may someday be as singular as *agenda*, which has traveled the same road. At this writing, however, good usage favors *data are*.

One of the boys (was) (were) absent

Watch out for the false association of verbs with nearby nouns that are not in fact their subjects. Number errors from this cause, which is sometimes called "attraction," are surprisingly common. The following examples are wrong:

> Bob's eating habits, like his way of speaking, *is* marked by little quirks.

> A timetable for arriving at workable arrangements *remain* to be discussed.

The subject of the first sentence is *habits*, not *way* or *speaking*. The subject of the second is *timetable*, not *arrangements*. Errors of this sort come from haste and should not survive a careful editing.

Note that *with* and its compounds (*together with, along with*) do not act like *and* to make a subject plural. The following sentences are both correct:

> Morgan and the two other rioters *were* fined $500 each.

> Morgan, along with the two other rioters, *was* fined $500.

POSSESSIVE PROBLEMS

Forming the Possessive

To form the possessive, use *'s* for the singular (*John's hat, the dog's dish*) and an apostrophe only for the plural (*the ladies' bridge club, the Smiths' car*). For words that do not form the plural in *s*, notably *men, women,* and *children*, add *'s* for the plural possessive (*the children's toys, the alumni's wishes, the people's choice*).

Some singular common nouns and many proper names end in an *s* or *z* sound. Most of these, along with all names ending in silent *s* or *x* (*Descartes, Malraux, Illinois, Arkansas*), form the possessive in *'s* just like any other singular noun:

Henry James's novels	for appearance's sake
Essex's plot	Degas's paintings
our hostess's husband	Columbus's crew
in Jesus's name	Alcatraz's first warden

A few such words, however, notably ancient Greek and biblical names of three or more syllables ending in a *z* sound, become too awkward to pronounce with the extra syllable added by *'s* and conventionally form the possessive with the apostrophe only: *Aristophanes' comedies, Socrates' wisdom.*

No apostrophe is used in the possessive pronouns *his, hers, its, ours, yours, theirs,* and *whose.* Errors on this point, particularly *it's* for *its*, are common in student writing. *It's* means *it is* or *it has* and nothing else (*It's a rainy day / It's been fun*); *who's* means *who is* or *who has* (*Who's there? / Who's seen Mary?*). The forms *her's, our's, your's,* and *their's* do not exist. Note, by the way, that *whose* may be used freely in place of the awkward *of which* irrespective of whether it refers to a person or a thing: *the house whose garden we admired* is standard English.

Misplaced Apostrophe

In some idiomatic phrases involving possessives, it is not immediately obvious where the apostrophe goes. Is it *state's rights*, for example, or *states' rights*? Is it *bull's-eyes* or *bulls'-eyes* or *bullseyes*, *hornet's nest* or *hornets' nest*, *doctor's orders* or *doctors' orders*? Try your dictionary on questions like this, or better yet an unabridged dictionary. If you can find no pronouncement one way or the other, your best bet is usually the singular. In proper names, the plural is the more common: *Reserve Officers' Training Corps*, *Professional Golfers' Association*.

Possessive apostrophes do not appear in some proper names (*the Veterans Administration, the Artists Workshop*), and this practice has been extended to some common compounds as well (*teachers college, citizens group*). There is no warrant, however, for extending it to all terms of this form. In particular, keep the apostrophe where dropping it would yield a nonexistent word like *mens* or *childrens*. For the same reason, take care to put the apostrophe where it belongs, not one letter away. It is *women's club*, not *womens' club*; *sheep's wool*, not *sheeps' wool*; *womens* and *sheeps* are not English words. The opposite error (*John Adam's presidency, the United State's viewpoint*) evokes nonexistent singulars: a president named *John Adam*, a country named *the United State*.

Do not add an apostrophe to a plural noun used as an adjective: it is *physics test*, not *physics' test* or *physic's test*. And never use an apostrophe to form the plural of a word that has a perfectly good plural of the normal form. Errors of this sort are common on signs: *Strawberry's for Sale*; *We Charge Battery's*. On doorplates we may find *The Jones's*, implying that some sinister figure known as The Jones lurks within, rather than an innocent family of Joneses. This last error in particular smacks of illiteracy: if it creeps into a first draft, it should creep no further.

Unwieldy Possessives

When *s's* and *s'* yield equally or almost equally unattractive alternatives, try to avoid the choice by rewording. Why make the difficult choice between *the metropolis's growth* and *the metropolis' growth* when you can say *the growth of the metropolis,* or *the growth of metropolitan Toronto?* Most words of four or more syllables whether or not they end in *s,* and many three-syllable words ending in *s* or an *s* sound (*wilderness, residence*), take the *of* form much more gracefully than the apostrophe. An especially awkward possessive is *United States':* *the United States' proposal* is not wrong, but might better be changed to *the American proposal* or *the proposal of the United States.*

Possessives of long phrases should also be avoided. *The man in the street's opinion* might just get by, but *the man in the fur coat's daughter* is too much. The *of* construction is better for both.

Compound Possessives

Short compound possessives of the form *John('s) and Mary's money* are harder to avoid. Whether to use *'s* after the last noun only or after each noun in the series depends on whether the thing possessed is more properly thought of as indivisible and thus jointly owned or as having components that are separately owned. The following four phrases are correct:

Mother and Dad's wedding anniversary
Mother's and Dad's summer clothing

Ed, Bill, and Charley's Bar
Ed's, Bill's, and Charley's responsibilities

OTHER CASE PROBLEMS

Apart from the possessive problems just described, case problems in English are few and are getting fewer. On the one hand, the generations of American farm boys and immigrant children who were exposed at home to the likes of "Me and her get along fine" have given way to the sophisticated television viewers who now fill our kindergartens. Today the basic rules of case in good spoken English are taken in early. On the other hand, teachers have reconsidered the old rules and discovered that some of the expressions they formerly condemned as ungrammatical are not so bad after all. Recent developments in linguistics and lexicography have had the same effect.

The result of all these developments has been a revolution in teaching and grammatical thinking. The fussy-sounding expressions *It is I* and *That is he* are no longer taught, and *Whom are you kidding?* is down to its last dozen defenders. Only a rare voice is still raised against T. S. Eliot's "Let us go then, you and I," on the ground that *I*, being in apposition to the objective *us*, should be the objective *me*. Many teachers no longer even object to *who* in *Who are they talking about?* The argument against these sentences is sound and logical: it can be grasped, diagramed, explained. The argument for them is simply that this is what most people, including educated people, would actually say.

TENSE PROBLEMS

Foreigners learning English find the tenses difficult to master, but for native-born writers only three kinds of decision consistently give trouble: between past tense and present in sentences like *She asked herself whether the law (is) (was) just*; between present and perfect in sentences like *He would have been glad to (go) (have gone)*; and between indicative and subjunctive in sentences like *If Reagan (was) (were) president, things would be different.* Although the subjunctive is technically a "mood" rather than a tense, the distinction has no practical effect.

The Past vs. the Present

In a clause following a past-tense verb or a verb in the conditional (*would* + verb), the verb should normally be in the past tense, not the present. The following sentences are correct:

She asked herself whether the law *was* just. (not *is*)

Professor Snyder explained what "atomic weight" *meant*. (not *means*)

One would think he *was* crazy. (not *is*)

The use of the past tense here is natural and idiomatic; the present tense, though not wrong, sounds unnatural. Note especially that the past-tense verb does not connote finality—in the second sentence above, for example, the choice of *meant* rather than *means* carries no suggestion that "atomic weight" means something different today. The present tense should be used only when the past would be awkward or misleading:

> The dispute was over what freedom *means* in the Soviet Union.

> The Senator explained what the Republicans stood for thirty years ago, and what they *stand for* today.

The Perfect

One verb in the perfect tense (*have* + verb) should not be subordinated to another: write *He would have been glad to go*, not *He would have been glad to have gone*. The following sentences are correct:

> She would have given anything *to be chosen*. (*not* to have been chosen)

> Gallman *has enjoyed being* Ambassador to Korea. (*not* has enjoyed having been *or* enjoys having been)

> It would have been easy for Myra *to make* her father happy. (*not* to have made)

The Subjunctive

The subjunctive takes three main forms: (1) the use of *were* for *was* in clauses introduced by *if* and *wish* and expressing hypothetical rather than factual conditions (*if I were king / I wish I were dead*); (2) the omission of *should* in clauses introduced by verbs expressing will, command, or desire (*I move that the meeting be adjourned / I insist that my money be refunded*); and (3) the use of infinitive rather than indicative forms in half a dozen old-fashioned expressions, notably *come what may, be that as it may, far be it from me*, and *suffice it to say*.

Much ink has been spilled in defense of the subjunctive in category (1) against the incursions of the indicative; but *if I was king* and *I wish I was dead*, though not yet accepted as proper by authorities on usage, are gaining inexorably and seem likely to prevail. Category (2), by contrast, is of recent growth and very vigorous, in large part because the use of *should*, though perfectly correct and natural to many Englishmen, strikes Americans as softening the intended meaning. In English usage, *I insist that my money be refunded* and *I insist that my money should be refunded* mean the same thing. In American usage, the first means "Give it back," the second "By rights I should get it back."

Category (3) offers no problems except to writers with a flair for the archaic, that minority in every generation who are prompted by their fondness for an older prose or poetry (*If this be treason / What care I how fair she be?*) to revive a form that is as foreign to modern writing as the casual use of Latin. The student who wrote *Whether his charge be true or false, it has the authority of his suffering* should have written *is* for *be*. As Fowler remarks, those who traffic in such archaic subjunctives run the risk "of having the proper dignity of style at which they aim mistaken by captious readers for pretentiousness."

10
SYNTAX

Good syntax is a matter of arranging or grouping words for maximum clarity to the reader. Five typical sentences in which the words are not properly arranged will illustrate the chief problems discussed in this chapter:

> The first stanza is serious, straightforward, and sets the theme of the poem.

> Lying in the gutter, Hannah found her lost watch.

> Seymour's brother asked the pitcher if he could play third base.

> The town, which I grew up in, had only one school.

> Like the AMA plan, private groups were to allocate the subsidies.

The first sentence is unparallel; having established the pattern of a series of adjectives, the writer has veered off before completing it. The writer of the second sentence has improperly attached the phrase *Lying in the gutter* to *Hannah* rather than to *watch*. In the third sentence, *he* has three possible antecedents. The fourth sentence may conceivably be correct, but would probably prove in context to require not *The town, which* but *The town that*; the issue here is that of restrictive versus nonrestrictive clauses, a basic distinction in the use of English. The fifth sentence misuses *like* as a conjunction. Either it should begin *As in the AMA plan,* or it should end *the new plan made private groups responsible for allocating the subsidies.*

PARALLELISM

According to Blake, there are three main states: innocence, experience, and a higher innocence. Their major symbols are the child, the man, the woman, and Christ. No good writer will subject his reader to such conundrums. A change to the *child, the adult, and Christ* is essential to make the two series parallel to each other, and hence coherently related to each other. Failing this change, the reader will either move on perplexed to the next sentence or have to spend time sorting out the two series. Either way he will be irritated, and with justice.

Although failures of parallelism are rarely so striking, the principle is of the first importance in good writing. Things related to each other in parallel construction are clearly related; where the parallelism is faulty, the relationship may or may not be clear. And where any chance for confusion exists, some readers will surely become confused.

The basic requirement for a parallel construction is easily stated: What is true of one element must be true of the others. If three horses are to be saddled, we need three saddles, not four or two. If one element of a series or comparison is a noun, the others must be nouns; if one is an adjective, the others must be adjectives; if one has a verb, the others must have verbs. In the next few pages we shall consider the most frequent departures from parallelism and the best ways of repairing them.

Series

The most common form of unparallel series is the one illustrated above: *The first stanza is serious, straightforward, and sets the theme of the poem.* Here are two others of the same sort:

Most uses of capital letters are conventional [*adjective*], easily understood [*adjective*], and cause [*verb*] no difficulty.

She made more sandwiches [*noun*], more hot chocolate [*noun*], and scraped [*verb*] out the last of the pudding.

To correct the faulty parallelism, either make the three terms of the series syntactically identical (*Most uses of capital letters are conventional, easily understood, and easy to apply*) or abandon the series as such (*She made more sandwiches and hot chocolate, and scraped out the last of the pudding*). The latter solution is always available, and is often the better. Some writers shrink from the second *and* ("The first stanza is serious *and* straightforward, *and* sets the theme of the poem"), but in our opinion it is a touch of elegance, a welcome sign that the writer knows what he is doing.

The second most common form of unparallel series is one in which an opening word—usually an article, a preposition, or a conjunction—appears before the first element in the series and again before the last element, but is dropped before some or all of the intermediate elements. Here are three examples of unparallel series of this sort, with the key words in italics:

The rules state that *a* hat, coat, and *a* tie must be worn.

Cortez was informed *that* the enemy forces numbered 2,000, they were heavily armed, and *that* their stone outworks were impregnable.

There is no life *on* the sun, the moon, or *on* the stars.

Parallelism requires that a preposition or a conjunction be used either before every term of a series or before the first term only: that is, either "*on* the sun, *on* the moon, or *on* the stars" or "*on* the sun, the moon, or the stars." The choice is a matter of taste. Articles are less flexible. For one thing, it is often better to put the article before each term in the series rather than just the first; in the first sentence above, for example, *a hat, a coat, and a tie* is better than *a hat, coat, and tie*, which tends to make a bogus unit or ensemble out of three clearly separate items. For another, a series may contain some terms capable of taking the article and some not, as in *the President, the*

Secretary of State, and General Abbott. In such cases, to make the series properly parallel the article must be repeated before each element to which it is appropriate.

There are many other possibilities of unparallelism in series, too many to be illustrated here. The main thing to remember is that parallel construction is a principle of order, a way of telling the reader economically what elements go together or have the same weight.

Correlatives

Parallelism in correlative pairs, like parallelism in series, requires that what is true of one element be true of the other. The four pairs in question are *either/or, neither/nor, both/and,* and *not only/but (also).* Errors made under this heading can often be fixed by merely switching the position of one of the correlatives, and can almost always be fixed in more than one way. The following sentences are defective, with alternative corrections indicated in parentheses:

> *Intransigent* dates in England from about 1880; being now established, it should neither be pronounced as French nor spelled -*eant* any longer. (*be neither pronounced;* OR *nor be spelled*)

> All-out war on two fronts was impossible: either we concentrated on defeating Germany or on Japan. (*or we concentrated on defeating Japan;* OR *we had to concentrate either on Germany or on Japan*)

> Smog is a problem both in the city and the country. (*and in the country;* OR *in both the city*)

> The Duke of San Lorenzo not only collected rare manuscripts, but also paintings and sculpture. (*collected not only;* OR *but also collected*)

In the first sentence, the rule says that if *neither* takes a verb phrase, *nor* should take a verb phrase; and that if *neither* takes a participle, *nor* should take a participle or some equivalent form of adjective. Similarly with the other sentences. In the second, for example, *either* is followed by a complete clause and *or* by a phrase.

Parallelism requires both words to be followed by clauses or both by phrases.

Correlative constructions in which both parts have not only the same subject but also the same verb may take any of three possible forms:

> *Either* it was a genuine Picasso, *or* it was a skillful forgery.
>
> It *either* was a genuine Picasso *or* was a skillful forgery.
>
> It was *either* a genuine Picasso *or* a skillful forgery.

In the first sentence the correlatives introduce complete clauses; in the second, verbs; in the third, nouns. Usually one of the possible choices sounds better than the other two: in our example, the third seems clearly the best choice. Once the various truly parallel possibilities are determined, the choice is a matter of taste. The problem is to avoid such unparallel alternatives as *It was either a genuine Picasso, or it was a skillful forgery.*

A surprisingly frequent error is the false pairing *neither/or*, as in *Neither the Army, the Navy, or the Marines favored American intervention.* Whether in pairs or in series of three or more, *neither* goes with *nor* and *either* with *or.* There are no exceptions.

Comparisons

You can compare apples and pickles, but you cannot intelligibly compare apples and sourness or pickles and red. The two or more terms of a comparison must be strictly parallel, both in syntax and in level of abstraction, if the comparison is to be understood. The parallelism is out of whack in these representative student sentences:

> There is a big difference between Chicago's *life-style* and its *suburbs.*
>
> The average *IQ score* of Irish farmers is lower than the average *white American.*
>
> She could not help contrasting her *experience* with her *mother and Aunt Jane.*

You can fix the second and third sentences easily by converting to the possessive: *white American's* (IQ score) / *her mother's and Aunt Jane's* (experiences). This change often does the job. For the other sentence, one of several possible fixes is *difference in life-style between Chicago and its suburbs.* Like other kinds of defective parallelism, this kind is easy to repair once you train yourself to spot it.

MISPLACED MODIFIERS

Just as an adjective normally comes immediately before or after the noun it modifies (*a blue car, a tale too sad for words*), so an adjectival clause should be placed as close as possible to its noun. Violations of this principle may produce the absurdities known as misplaced modifiers, of which the largest single class goes by the name of dangling participles.

Dangling Participles

A participle is the adjective form of a verb, ending either in *-ing* (present participle) or in *-ed*, *-en*, or *-t* (past participle); for all practical purposes, it may be treated exactly like an adjective. When a participle begins a sentence, it must modify the subject of the independent clause that follows. The following sentences are accordingly correct:

> *Ravaged* by illness and starvation, Mola's *regiment* had no choice but to surrender.

> *Shrieking* wildly, the *children* ran toward the lake.

The classic error is to place the modified noun or pronoun in some subordinate position, or to leave it to inference:

> Restlessly pacing the floor, her thoughts were of George's promise.

> After crossing the threshold, Brooke's room is on the left.

> Measuring 6'4'' and weighing over 200 pounds, you could tell at a glance that he was an athlete.

The first sentence has *her thoughts* doing the pacing, not her; the second has *Brooke's room* crossing the threshold;° in the third the athlete is *you*, not *he*.

Sentences of this sort can usually be corrected in either of two ways. One is to keep the participle or gerund construction but give the independent clause a suitable subject: *Restlessly pacing the floor, she thought of George's promise* / *After crossing the threshold, one finds Brooke's room on the left.* The other is to leave the independent clause as it stands but abandon the participle construction: *As she restlessly paced the floor, her thoughts were of George's promise* / *As one enters the front door, Brooke's room is on the left.* The choice between these alternatives is a matter of taste.

The word modified by a participle must be a full noun or pronoun, not a possessive form, and must be complete in itself, not part of a compound subject or buried in a verb. The following sentences are wrong:

> *Surprised* at the compliment, her *eyes* sparkled with pleasure.
>
> *Being* the oldest, his *word* was law.
>
> *Having borne* him two boys, *Mrs. Lincoln and her husband* were hoping for a girl.

Her eyes were not surprised by the compliment; *she* was. *His word* was not the oldest; *he* was. As for Lincoln, his part in the bearing of his sons was no doubt as large as a loving husband could make it, but the equal of Mrs. Lincoln's it was not.

Other Danglers

Not only participles may be wrongly placed, but other adjectives and adjective phrases as well, as in these sentences:

> Twice the size of her brother, they called her Big Bertha.
>
> While out for a stroll one morning, a thief broke into my apartment.

° *Crossing* is a gerund, not a participle (see p. 276), but the distinction makes no difference in this context.

Sad and bitter at first, Chopin's good spirits soon returned.

As an orphan, Hardy has made Jude even more susceptible to the modern anxieties.

The remedy here is the same as for misplaced participles. Either convert the opening phrase to a subordinate clause, or see that the independent clause begins with a suitable noun:

Twice the size of her brother, she was known as Big Bertha.

While I was out for a stroll one morning, a thief broke into my apartment.

Sad and bitter though Chopin was at first, his good spirits soon returned.

As an orphan, Jude is even more susceptible to the modern anxieties.

Adverbial phrases can also be misplaced, as in the following examples, the first from a student paper, the second from a magazine:

In his fiction, Forster portrays men who sweep streets from a godlike height.

He denounced another critic, Martin Luther King, at a 1964 news conference with women reporters as a notorious liar.

In the first sentence, *from a godlike height* makes a false sense unit with *sweep streets*; in the second, *as a notorious liar* is too far from *Martin Luther King* for the connection to be made without difficulty. Both sentences need reshuffling to bring the adverbial phrases nearer to what they modify:

In Forster's fiction, men who sweep streets are portrayed from a godlike height.

At a 1964 news conference with women reporters, he denounced another critic, Martin Luther King, as a notorious liar.

Participle Prepositions

A number of participles have acquired the status of prepositions in some conventional uses, and thus can be placed without concern for how they relate to the nearest noun. For example:

Given Byrd's view of the chances of success, how can we blame him for seeking help?

Barring acts of God, no more money should be spent on welfare measures.

Six more votes remained to be cast, not *counting* those of the New York delegation.

Some two dozen participles have entered this category, in the wake of such earlier participle prepositions as *according* and *concerning;* and more will no doubt follow. Most, however, are untouched by this trend and seem likely to remain so. When in doubt, attach participles carefully to suitable nouns or pronouns, or avoid the participle construction altogether.

One participial phrase for which preposition status is hotly disputed is *due to.* It is correct to say *His success was due to hard work,* but can we say *Due to hard work he succeeded?* That is, can the phrase be used adverbially as well as adjectivally? *Due to* in this adverbial use is gaining ground, but is not yet generally accepted. Our advice is to use *owing to, thanks to,* or *because of* where an adverb is needed and restrict *due to* to its undisputed adjectival use. A rule of thumb favored by some editors is to use *due to* only where *caused by* would not sound foolish.

ANTECEDENTS

Ambiguous Antecedents

The noun to which a pronoun refers should be unmistakable. Such a farrago of pronouns as *He told him that his father had lost his shoes* is impervious to rational analysis, but a sentence with only one pronoun may be just as baffling. *During the war between China and*

Japan, their industrial output increased 20 percent. Whose industrial output? Both countries'? And if so, both equally, or is the 20 percent some kind of average? And does it make sense to quote a joint statistic like this for two countries that are fighting each other? Clear antecedents spare the reader puzzlements of this sort.

The main thing to avoid is pronouns that can refer to any of two or more possible antecedents. In the following sentences, the ambiguous pronoun is italicized and the ambiguity is elaborated in parentheses:

Cliff asked Jack if *he* could go. (*who?*)

Brad bought the car with money from his summer job, *which* occasioned some bitter remarks among the neighbors. (*the money? the job? the car? buying the car?*)

Oakland is losing population to San Francisco and *its* suburbs. (*Oakland's suburbs or San Francisco's?*)

They spend a lot of time drinking, and *that* is something I don't approve of. (*drinking in general, or spending so much time drinking?*)

Sometimes a mishandled antecedent makes for a sentence whose meaning is clear enough, but only on a second reading. The first of the following examples is from Gowers; the second, courtesy of the *New Yorker*, from a translation of Alexander Solzhenitsyn's *August 1914*:

If the baby does not thrive on raw milk, boil it.

He ate the porridge rapidly with a broad wooden spoon which forced his mouth wide open, wound up his pocket watch, put on his belt, greatcoat, binoculars, and then stopped to think: where ought he to go?

The *New Yorker* commented, "They don't make spoons like that any-more."

Omitted Antecedents

Another error is to bury the antecedent in an adjective, or to leave it to inference:

> *French* cooking is *their* chief claim to fame.

> The Dean's Office welcomes *student* inquiries about *their* financial problems.

> The Hawks *fumbled* five times but recovered four of *them*.

Often the best way to correct sentences of this sort is to get rid of the pronoun altogether: "French cooking is *France's* chief claim to fame." Alternatively, the pronoun should have a legitimate and unmistakable antecedent: *"students'* inquiries about *their* financial problems"; "had five *fumbles* but recovered four of *them*."

Ideas and Phrases as Antecedents

Which, this, or *that* may refer to a general idea or statement rather than to a specific noun antecedent, provided there is no ambiguity in the reference. It is essential, however, that this condition of no ambiguity be fulfilled. The following sentences are good English:

> Few blacks voted, *which* is understandable in the circumstances.

> Thirty-five people were killed and two hundred wounded; *that* is all we know.

The following sentences, by contrast, contain ambiguities (indicated in the parenthetical questions), and are accordingly unacceptable:

> The audience booed and threw fruit, *which* caused the manager to lower the curtain. (*the audience reaction in general, or the fruit in particular?*)

> The commission vetoed the mayor's plan to ban weekday traffic on midtown streets; for my part, I think *this* was the right thing to do. (*what? ban traffic or veto the plan?*)

RESTRICTIVE AND NONRESTRICTIVE CONSTRUCTIONS

In a celebrated example from Gowers's *Plain Words*, a writer intending the first of the following sentences mistakenly wrote the second:

Restrictive

Pilots whose minds are dull do not live long.

Nonrestrictive

Pilots, whose minds are dull, do not live long.

The writer intended *whose minds are dull* as a restrictive clause, a clause defining what particular pilots he was talking about and implying the existence of an opposite class of pilots, those whose minds are sharp and who live longer. By adding the commas he gave us instead a nonrestrictive clause, a clause not restricted to certain pilots but commenting on pilots in general, telling us that they all have dull minds and do not live long. The commas make the difference between restrictive and nonrestrictive, between defining and commenting; and between sense and nonsense.

If you find the distinction between restrictive and nonrestrictive hard to grasp, you are in surprisingly good company, always supposing you consider writers and English professors good company. But you must do your best to grasp it if you want to write clearly. The following sections, which discuss the three main kinds of choice between restrictive and nonrestrictive, should help.

Nouns in Apposition

Apposition is a construction in which two nouns or noun phrases, usually adjacent, refer to the same thing. Consider the following examples:

Nonrestrictive

I have a brother and a sister. My brother, *a priest*, lives in New York.

Restrictive

I have two brothers. My brother *John* lives in New York.

In the first example, *my brother* is enough to tell the reader precisely who is meant, since he knows I have only one brother. My addition of *a priest* does not restrict or alter the meaning of *my brother*, but simply adds a piece of parenthetical information—a comment—to a sentence that makes perfect sense without it. In the second example, *my brother* alone would not tell the reader who is meant; he knows I have two brothers, and cannot know which one I refer to until I add a name. My addition of *John* accordingly restricts the meaning of *my brother* to the particular brother I have in mind: it defines that brother as my brother John, not my brother Elmer. Without the addition the sentence is unintelligible in its context.

Here, as in our pilot example, the distinction between restrictive and nonrestrictive is made with commas: the restrictive takes no commas, the nonrestrictive two commas (one if the noun comes at the end of the sentence). The usual error is to add commas where they are not wanted, as in the following sentences:

> Mailer's novel, *The Naked and the Dead*, shows his obsessive concern with the details of sex.

> A good place to begin is with Marx's critique of the reformist economists, Carey and Bastiat.

The commas in the first sentence imply that *The Naked and the Dead* is Mailer's only novel; the one in the second sentence implies that Carey and Bastiat alone in history, or at least in Marx's time, can properly be called "reformist economists." Neither implication conforms to the facts. Such constructions should be made either unmistakably restrictive (*Mailer's novel* The Naked and the Dead *shows* / *the reformist economists Carey and Bastiat*) or unmistakably nonrestrictive (*Mailer's first novel*, The Naked and the Dead, *shows* / *two reformist economists, Carey and Bastiat*).

Neat as this distinction is, it must sometimes be ignored. The following sentences, which ignore it, are correct:

> His wife Grace was the first to volunteer.

> The bond issue was floated by that notoriously corrupt and incompetent subsidiary of Amco International, the General Bionics Corporation.

Our erstwhile ally and friend in the Far East, General Pham Vong, was listed among the wounded.

Since a man has only one wife, *Grace* is clearly nonrestrictive; yet commas would place more emphasis on this name than the context warrants, and they may accordingly be dropped. In the other two sentences the apposition is basically restrictive, as we can see from the simple analogous constructions *that rascal Arthur* and *my friend Flicka*; but the components are too long and complex to hold together without commas, which are accordingly added.

The exceptions, it is clear, come at the extremes of simplicity and complexity. For the 90 percent or more of all appositive constructions that fall between these extremes, the rule holds: comma or commas for the nonrestrictive, no comma for the restrictive.

Adjectives in Sequence

Different red socks is a restrictive construction; it means *different* red socks, not the same red socks as before. *Different, red, socks* is nonrestrictive; it means different socks, this time red ones. Often, as in *big brown dog*, this distinction need not concern us (see p. 196), and sometimes we lack the information to make it, e.g. the color of the original socks. But just as often restrictiveness or nonrestrictiveness is inherent in wording itself. Thus, in Francis Christensen's example, to think of a pigeon *standing on its favorite right foot* is an absurdity, implying as it does that the bird has at least two right feet.

The following passages, though not as patently absurd, are ambiguous in the same way and need revision for clarity:

My baby sister can't read yet, but my *other older* sister reads to her every evening.

His two comments canceled each other out. The *first positive* comment was that we had played well and deserved to win. The *second negative* comment was . . .

It was sunny this time, but we remembered what the lake had looked like on the *earlier stormy* day.

In the first sentence, *other older sister* implies the existence of yet a third sister, also older, who does not read to the little girl; if only one older sister is meant, as seems likely, the phrase is *my other, older, sister*. Similarly *first positive comment* implies the first of two or more positive comments, which does not fit the facts. Commas are again the answer: *The first, positive, comment.* Similarly *the earlier, stormy, day*.

If you find the two commas awkward, the remedy is not to settle for the ambiguity of no commas or opt for the halfway house of a single comma, but rather to drop one of the adjectives if you can without loss (*my other sister / The first comment*) or reword (*my other sister, who is older / had looked like earlier, on a stormy day*).

Relative Clauses

The choice between restrictive and nonrestrictive is most difficult with relative clauses (clauses introduced by *who, whom, that, which, of whom, to which,* etc.). In the following correct passage, the first italicized clause is restrictive, the second nonrestrictive:

> Some literary critics have critical principles *that can be adequately summarized in a single word or phrase.* Such simple principles, *which do not concern us here,* have their use, but they rarely if ever do justice to the complexity of a literary work.

In the first sentence the restrictive wording *principles that* limits our concern to the particular class of principles that can be adequately summarized in a word or a phrase, as opposed to those that cannot be so summarized; the nonrestrictive wording *principles, which* would have falsely implied that *all* principles held by literary critics could be simply summarized. In the second sentence the nonrestrictive wording *principles, which* indicates that the whole class of *simple principles* does not concern us here; the restrictive wording *principles that* would have falsely implied the existence of a subclass of simple principles that *do* concern us.

Few distinctions are more important to good writing than this one, yet few are harder for the beginning writer to master. In our experience examples help, and we accordingly present six representative pairs of examples below. Only the first three involve relative clauses;

the next two involve adverbial clauses and the last an adverbial phrase. In each case the first member of the pair is restrictive, the second nonrestrictive. Note that the distinction is always made by using a comma for the nonrestrictive (two commas if the clause is in the middle of the sentence rather than at the end), and no comma for the restrictive. All the following sentences are correct:

R Why should I keep ice skates that are too small for me?
N I sold my old ice skates, which were too small for me.

R Senator Church is one senator whose views on this subject are known.
N Senator Church, whose views on this subject are known, did not vote.

R Clean government is a goal to which most officials give only· lip service.
N Kavanaugh's goal was clean government, to which most officials give only lip service.

R The headings should not be numbered as they are now. (*they should be numbered some other way*)
N The headings should not be numbered, as they are now. (*the numbers should be eliminated*)

R Sir William Craigie makes his home in the town where Dr. Johnson was born.
N Sir William Craigie makes his home in Lichfield, where Dr. Johnson was born.

R We had only one bad hurricane in 1969. (*but some years we have more than one*)
N We had only one bad hurricane, in 1969. (*and none before or since*)

It is not always easy to determine whether a sentence should be restrictive or nonrestrictive. How does one choose between *I have a lawn mower that needs sharpening* and *I have a lawn mower, which needs sharpening*? Between *There was a drought one summer that dried up the lake* and *There was a drought one summer, which dried up the lake*? None of these alternatives is wrong, and our advice in borderline cases of this sort is simply to take your pick. When in doubt, choose the restrictive. In ordinary speech the restrictive (*that*) construction is six times as common as the nonrestrictive (*which*); the ratio in writing is much lower, but is probably at least two to one.

That and *Which*

In the preceding examples we have recommended using *that* for the restrictive and *which* for the nonrestrictive, following the practice of most good writers and the almost universal pattern of spoken English. Another characteristic of spoken English is to omit *that* altogether when it serves as the object (as opposed to the subject) of a restrictive clause. Here again we recommend making writing conform to speech:

Awkward

the first books *which* Dickens wrote

Acceptable

the first books *that* Dickens wrote

Better

the first books Dickens wrote

If you would omit *that* in speaking, we think you should omit it in writing. Similarly in the following:

the security which it gives	the kind of person which she was
the security that it gives	the kind of person that she was
the security it gives	the kind of person she was

Even writers who reject the highly formal *which* in such phrases sometimes retain an unnecessary and faintly irritating *that* in deference to the supposed requirements of formality. Formality has its requirements, to be sure, but this is not one of them.

MIXED CONSTRUCTIONS

In Chapters 6 and 7 we discussed the dangers of mixing clichés and mixing metaphors. An equally common shortcoming of hasty writing is mixing two standard constructions, either of which would have served but which clash with each other. These examples, all from student writing, are followed by suggested fixes in parentheses:

> The more emotional he becomes, his arguments for getting Dooley to fight become less logical. (*As he becomes more emotional*)

> His tie didn't match his shirt, and neither of which matched his coat. (delete *of which*)

> It was about a week after my first meeting with her did I begin to realize what an excellent teacher she was. (*that I began*)

> The court should fine these people a large sum and be put on parole for two years or more. (*These people should be fined*)

The writers of these sentences may have switched syntax in mid-sentence without ever looking back, or they may have edited part of the sentence without considering the other part. Either way only careless writers would permit such blatant departures from good English to find their way into a final draft.

TWO SYNTAX CONTROVERSIES

Over the years teachers of English have developed a number of simple principles of syntax in an effort to come to some sort of workable terms with the complexities of a living language. Some of these principles are sensible and to the point: the main ones have been dealt with earlier in this chapter. Others have been ill served by oversimplifiers or eroded by contrary usage; if they are still worth heeding, their claims must be convincingly restated. Still others were nonsense from the start, having nothing but their simplemindedness to recommend them.

With these last we need not concern ourselves. It was never incorrect to begin a sentence with *But* or *And*; it was never incorrect to write sentences without verbs; and if it was ever incorrect to end a sentence with a preposition, that stuffy day is long past. Other practices, however, remain controversial, with traditionalists on one side and modernists on the other. Probably the two leading members of this class are the split infinitive and the use of *like* as a conjunction.

The Split Infinitive

The split infinitive can be traced back to the fourteenth century. Its chief modern forms appeared in the early seventeenth, and in the past hundred years there has been scarcely a major writer in the United States or England whose works are free of it. Is the form then completely acceptable? No, say the traditionalists. Yes, say the impatient. Not quite, is the advice here.

There are three possible positions for the adverb modifying an infinitive: before it (*completely to understand him*), splitting it (*to completely understand him*), and after it (*to understand him completely*). The last is recommended as natural:

In the end she decided to live *openly* with Paul.

They were too busy to look after the children *properly*.

Captain Larsen requested permission to explore the matter *further*.

The first position, before the infinitive, is less often natural, but should be preferred to splitting when it is not objectionable: "I do not want you *ever* to take such chances," "*Even* to wish for mercy would be cowardice." Only if neither outside position will do justice to the meaning should the infinitive be split:

The glare caused the men to *half* close their eyes.

He appeared to *suddenly* lose all control of the boat.

Mother had to *simply* take over the accounts.

The chief difficulty with split infinitives today is not that conservatives oppose them absolutely, but that radicals split them too freely. The battle for permission to split has long been won; the issue today is where to draw the line. Rightly or wrongly, split infinitives make many readers uneasy. Since the last thing you want to do is make your readers uneasy, you should split infinitives only when any alternative arrangement would be even less attractive.

Like and As

The distinction between *like* and *as* is easily made. *Like*, a preposition, compares nouns, pronouns, and noun phrases: *I am like my father / Like the women who had brought him up, Neil hated braggarts. As*, a conjunction, compares adverbs, adverbial phrases, and clauses: *For Johnson, as for Kennedy, there were no easy answers / Mme. de Sévigné was afraid of mice, as many women are. As* has other uses as well, some of which are discussed on pp. 263–264. We confine ourselves in this section to uses of *as* that bring it into conflict with *like*.

The classic error is to use *like* to introduce a clause. The following sentences illustrate this error:

Harry drives like Jack does.

These recurrent symbols clarify the poem's meaning, much like the action of a Greek drama is clarified by the chorus.

The patient sits before a screen that looks like it came from a television set.

The more vocal champions of *like* apparently consider the correct use of *as* in these sentences (*as if* in the third) affected or snobbish. However this may be, *like* is now routinely used to introduce clauses by perhaps half the English-speaking world, and bids fair in the end to drive *as* from the field.

The advice here, nonetheless, is to hold the line. The distinction between *like* and *as* is easily learned, and discriminating people consider it basic to good English. If you shrink from using *as* to mean *in the way that*, for example in *Harry drives as Jack does*, use *the way* instead: *Harry drives the way Jack does*.

What goes for *like* goes also for *unlike*, a word often misused out of desperation because there is no word *un-as* and no good equivalent. *Unlike* can only compare nouns, pronouns, or noun phrases: *Unlike*

Pete, I was tired / Elizabeth Taylor, unlike most people, spends $20,000 a month. The following sentences are wrong (suggested revisions in parentheses):

> Unlike the previous election, few charges of fraud were made. *(Unlike the previous election, this one evoked few charges of fraud.)*

> Unlike what both sides had expected, the game was soon over. *(Contrary to what both sides had expected, the game was soon over.)*

Finally, take care not to write *as* erroneously for *like*. A sentence like *Byron, as Keats and Shelley before him, died young* is apparently due to the writer's excessive fear of falling into the opposite error, that of using *like* for *as*, which is by far the more common and the more loudly deplored. *As* for *like*, with its prissy, toe-in-the-water effect, seems if anything the more deplorable slip of the two.

As this chapter has suggested, good syntax is not just a matter of rules, though rules are its necessary point of departure. It is also a matter of judging when and to what extent the rules apply, when and to what extent time and usage have passed them by, when convenience may properly be indulged at the expense of fastidiousness, and when the line should be held. The best arbiters of such matters, we think, are professional writers and editors, whose sense of the language is constantly elaborated and modified by their work. Their current practice has been the basis for our pronouncements in this chapter.

Several dozen errors and pitfalls of syntax are discussed briefly in the Index to Current Usage, pp. 259–303.

11

ORTHOGRAPHY

Words must be not only correctly chosen (see Chapter 6) but correctly written, which is to say correctly spelled, divided, capitalized, and italicized as general usage or a specific context may require. Questions of orthography are generally less interesting than questions of diction, but they can be just as important to the writer's message. Small, even niggling, as most of them are, you cannot ignore them or answer them carelessly except at the expense of your reader's understanding.

SPELLING

For spelling, there is only one rule: if you are not absolutely sure how a word is spelled, look it up in the dictionary. If you are not allowed to use a dictionary—for example, during a test—you are on your own. English spelling is so irregular that no one should be required to memorize the spelling of more than a thousand or so of the most familiar words. A teacher who does not allow you to use a dictionary on a test will probably allow you a spelling error or two without penalty.

A dictionary can also correct any tendency you may have to write single-word compounds as separate words. To be sure, a word like *bedroom* was originally formed by conjoining *bed* and *room*, but it has by now been a single word for so long that the spelling *bed room* smacks of illiteracy. So do the following specimens from student papers, the last of which magnifies the error by changing *scape* to *escape*:

> Most of us considered Mike a *loud mouth*.

> His *wise cracks* were rarely appreciated.

> Often the parents are used as the *escape goat*.

Further comments on compounds appear on pp. 177–178.

An occasional spelling error is understandable, but there is no excuse for confusing your readers with *or* where you mean *of* or *on*, with *an* where you mean *in* or *and* or *as*, etc. And there is no excuse whatever for handing in garbage like this:

> We worked together, drank together, sang togehter, sometimeds all a once. He had a bery serious relationship with an old girl-friend of mine.

Whenever time pressures tempt you to type a paper at top speed and not proofread it afterward, remember that it will be read under other conditions. If, like the student just quoted, you come through sounding drunk, you will be judged accordingly.

HYPHENATION

The hyphen has four uses: to divide words at the end of a line (*Mac-/beth, syca-/more*), to divide prefixes from certain root words (*un-American, anti-imperialist*), to pull together compounds of two or more words into visual units (*brown-and-serve muffins, a great get-together*), and to avoid repeating part of a word or a hyphenated compound (*pre- and postwar statistics*).

Word Division

To divide words properly simply follow your dictionary, which indicates all possible word divisions for a given word. Thus the dots in **syc·a·more** show that the word may be divided either *syc-/amore* or *syca-/more*. Proper names and words not in a dictionary should be divided between syllables; if you cannot tell for certain where a syllable ends, your best guess will probably serve. Never divide a one-syllable name or word, and never divide after the first letter or before the last.

Prefixes

The use of a hyphen with prefixes is easily learned. (1) If the root word begins with a capital letter, use a hyphen (*pre-Christian*). (2) If the prefix ends with a vowel and the root word begins with the same vowel, check your dictionary. Some such words are unhyphenated (*cooperate, preeminent*); others are hyphenated (*co-opt*); others do not appear in the dictionary, in which case use a hyphen (*co-owner, pre-educate*). (3) Otherwise do not hyphenate, save where a hyphen distinguishes one reading of a word from another; thus *re-cover*, "to cover again," is distinguished from *recover*.

Compounds

The third use of the hyphen—to pull together compounds of two or more words into visual units—is the most important and the most complex. The two main classes of such compounds may be illustrated as follows:

Noun compounds	Adjective compounds
a *sergeant first class*	a *life insurance* salesman
an *air-conditioner*	*hard-to-get* parts
a better *mousetrap*	a *clearheaded* woman

Observe that some members of each class are unhyphenated phrases, some are hyphenated compounds, and some are unhyphenated words. For noun compounds alone, *Webster's Third* prescribes the following bewildering variety of forms:

pocket-handkerchief	half-wit	off-season
pocket battleship	half brother	off year
pocketknife	halfback	offshoot
birthrate	makeup	vice-president
death rate	shake-up	vice admiral

How in the world, then, is one to know whether a compound should be hyphenated, run as two separate words, or made into a single word? For noun compounds the answer is easy: look up the compound in the dictionary. If you find it, use its dictionary form; if you don't find it, write it as separate words unless a hyphen seems necessary to eliminate a possible misreading.

Adjective compounds are harder to handle. Most are not listed in the dictionary at all, or are listed in their noun form only. We know, for example, that we should write *high school* thus as a noun, but should we hyphenate it or not as an adjective compound in the phrase *high school teacher*? The dictionary does not say. In effect, usage on this point is in transition, but the following broad guidelines may help.

If an adjective compound appears in your dictionary as a consolidated or hyphenated word, use the dictionary form: thus *Webster's New Collegiate* shows *fainthearted, hardworking, clear-sighted,* and *hard-boiled.* If an adjective compound is not listed in your dictionary, either hyphenate it or write it as two (or more) words. Hyphenate number compounds (*a twenty-year period, a third-floor apartment*); participle compounds (*a card-carrying Communist, porcelain-capped teeth*), except with adverbs ending in *-ly* (*a recently built factory*); preposition compounds (*a made-up story, an after-dinner speech*); compounds of coequal nouns (*the second Clay-Liston fight, the mind-body problem*); compounds expressing degree (*a large-scale enterprise, middle-class morality*); and compounds of three or more words (*a door-to-door salesman, a high-silicon-content alloy*). Write other adjective compounds as two words: *high school teacher, senior class party, civil rights agitation.* A hyphen would not be wrong in such expressions, but it may seem a bit too formal.

Hyphenation to Avoid Repetition

Hyphens are sometimes used to avoid repeating part of a word or a hyphenated compound: *pro- and anti-Chinese writing / over- and underrated products / full- or part-time work / the food-preparing and -packaging industries.* Although Gowers calls this construction "a clumsy device that should be avoided if possible," there is often no better way to write what would naturally be said in speech. The problem is not so much to avoid the construction as to remember to add the essential hanging hyphen. Leaving it out will always produce imprecision: thus *full* for *full-* in the third example above would yield not *full-time work* but the meaningless *full work.* And it may cause deeper confusion: thus *packaging* for *-packaging* in the last example would yield not *the food-packaging industry* but *the packaging industry* in general, a very different thing.

Are good writers tending to use fewer and fewer hyphens? There are signs they are. We know that British literate usage favors more hyphens than American literate usage, which in turn hyphenates more freely than American literate and scientific usage. At the same time, we find influential British writers like Winston Churchill spurning the hyphen as "a blemish to be avoided wherever possible," and Gowers echoing this judgment to the point of recommending consolidated forms like *aftereffects* and *panicstricken* without turning a hair. The Merriam-Webster editors go even further, endorsing such extreme specimens as *radiobroadcasting* and *fluidounce.* When British grammarians and stylists agree with American illiterates, scientists, and lexicographers, who can stand against such overwhelming odds? Our guess is that the hyphen is on its way out.

THE APOSTROPHE

In addition to forming possessives (see pp. 148–149), the apostrophe is used to form certain plurals and to form contractions.

Plurals

You may use an apostrophe to form plurals of numbers (*the 1960's, two size 9's*), letters (*two A's and three B's*), and abbreviations (*six-*

teen Ph.D.'s, some MP's), and to form plurals of words used as words, book titles, and the like (*do's and don't's,* and*'s instead of* but*'s, a dozen* David Copperfield*'s*). Apostrophes should not be used to form other plurals. As we have seen, Mr. Jones's family is *the Joneses,* not *the Jones's.* Similarly, the plurals of *Rolls-Royce* and *New York,* for example, are not *Rolls-Royce's* and *New York's* but *Rolls-Royces* and *New Yorks: Two New Yorks would be one too many.*

Contractions

Contractions are formed by substituting an apostrophe for some part of a word that is not pronounced in informal speech. The words most commonly contracted are *not* (*isn't, don't*) and the various forms of *have* (*he's been, you've gone*), *will* (*I'll stay, they'd complain*), and *be* (*I'm, you're*). Although the standard contractions of *have, will,* and *be* involve pronouns, other contractions of all three are possible in dialogue: *I wouldn't've dared / The sun'll be up soon / The sky's the limit.* In writing contractions, take care to get the apostrophe in the right place (*hadn't,* not *had'nt*) and not to leave a space before or after it (*you'll,* not *you' ll* or *you 'll*).

Contractions like *'teens* (as in *girls in their 'teens*) and *'seventies* (meaning the 1970's), where the apostrophe indicates that part of a word is being used for the whole, are increasingly, and we think properly, written without the apostrophe. Some earlier travelers along this path were *'bus* for *omnibus* and *'coon* for *raccoon.*

On the status of the standard contractions in formal writing, see p. 103. Cute spellings like *ham 'n' eggs* are discussed on p. 104.

CAPITALIZATION

Capitalization is the bane of many a writer. The basic rules—to capitalize the first word in a sentence and such proper names as Henry Smith, Thursday, *War and Peace,* and the Chicago Bears—are easily learned, but once beyond the basics even the most experienced writer encounters difficulties. In this section we shall discuss some of the more persistent problems.

Sentences Within Sentences

When a direct quotation makes a complete sentence within a sentence, you may either capitalize or lowercase the first word, depending on how the quotation relates to the rest of the sentence and without regard to whether or not the word is capitalized in the original. Thus, the same quotation may properly be begun with a capital letter in one context and a lowercase letter in another:

> The Bible says: "Look not upon the wine when it is red."
> The Bible asks that we "look not upon the wine when it is red."

> In the words of Harold Wilson, "The worst is over."
> Harold Wilson argues that "the worst is over."

When a sentence within a sentence is not in quotes, do not capitalize the first word:

> According to Harold Wilson, the worst was over.

> The truth was plain: we had been deceived.

> Art's job (he was test-flying helicopters) was classified as hazardous.

A capital letter may follow a colon when the colon introduces a formal or weighty pronouncement, even if no quotation marks are used. For example, *He had his own version of the Golden Rule: Do unto others all you can get away with.* When in doubt, however, lowercase after a colon.

Proper Nouns and Adjectives

Students are often unsure whether to capitalize familiar short forms of brand names and other formal designations. Is it *a chevvy* or *a Chevvy, a mountie* or *a Mountie*? Is Capitol Hill (meaning usually Congress) *the hill* or *the Hill*, the House of Representatives *the house* or *the House*? We prefer the capitalized form in all the above examples as making one's meaning more immediately clear. This reason is perhaps especially compelling when a lowercase form carries another meaning altogether, as in *cad* for Cadillac, *met* for Metropolitan Opera, or *coke* for Coca-Cola. *Coke* is in fact a trademark, as are also, surprisingly enough, such other words as *Jeep* and *Laundromat,* which means that you use the lowercase form in print at the risk of a stern letter from the proprietor's lawyers.

Another troublesome category is courses of study. Do we say *a history class* or *a History class*, *a professor of history* or *a professor of History*, *a French literature examination* or *a French Literature examination*? We think one way is as good as the other. Take your pick, but then stick with it: don't write *a professor of French Literature* and *a history professor* in the same paper.

French, German, and other languages do not capitalize proper adjectives, but English does: thus *Swedish diplomat*, *Catholic mass*, *Jewish rye bread*. Confusion arises chiefly where a capitalized form has a legitimate lowercase form with a very similar meaning: is it *the Protestant ethic* or *the protestant ethic*, *a Socialist program* or *a socialist program*, *the Roman alphabet* or *the roman alphabet*? A good dictionary sometimes makes the choice clear: the *Roman* alphabet as opposed to the Greek or the Cyrillic, the *roman* alphabet as opposed to the italic. When in doubt, capitalize.

Personal Titles

Good writers capitalize personal titles when they are attached to names (*General Bert Guano, Professor Rainier*), but lowercase them when they are used alone (*Bert Guano was promoted to general / Mr. Rainier is a professor of French*). The problem comes when a title is used in place of a specific name. In a specific reference to General Guano, for example, should we write *The General called for volunteers* or *The general called for volunteers*? Both forms are common; neither is wrong. If current usage has any pattern at all, it is that the most eminent titles are the most frequently capitalized: few if any writers lowercase *the Pope, the President of the United States, the Queen of England*. For slightly less eminent titles, though lowercase is increasingly common, capitalization remains usual: *the Secretary of State, the Governor of Alaska, the Prime Minister, the Archbishop, the General*. At lower levels of eminence lowercase prevails: *the president of General Motors, the major, the professor, the judge, the coach*.

Parts Standing for the Whole

Eminent titles apart, it is usual to lowercase key words substituted for formal proper nouns. Thus, after an initial reference to the Mississippi River, we refer to it as *the river*, not *the River*; we refer to the Second World War as *the war*, to the Chinese Communist Party as *the party*, to the Chicago Public Library as *the library*, to the University of Wisconsin as *the university*, and so on. Naturally, this practice applies only when the lowercased word faithfully conveys the meaning of the full expression: a restaurant named the Old Barn cannot be referred to as *the barn*, or the Chicago Bears as *the bears*.

Points of the Compass

North, east, south, west, and their derivations cause all sorts of trouble. Should it be *Western Europe* or *western Europe*? *In the north* or *in the North*? Probably the most workable rule is to capitalize these words when they stand for a formal or semiformal political or geographic unit, and to lowercase them when they are used in a general geographical sense or merely to indicate direction. Thus *Southeast Asia* designates the area south of China and east of India and politically independent of both, whereas the geographical region *southeastern Asia* would include much of China and part of India. Similarly, *the East* refers to New England and the Central Atlantic states, or in another context to the Orient; *the east* refers to where the sun rises. A few more examples may make the distinction clearer:

Semiformal	General
West Germany	a west wind
South Korea	the south of France
North Africa	drive north to Seattle
the Far East	the east bank of the Rhine
the Southwest	southwestern Arkansas

By a semiformal name, we mean one that is sanctioned by usage (*West Germany*) or convenience (*North Africa*) rather than by formal political decree. *West Germany* is the common name for the Federal Republic of Germany, as *South Korea* is for the Republic of Korea; *North Africa*, *the Far East*, and *the Southwest* are convenient names for areas having no formal unity. Although not formal in the sense that *West Virginia* and *Northern Ireland* are formal, these names are in practice treated formally. The distinction between semiformal and general is more important, and is not always easy to make. When in doubt, lowercase. Adjectives derived from capitalized nouns in this class should themselves be capitalized: *Far Eastern policy, Middle Western roads, Southern hospitality.*

Historical Terms

Capitalize the names of historical eras and other historical phenomena when lowercasing would suggest a different or more diffuse meaning than the specific one you have in mind:

the Stone Age
the Reign of Terror
the Industrial Revolution
the May Thirtieth Movement

the Fourth of July
the Lost Generation
the Iron Curtain
the Great Proletarian Cultural Revolution

Where lowercasing would not convey a different meaning, either form is usually acceptable:

the Roman Empire/empire
the Bolshevik Revolution/revolution
the Pre-Raphaelite Movement/movement

the Treaty/treaty of Versailles
the French Impressionists/impressionists
the Augustan Age/age

An exception is *War*, which is conventionally capitalized when the name of a war is given in full: *the Sino-Japanese War of 1894-95, the Second World War, the War of the Roses.*

Book and Article Titles

In titles of books, magazine articles, songs, and other formal compositions, and in the titles and subheadings of papers that you write, capitalize the first and last words and all other words except (1) articles and (2) prepositions and conjunctions of five or fewer letters:

What Is an American?
"The Light Behind His Eyes"
Of Mice and Men

"When the Saints Come Marching In"
Love in a Cold Climate
"What It Means to Be Ill"

ITALICS

Titles of Publications and Compositions

Italics are indicated in manuscript or typescript by underlining. Underline the names of newspapers and magazines; the titles of books, plays, and other longish pieces of writing, especially if published separately; and the names of movies, paintings, and long musical compositions:

the *Washington Post*	*Paradise Lost*
Time magazine	movies like *Pygmalion*
The Sun Also Rises	Cézanne's *View of Auvers*
The Merchant of Venice	Mozart's opera *Don Giovanni*

Do not underline the titles of newspaper or magazine articles, short stories, poems, songs, and other shortish pieces of writing, or of unpublished works. Use quotation marks:

"Chaos in Laos," editorial in the *San Francisco Chronicle*, August 1, 1971, p. 26

a senior thesis entitled "The Early English Stage"

Milton's "Lycidas"

the "Dear Abby" column

Roth's short story "Epstein"

Cole Porter's "Begin the Beguine"

When in doubt, use quotation marks rather than underlining.

Foreign Terms

Underline only the most unfamiliar foreign words, not relatively common terms like ruble, fiancé, and prima donna. If a foreign expression is in quotation marks, underlining is unnecessary unless foreign and English words are mixed:

"Bonjour," said the man uncertainly.

Tolstoy's "Utro Pomeshchika" is another of his stories about peasants.

BUT: "Time to go now, *nicht wahr?*" said Charlie.

Do not underline foreign proper names:

> The Comuneros and the Alumbrados joined forces in 1534.

> I met her at the Piazza San Marco.

> The Jeunesses Agricoles is a sort of French 4-H club.

The whole idea of underlining a foreign expression is to set it off clearly from the surrounding English. If quotation marks or capital letters accomplish this purpose, underlining is superfluous.

Emphasis

Underlining for emphasis is almost always a mistake; if you have this tendency, do your best to suppress it. Writers who underline for emphasis usually do so for one of two reasons. One is the desire to clarify a badly constructed sentence for the reader without going to the trouble of reconstructing it:

Clumsy

> It was not so much the things she *had* done that made people annoyed with her as the things she had *not* done.

Rewritten

> What she had done annoyed people much less than what she had not done.

The other is the desire to give writing some of the body English that intonation and gesture give to speech. Novelists sometimes use italics effectively in dialogue to convey kittenishness and other unprepossessing (or at best amusing) characteristics: "In *Ho*llywood! How *mar*-velous! What's he *doing*?" exclaims a girl in *The Catcher in the Rye*, and we know immediately what sort of girl she is.

In nonfiction, it is usually the writer that ends up sounding foolish. Here are three examples of excessive underlining from student themes:

Dogged

> I feel that punishment *can* be detrimental to a child's character or that it *could* cause damage to his psyche, but I do not think it usually *does*.

Strident

> Some people *really* have *no idea* that their parents were ever young.

Posturing

> His giggle nearly drove me *crazy*, and I thought to myself, "How am I *ever* going to survive this *ghastly* picnic?"

The temptation to underline can be very strong, particularly when you are exasperated at not being able to get the kind of emphasis in writing that comes so easily in speaking. But there is almost always a better way to get the reader's attention than by shouting at him. A change in wording will usually do the trick.

NUMBERS

The Twenty/21 Rule

Other things being equal, a good general rule is to spell out numbers up to twenty and use figures for 21 and over:

twelve o'clock	a sixteen-year-old	ten minutes
140 men wounded	a 21-year-old girl	45 minutes

Several exceptions to this rule are commonly made. One is that when figures for a number over 21 would suggest an exactness belied by the context, the number can be spelled out:

> about a hundred years ago (*not* about 100 years ago)
>
> sixty or eighty policemen (*not* 60 or 80 policemen)
>
> a thousand times as good (*not* 1,000 times as good)

For numbers in four, five, or six figures this exception conventionally applies only to 1,000 and 10,000; other round numbers in this range are assumed to be approximate even if presented in figures: *an army of 80,000 men / 200,000 years ago.* For millions and billions mixed treatment is usual (*a population of over 14 million / a deficit of $163.1 billion*), with the first number often spelled out if it is one to ten (*two million beggars*).

A second exception commonly made to the twenty/21 rule is to use figures invariably before *percent*: thus *1 percent, 10 percent*.

A third exception is to spell out any number that begins a sentence:

> *not* 16 percent were Catholic *but* Sixteen percent were Catholic *or* Some 16 percent were Catholic

> *not* 75 men showed up *but* Seventy-five men showed up *or* Only 75 men showed up

> *not* 1865 was a memorable year *but* Eighteen sixty-five was a memorable year *or* The year 1865 was a memorable one

This convention, which grew up because numbers do not have capital and lowercase forms like letters, no longer makes sense to many writers and editors. As the 1865 example suggests, the alternatives are particularly unsatisfactory for dates; nor is it easy to stomach something like *One thousand four hundred and eighty-one men were killed and wounded.* In the circumstances, we recommend following the convention when you can and violating it when you must.

Finally, a sequence of numbers that are essentially equal in weight or parallel in syntax should be treated the same way: either all spelled out or all in figures. Thus instead of writing *I am 22, my sister Joan is eighteen, and my brother Dick is twelve,* either spell out *twenty-two* or run *18* and *12* in figures.

The twenty/21 rule does not apply to tabular presentation, scientific and technical writing (*carbon 14 / a factor of 2*), reference numbers (*Chapter 6 / Theorem 12*), dates (*15* B.C. */ April 3*), sports scores (*Amherst 7, Williams 6*), or any other area in which numbers are conventionally given in figures irrespective of context. It applies only where convention permits spelling out and where doing so may solve a problem or avoid an irritation.

Other Number Conventions

Numbers linked by a hyphen to indicate a span (*pp. 326–328 / 1970–1971*) should be treated consistently: if you write *pp. 326-8* in one footnote, you should not write *pp. 205-06* in another and *pp. 171-179* in a third. The easiest way to be consistent is always to give the second number at full length, as is done in this book. If this seems a bit ponderous for dates, treat them as a separate category; the convention is *1976-77*, not *1976-7*.

A comma is conventional in four-figure numbers (as well as numbers of five and more figures) except for dates and page numbers of long books and journals. The comma is used not only in numbers like 1,234 that are read with a natural break at the comma position ("one thousand / two hundred and thirty-four") but also in numbers like 1,500, in spite of their being customarily read as "fifteen hundred" rather than "one thousand / five hundred."

Fractions are conventionally spelled out and hyphenated: *two-thirds*, not *two thirds* or *2/3* or *2/3rds*. The hyphen is standard even where the denominator can be read as a noun: *Two-thirds of my money was gone*, not *Two thirds*. Only *half* has achieved sufficient independence as a noun to drop the hyphen occasionally, as in *I took one half and gave George the other*. *Quarter* (the coin), *fifth* (the whiskey measure), and other such fraction-derived nouns do not of course come under these rules for fractions.

Numbered Lists

In numbering lists, most writers use periods when each numbered item begins a new line, thus:

1. The dean of women should report directly to President Schweinkopf.
2. An assistant dean of women should be appointed to process applications by women for admission to graduate school.
3. Women should be granted access to the gymnasium on an equal basis with men.

When a numbered list is given in running text, double parentheses are usual, thus: *The petition asked (1) that the dean of women report directly to President Schweinkopf, (2) that an assistant dean of women be appointed*, etc. Other writers use double parentheses or single parentheses—1), 2), 3)—for both separate-line lists and lists in running text. The important thing is to be consistent: not to use (1), (2), (3) in one list and 1), 2), 3) or (*a*), (*b*), (*c*) in an analogous list several pages further on.

Prominent as the word *consistent* is in the last few paragraphs, consistency is no more important for numbers than for the other subjects covered in this chapter. Whether or not you hyphenate *junior college transfer* or capitalize *the Senator* or italicize a song title matters less than whether you write it the second time the same way you did the first. Four hundred years ago inconsistency was the norm; Shakespeare signed his name half a dozen different ways, and his contemporaries invented as many more. But today's writers are more orderly. A foolish consistency may be what Emerson called it, the hobgoblin of little minds; but between reasonable consistency and potential confusion there can be only one choice.

12
PUNCTUATION

Punctuation has one purpose only: to clarify the writer's meaning. Poor punctuation can and often does mean poor communication, as in the following sentences from student papers, all of which use commas ineffectively to do the work of stronger punctuation marks:

> Whenever we had a problem about anything, we could always talk to Jim, whether he had a solution or not was not the most important thing, it was the idea of having someone older, and experienced listening with an open mind.

> I always thought that was simply the way her features were molded, after all, some of the happiest creatures I knew had that look.

> Needless to say, common sense or the lack of it, is responsible for these traits.

In the first sentence, the first comma is right but the others should be changed to a period, changed to a semicolon, and eliminated, respectively:

Whenever we had a problem about anything, we could always talk to Jim. Whether he had a solution or not was not the most important thing; it was the idea of having someone older and experienced listening with an open mind.

In the second sentence, we don't know how to read *after all* until one or the other comma is changed to a period or a semicolon:

I always thought that was simply the way her features were molded; after all, some of the happiest creatures I knew had that look.

In the last sentence, dashes make the meaning clear:

Needless to say, common sense—or the lack of it—is responsible for these traits.

Good punctuation is partly a matter of rules and partly a matter of taste. Those who would make it altogether a matter of rules paint themselves into a corner: no rules can anticipate the millions of possible combinations of words that a writer may be moved to use, or his need to relate words in various ways for various effects, or his desire to slow down or quicken the reader's pace. Those who would make it altogether a matter of taste make an even more serious mistake. There are, after all, certain well-established rules or conventions for relating words, phrases, and clauses to each other, and most readers expect to see them followed, at least for the routine connections and separations.

THE PERIOD

A sentence has a subject and a predicate: *Dogs bark / Did you see Henry? / [You] Get lost!* A sentence fragment lacks either a subject or a predicate or both. It is often the answer to a question (*Tomorrow or the day after / Tommy's sister*), or a question itself (*Who? / Why not?*), but it can be any combination of words that make a separate unit of thought (*Feeling good today / Nuts to you!*).

A sentence or sentence fragment should end with a period unless it ends with a question mark or an exclamation point. A sentence occurring within another sentence must be punctuated according to the needs of the larger sentence: *She said "I am tired," but she didn't mean it / Bill spoke crossly (he was tired)*. Periods are misused chiefly in making an illegitimate sentence fragment out of what is properly a subordinate clause in the preceding sentence:

Wrong

> He always goes fishing on August 1. Which is his birthday.

Right

> He always goes fishing on August 1, which is his birthday.

Right

> He always goes fishing on August 1. That is his birthday.

Another difficulty is the converse of this last, namely, making what is properly two sentences into one:

Wrong

> He always goes fishing on August 1, that is his birthday.

Poor

> I was hungry, I wanted some lunch.

Right

> I was hungry. I wanted some lunch.

You may use a semicolon if a period seems too abrupt: *He always goes fishing on August 1; that is his birthday / I was hungry; I wanted some lunch*.

Notice that the sentence *I was hungry, I wanted some lunch*, which connects two independent clauses with a comma rather than a semicolon or a period, is labeled *poor*, not *wrong*. For many years this punctuation—known as the comma splice or comma fault—was anathema to teachers and editors, a sign of gross illiteracy; in some colleges it was grounds for an automatic F on a paper. But good writers persisted in using the construction, especially for certain effects of nervousness, tentativeness, and haste that no other punctuation could quite capture; and gradually it became acceptable in principle, however greatly abused in practice. The sentence fragment has come the same road, from outright rejection to qualified acceptance. Both constructions, the comma splice and the sentence fragment, have their unique uses. The problem is not how to avoid them altogether, but how to use them well.

A particular source of difficulty with the comma splice is the handling of direct quotations:

Wrong

"I am hungry," Marie said, "I want some lunch."

Right

"I am hungry," Marie said. "I want some lunch."

Right

"I am hungry," Marie said, "and I want some lunch."

The writer of the first sentence has punctuated it as if it were the third; that is, he has mistaken two sentences for one. In the second sentence, a semicolon rather than a period may be used; but a period is usual, perhaps because semicolons seem too formal for informal dialogue.

THE COMMA

The comma is the most important punctuation mark; as befits this status, its proper use is both complex and hotly disputed. The disputants come largely from two schools of thought. One is the old-fashioned or rhetorical school, which concerns itself with marking the natural pauses in a sentence as it might be spoken by an able speaker, and which accordingly caters to the ear. The other is the modern or logical school, which concerns itself with clarifying the sense units of a sentence and bringing out their proper relationship to one another; this school caters primarily to the eye. Current usage draws on the insights of both schools, with most authorities favoring the modern school in cases of out-and-out conflict.

The following discussion begins with some basics (use of the comma in appendages, series, compound sentences), moves on to more difficult matters (introductory phrases, parenthetical phrases, confluences), and ends with some general remarks on over- and underpunctuation. The basics are both the most important and the easiest to learn, but the later material is indispensable to a mastery of the comma.

Appendages

Most appendages preceded by a comma are also followed by a comma in running text:

Washington, D.C., is	June 14, 1947, was
Athens, Ohio, is	Sunday, June 14, was
The University of California, Berkeley, is	Trinity College, Oxford, is

The chief exceptions to this practice are *Jr.*, *Inc.*, and academic degrees:

Alexander H. Jones, Jr. is	Textron, Inc. is
Robert Abrams, M.D. is	Unilever, Ltd. is

There are also, of course, appendages that take no commas at all:

John D. Rockefeller III is	8:30 A.M. is
The fifth century B.C. is	Queen Elizabeth II is

Still others take parentheses: *12:15 P.M. (EST) is.*

All these last cause no problems. The hard thing to remember is the comma *following* appendages of the sort illustrated in the first examples above.

Series

In a list or series of three or more members, put a comma after every member but the last:

Lenin, Gandhi, and Mao Tse-tung are mentioned most frequently.

Detectives were stationed in the drawing room, on the patio, and in the garden.

Landis was a big, fat, slovenly, but extremely agile man.

When two adjectives precede a noun, use a comma if they modify the noun independently: that is, if their relationship is an *and* relationship. *A big, funny-looking dog* is a dog that is both big and funny-looking. If the first adjective modifies the unit composed of the second adjective and the noun, omit the comma. *A wild young man* is a young man who is wild; we read *young man* as a single unit. Most people find this distinction hard to apply, and it is accordingly breaking down, with the no-comma form increasingly favored. (See also pp. 167–168.)

Compound Sentences

In general, put a comma before the conjunction (*and, but, or, for, nor, yet, so*) in a compound sentence:

I sat with Jack, and my sister sat in the balcony.

The reason was not altogether clear, but clarity was not altogether desirable.

The President never notified Secretary Butz, nor did he call a Cabinet meeting to discuss the charge.

The comma enables the reader to divide the sentence instantly into its two components. Sometimes it may eliminate false trails: for example, *Jack and my sister* in the first sentence. But even where such ambiguities are no problem, as in our second sentence, the comma offers the most economical possible clue to the sentence structure. The reader confronted with an unpunctuated sentence like *The reason was not altogether clear but clarity was not altogether desirable* must in effect hunt down the turning point for himself and put in his own mental comma, a labor the writer should have spared him.

Four exceptions may be noted. First, a compound imperative sentence does not usually take the comma: *Shoot and be damned / Go down to the drugstore and get some aspirin*. Second, a short compound sentence with an introductory adverbial phrase governing both verbs is sometimes more clearly punctuated with a single comma after the opening phrase:

> In Montaigne's opinion, Medina Sidonia was right and Sir Francis Drake was wrong.

> As my grandfather used to say, most people are fools and the rest are swine.

Third, the comma can be omitted in a very short sentence (except before *for*): *Anne forgot and so did Mary / He went but she stayed home*. Fourth, in a very long compound sentence, or one with internal punctuation in one or both of its clauses, a semicolon is usually better than a comma. A semicolon is of course obligatory if there is no coordinating conjunction, save where the comma splice is deliberately used for a special effect (see pp. 193-194).

Opening Phrases

Many writers put a comma after an opening phrase or clause only if it is seven words long or longer:

> In the Sudan there are very few large cities.

> Among the Wolagusi warriors of the northern Sudan, property squabbles are frequent.

> When Aunt Laura arrived the fun began.

> When Aunt Laura and Uncle Harry arrived, the fun began.

Other writers put a comma after all introductory phrases, regardless of length: *In 1917, the Bolshevik Revolution occurred / When Lincoln died, the nation mourned*.

These practices are equally acceptable; our advice is to choose one or the other and stick with it. In borderline cases let your ear be your guide. When single words like *however* and *incidentally*, short phrases like *for example* and *in other words*, begin a sentence, they are commonly followed by a pause in speech, and hence by a comma in writing. Other single words like *thus* and *therefore*, other short phrases like *in some ways* and *at one time*, are commonly followed by little or no pause in speech, and normally by no comma in writing. If you simply cannot decide, add the comma.

When an opening phrase or clause ends with a preposition, always add a comma to keep the preposition from being read as part of what follows it: *To begin with, the overture is weak / From late June on, the beach is crowded.*

Parenthetical Phrases

Place commas before and after a phrase or clause in a sentence that would be complete and coherent without that phrase or clause:

> Mother was amused, oddly enough, and so was Dad.

> "You are a traitor," she said quietly, "and a coward."

> Only Ravenna, the home of Andrea del Sarto's *Last Supper*, was spared.

Neither comma may be omitted without sending the sentence off the rails. In these student sentences necessary commas were inadvertently left out at the points marked by brackets:

> The three of us, Steve, Grandma, and I [ ] used to sit at one end of the table and play cards.

> Before I spring that surprise [ ] though, I want to describe his background.

If a parenthetical word or phrase ends the sentence, a comma should precede it: *Oveta Culp Hobby was the first WAC colonel, if I am not mistaken.*

This convention applies only to truly parenthetical or nonrestrictive phrases, phrases that might as readily have been put between parentheses as between commas: *Mother was amused (oddly enough), and so was Dad / The total was under ten dollars (I think).* The convention does not apply to defining or restrictive phrases, phrases that could not be placed in parentheses without distorting the intended meaning. (For a fuller discussion of restrictive and nonrestrictive constructions, see pp. 165–170.) In the following sentences, a comma at any of the points indicated by brackets would be wrong:

He was a friend of the poet [ ] Matthew Prior.

Stores [ ] with high reputations [ ] often overcharge.

A man [ ] who would do that [ ] would do anything.

Here the phrases following the opening brackets do not merely comment parenthetically on the preceding words but complete them. *Stores (with high reputations) often overcharge,* for example, would be nonsense; not all stores are in question, only *stores with high reputations.*

In some sentences, notably those in which a conjunction is followed by a longish introductory phrase or clause, the distinction between parenthetical and nonparenthetical expressions is hard to apply, largely because the ear and eye approaches to punctuation clash. The following sentences, with brackets where commas are possible, illustrate the problem:

The repairman said that [ ] for all practical purposes [ ] the heating system could be regarded as adequate.

Cromwell had made his preparations, and [ ] if the bad news proved to be true [ ] he was ready.

The logical school would plump for two commas in each case, to telegraph the construction of the sentence clearly. The rhetorical school would omit the opening commas, on the ground that since there would be no pause in speech after *that* and after *and,* a comma after either would be irritating.

We incline to the rhetorical school here. If the phrase is too long to leave without commas, put a comma at the end but do not slavishly add one at the beginning. Follow your ear. In the following sentences one comma seems adequate:

Mrs. Edmunds said that *whatever the judge's decision might be,* she would accept it.

Abbott was angry at first, but *when he remembered what Ginny had told him about bears,* he started smiling.

Confluences

"Confluence" is Fowler's term for a construction in which two syntactically parallel elements, one following the other, flow simultaneously into the sentence somewhere short of its end:

Some, if not all [,] of the teachers were on strike.

Anne's approach was more delicate, more ingenious [,] than mine.

Ney's courage was his foremost, perhaps his only [,] virtue.

Many people are opposed to, or at least annoyed by [,] the new zoning regulations.

The question is whether the comma shown in brackets should be added or not. We think it should be, so as to connect the first element of the sequence more securely with the words that follow the second. Without the comma the construction is not immediately clear.

Clarity

Consider the following sentence:

The headmaster of the academy would on ceremonial occasions refer to the school as a patriotic institution [,] and to the boys and the recent alumni as their nation's best hope for a glorious future.

Although this is not a compound sentence, to add the comma shown in brackets is a service to the reader. It converts an unwieldy mass of 34 words into two more manageable units of 17 words each; and it adds weight to the *and* immediately following it, which might otherwise appear to be coequal with the lesser *and* four words farther on.

In the following sentences, the commas help to separate units of thought that might otherwise be muddled by the abundance of *and*'s:

> There are two kinds of great men: men of wit and wisdom [,] and men of power.

> She distrusted the Americans [,] and the Canadians and the English as well.

> They disallowed my vote for Ralph Nader and John Lindsay [,] and Oliver's vote for Bill Cosby and Shirley Chisholm.

Commas must not, of course, be added indiscriminately simply to break up a long sentence for the eye, or to distinguish one weight of *and* from another. In the following sentence it would be wrong to add commas at the bracketed points:

> Whether it is right or wrong to imprison for life a man [ ] who has committed four or more relatively trivial offenses [ ] has been for years a subject of debate in the law schools.

Although the sentence is long and some division of it for the eye would be welcome, none is possible; commas at the indicated places, by making the *who* clause parenthetical rather than defining, would make the sentence unintelligible. The sentence must be either left as it is or rewritten.

Over- and Underpunctuation

In the end, there remains a great region of discretion in which writers may use commas or not as strikes their fancy. Within this region of discretion, some like their punctuation heavy, some medium, some light. We like ours medium.

A distinguished exponent of heavy punctuation is the *New Yorker*, from which the following extract is taken:

> During the morning, more or less as Toperih-peri had predicted, the Turkana, avoiding the pass, which, as Toperih-peri could have told them, was sure to be guarded, had entered the district between Moru-kore and Kalapata and, turning north instead of south, raided a neighborhood on the plain.

Here we agree with Fowler: "Any one who finds himself putting down several commas close to one another should reflect that he is making himself disagreeable, and question . . . whether it is necessary."

As an example of light punctuation, here is James Joyce's *Portrait of the Artist as a Young Man*:

> His heart trembled; his breath came faster and a wild spirit passed over his limbs as though he was soaring sunward. His heart trembled in an ecstasy of fear and his soul was in flight. His soul was soaring in an air beyond the world and the body he knew was purified in a breath and delivered of incertitude and made radiant and commingled with the element of the spirit.

Underpunctuation of this sort causes the very trouble, especially with *and,* that we have mentioned earlier as a reason for adding commas; many of Joyce's sentences have to be read a second time to be read properly. Where a Joyce leads we gladly follow, but few would be so quick to indulge a lesser writer.

In short, the extremes of heavy and light punctuation seem to us excessively hard on the reader: the first belabors him to no purpose; the second ignores his need for signposts. We accordingly recommend medium punctuation. We close this section with a brief passage from the *New Yorker,* first as that magazine printed it, next as Joyce might have punctuated it, and finally as we would punctuate it:

Heavy punctuation

> But the people had delayed, and, seemingly by accident, had speared the ox just as the Turkana were coming in. Moreover, the ox, of its own volition, had run in a circle for almost a mile.

Light punctuation

> But the people had delayed and seemingly by accident had speared the ox just as the Turkana were coming in. Moreover the ox of its own volition had run in a circle for almost a mile.

Medium punctuation

> But the people had delayed, and seemingly by accident had speared the ox just as the Turkana were coming in. Moreover, the ox of its own volition had run in a circle for almost a mile.

THE SEMICOLON

The semicolon weighs about twice as much as a comma and half as much as a period. From its weight we may infer its two main uses: as a strong comma, and as a weak period. As a strong comma, it is used chiefly between phrases with internal commas:

> Those missing were R. A. Abramovitz, the director of the bank; Elma Snyder, the chief cashier; and two tellers, Joseph J. Petrullo and Louise Kreps.

> Despite the news from the northern front, the invasion was not canceled; but weekend passes were given out, at least to some of us.

Use a semicolon only where something stronger than a comma is needed. The semicolons in these student sentences should have been commas:

> He uses several different appeals to Lafferty's conscience and emotions; trying to get some kind of emotional response from Lafferty.

> This man is not a traitor; and therefore should not die.

As a weak period, the semicolon connects independent clauses that are too closely linked to be separated by a period, or too short and undramatic to stand by themselves:

> Such sentiments are not rare; on the contrary, they are very common, especially among policemen.

> *Probe* is a good word for headlines; it takes less space than *investigate.*

Since an excess of semicolons gives writing a stuffy look, they are inappropriate in informal dialogue and should be used sparingly in other informal prose. Some writers and teachers have gone further and argued that periods should replace semicolons wherever possible, as in this passage:

> In Watergate nobody ever discussed a subject. It was always subject matter. . . . Things were not said. They were indicated. Things were not done. They were undertaken. If something was undertaken, it was never after the indications about the subject matter. It was subsequent to them.

This kind of jerky, insistent writing may be all right for Hard-Hitting Harry, a tough reporter with no interest in subtle effects. But most writers need semicolons as well as periods, as in this fine passage from J. Bronowski's *Common Sense of Science*:

> The order [we impute to the universe] is what we find to work, conveniently and instructively. It is not something we stipulate; it is not something we can dogmatize about. It is what we find; it is what we find useful.

Replacing the two semicolons with periods would make five units out of what Bronowski instinctively, and in our view rightly, thinks of as three.

To sum up, then, we consider the semicolon indispensable to standard expository writing. Its chief virtues are two. It makes possible the clear and orderly grouping of complex units, especially in series; and it helps make possible the pleasing variation of pace and rhythm that is essential to good writing.

THE COLON

Centuries ago, the colon was nothing more than a strong semicolon, halfway in weight between a semicolon and a period. Today its use is very different. In Fowler's phrase, the colon "has acquired a special function: that of delivering the goods that have been invoiced in the preceding words." The colon in its modern use is the equivalent of *namely* or *that is*:

> I have seen every National League team but three: the Giants, the Braves, and the Mets.

> The message was clear: our views were not welcome.

> I remember her words: "May God forgive these men!"

As remarked in Chapter 11, a normally lowercase word following a colon should not be capitalized even when it begins a complete sentence, unless the sentence is either in quotation marks or especially formal or weighty.

There are three restrictions on the use of the colon. First, do not subordinate a colon to a lesser piece of punctuation. A colon yields only to a period: the goods it delivers must accordingly consist of all the words from the colon to the end of the sentence. Not some; all. The following sentences improperly subordinate colons to a comma and a semicolon, respectively:

> If he said: "I am innocent," he was lying.

> There were three men: Taylor, Adams, and Szyszniewski; and two women.

The first sentence can be fixed by simply deleting the colon, the second by changing the colon and the semicolon to parentheses or dashes. Alternatively, *There were two women and three men: Taylor, Adams, and Szyszniewski.*

Second, do not subordinate a colon to another colon; in other words, never use more than one colon in a sentence. The following sentences violate this restriction:

> The American delegation was distinguished: Rockefeller, Kissinger, and two Senators: Kennedy and Mansfield.

> The vote was as follows: California: aye, 85; nay, 15; Oregon: aye, 60; nay, 7.

The colons in sentences like this are visually equal but syntactically of different weight. The writer knows how they dovetail, but the reader is left the work of sorting things out for himself.

Third, a period should not be subordinated to a colon. Consider the following examples:

> We listed three reasons: the garage had no roof. The bathroom had no fixtures. And the yard was piled high with junk.

Remember two things: first, the dependent countries will be hard hit; their coal supply may be cut in half. Second, the rich industrial countries will benefit most.

In each example, the first period, which the reader expects will mark the end of what the colon has promised to deliver, marks instead a mere halfway point. The first example can be fixed simply by changing the periods to commas. In the second, since there is no apparent way of delivering the invoiced goods without an internal period, we recommend making "Remember two things" a separate sentence.

THE DASH

The overuse of dashes gives writing a breathlessness that is rarely appropriate, and in some cases a bogus dramatic quality. Dashes may legitimately be used for emphasis (for example, to bring out a paradox), or in pairs for long or complicated parenthetical insertions. They should not be used where commas would serve as well.

There are two dash constructions: the double dash (*Johnny ran away again—he does every Sunday—and was brought home by Chalmers Johnson*) and the single dash (*We were broke—not a penny left*). In a given sentence neither of these constructions may be used more than once, nor may the two be used together. The following sentences are all unacceptable:

Two double dashes

For Austria—Hitler's fatherland—not a penny; for Hungary— the cradle of freedom—all possible aid.

Double dash plus single dash

He loved his work—he lived for nothing else—but he was fired—no one ever knew why.

Two single dashes

Napoleon was his idol—the greatest man of the age; but Guizot was his master—the man of the moment.

The single dash, like a colon, governs everything from itself to the end of the sentence; the first of two dashes governs everything up to the second. If dashes are used with a semicolon, the semicolon should be subordinate, as in this sentence from the *New Yorker:* "I found myself getting annoyed with Gould, not because of his gloating over the settling of old scores—that was all right with me; I believe in revenge—but because of his general air of self-satisfaction." Compare this correct sentence with the incorrect Napoleon sentence above, in which the sequence of punctuation is identical.

PARENTHESES

In the nineteenth century and earlier, commas and semicolons were used in immediate conjunction with dashes, but in modern usage no punctuation may immediately precede or follow a dash. Parentheses, which do not suffer from this restriction, can sometimes clear away ambiguities that pairs of dashes or commas cannot handle. In the following ambiguous sentences parentheses are the obvious remedy:

> The card featured Peterson, Gilroy—known as the "Terre Haute Tiger"—Morse, and Martin.
>
> Three vegetables—carrots, beans, and brussels sprouts—and two fruits—avocados and raspberries—were particularly vulnerable to "smog fallout."
>
> The chief culprits were Mr. Ward, the sales manager, and Mr. Tyler.

In the first sentence, parentheses would rule out the possibility that we are talking about somebody named Gilroy Morse: *The card featured Peterson, Gilroy (known as the "Terre Haute Tiger"), Morse, and Martin.* In the second, parentheses would bring order to a badly fragmented sentence: *Three vegetables (carrots, beans, and brussels sprouts) and two fruits (avocados and raspberries) were particularly vulnerable.* In the third, parentheses would show us that two men were involved, not three: *Mr. Ward (the sales manager) and Mr. Tyler.*

Beginning writers make two errors in using parentheses. One is overusing them: their residual connotation of a whispered aside makes them irritating in large quantities. The other is making them enclose too long a parenthetical passage, especially one so long that the reader loses his bearings before he gets to the end of it. Make your passages in parentheses few, and make them short.

A sentence with parentheses in it is punctuated exactly as it would have been if the words in parentheses had been omitted. The punctuation follows the closing parenthesis except when the passage consists of a whole sentence or several sentences, in which case the final period is placed inside the closing parenthesis. Thus:

> There were only two of us (me and my sister).

> (There were only two of us, me and my sister.)

QUOTATION MARKS

Quotation marks have two main uses: to set off passages attributable to speakers or writers other than the present writer at the time of writing, and to alert the reader to words or phrases that are being used in some unfamiliar or unusual sense.

Punctuation and Capitalization with Quotation Marks

Always put a comma or a period *inside* the closing quotation mark, a semicolon or a colon *outside*. This is one of the very few rules of writing that have no exceptions, and at the same time one of the rules most frequently violated in student writing.° For other punctuation, use your common sense: a question mark or an exclamation point, for example, goes inside the quotation marks if it is part of the quotation, otherwise outside. If a quotation runs to more than one paragraph, all paragraphs should begin with quotation marks, but only the last should end with one. With this exception, all quotation marks come in pairs.

Quotation marks following *said* and equivalent words may be preceded by no punctuation, by a comma, or by a colon, depending on the context and the writer's taste. The following sentences are all acceptably punctuated:

° Perhaps students are led astray by older books and books printed in England, many of which follow a different system for commas and periods. The system recommended here is all but universal in current American publishing.

She said "I dare you!"

He replied, "I'll do my best, but I can't promise anything."

The ad read: "Experienced waitress wanted; age 21–45; short hours; no Sundays."

No punctuation should follow a preposition or conjunction introducing a quotation; nor, as we have seen (p. 205–206), should a colon introduce a quotation that ends before the end of the sentence. In the following sentences the punctuation preceding the quotations should be omitted:

His reason for resigning was that, "Birmingham cannot afford a symphony orchestra."

When she said: "Aunt Roxie is here," I thought she must be mistaken.

Single quotation marks are used exclusively for quotations within quotations: *"That's unfair," said his wife. "All I said was 'You're wrong.'"* Note that the closing quotation marks both go outside the period.

If words in quotation marks make a full sentence, or a sentence fragment or exclamation used as a sentence, the first word quoted should be capitalized. Otherwise a normally lowercase word should be left lowercase:

According to Schlesinger, Kennedy replied "Never again."

When he said "Where's the food?" everyone laughed.

Red Smith calls the 1927 Yankees "the greatest baseball team of all time."

Superfluous Quotation Marks

Verse quotations of more than one line, and prose quotations too long to be incorporated conveniently in one's text, are conventionally set off like the Bronowski passage on p. 204. In such cases quotation marks at the beginning and end are superfluous. Internal quotation marks, for example in dialogue, should be retained, and should be double rather than single.

Quotation marks should be used sparingly to set off words and short phrases from their context. If you use a word in an unusual sense, or if you coin a new word for some special use, explain matters clearly the first time you use the word and thereafter write it without quotation marks. If you use slang, use it boldly; quotation marks make slang look defensive and self-conscious. In general, if quotation marks do not make any distinction worth making, drop them. In the following sentences, the quotation marks should be eliminated:

> When I was little, my family called me "Bobo."
>
> "Communism" has a different definition in every country.
>
> I always wanted to "show off" when I knew he was watching me swim.
>
> In the summer Mario offers "guided tours" to visitors.

As the last example suggests, quotation marks may be worse than superfluous; carrying as they do the connotation of something-fishy-here, they may actually suggest the opposite of what the writer intends. Thanks to the quotation marks, we get the feeling that Mario is up to no good and that a wise visitor will look elsewhere for a guide.

PART 4
THE RESEARCH PAPER

13

RESEARCH AND NOTE-TAKING

Every educated person should be able to investigate a subject, evaluate the facts and opinions he encounters, and present his findings in a reasonable and orderly way. Training in how to do this is what the research paper is all about. It is a practical as well as an academic exercise. As our society grows more complex, it places increasing demands on its educated citizens to sift out from the glut of available information the information relevant to a particular need, and to report that information reliably to others. The day when an engineer or businessman could make it through life without ever reading or writing a serious word is over. Professional men and women in particular are often called on to write papers and deliver them at professional meetings. But whoever you are or might become—rotarian, revolutionist, scoutmaster, PTA activist, or mere writer of letters to the editor—you will need training of the sort the research paper provides.

Some writing courses require a so-called "critical" paper rather than the traditional "research" paper, the difference presumably being that in a research paper you just gather, sort, and order a body of information on a subject, whereas in a critical paper you also *think* about that information, evaluate it. We think the distinction is useless because research and evaluation are inseparable. You can't write a research paper without deciding first what information to gather, and later what to put in and what to leave out. All these decisions are acts of evaluation.

To assist the student in writing a critical paper, some teachers rely on sourcebooks or casebooks like David Levin's *What Happened in Salem?*, a gathering of testimony from five Salem witchcraft trials in 1692. There are dozens of books like this—on novels and poems, historical events and literary genres, scientists and artists. With the help of such books, both teacher and student can master a limited body of knowledge with minimum inconvenience, and hence devote themselves to discussion, thinking, and writing rather than to leg-work, often futile, in the understocked college library.

But for all its conveniences, this approach has its shortcomings. The library is your prime educational resource: you should discover its pleasures and treasures for yourself. This is perhaps especially important if you habitually look to television or mass-circulation magazines for information about the world rather than to books. Even if a casebook or sourcebook is assigned, you would do well to go beyond it and examine some of the library's books and articles on your subject. It is better to explore the library as a freshman than as a junior—or as an aging graduate lost in a labyrinth that should long ago have become familiar.

The first step in writing a research paper is finding a subject, sup-posing one has not been assigned. Our earlier advice (pp. 13–14) was to choose something that interests you, some question whose answer you really want to know. But how do you know in advance what will both interest you and generate three or four thousand words worth reading? Maybe you don't; you must play some hunches. Let us say that your teacher has tossed out the following suggested topics for those who have not found something on their own:

The grossness of the gross national product

"Redundancy" as a loaded term for unemployment

Violence as a way of "doing your thing"

The puritanism of the Watergate criminals

Pornography and pollution of other kinds

Marijuana and the generation gap

After mulling it over, you decide on the last topic. Perhaps you have tried marijuana; perhaps you have been in arguments about it and wished you had more evidence to support your claims; perhaps you simply welcome the opportunity to find out what the fuss is all about. At any rate, you settle on "Marijuana and the generation gap." Why, you have heard people ask, are there strict laws against marijuana when other drugs like tobacco and alcohol are perfectly legal? Are there solid reasons for the difference, or is it because, as some say, tobacco and alcohol are the vices of the old and marijuana is the vice of the young? Armed with tentative questions like these, you approach your problem.

BOOKS

Your first step is to consult the card catalogue of your college or university library. You look up "Marijuana" there and find nine books listed, six of them in the "locked stack." Why they should be so sequestered puzzles you, especially since two of them are on the chemistry and pharmacology of marijuana and two are in Spanish; they seem hardly likely to corrupt young minds! But some of the books look interesting and you make a note of them, hoping you will be able to get them out of hock.

Of more immediate interest, however, is a cross-reference leading you to "Marihuana," where you are staggered to find a total of thirty books listed (including all the "Marijuana" books) and four bibliographies. All but two of these books were published since 1968—an indication of how interest in the subject has mushroomed since that time. You cannot see why the titles of most of the entries under "Marihuana" use the spelling "Marijuana"; obviously either spelling is acceptable, so you leave that mystery unsolved. Here are some entries that you think might be useful:

Goode, Erich. *Marijuana.* New York: Atherton Press, 1969.
Grinspoon, Lester. *Marihuana Reconsidered.* Cambridge, Mass.: Harvard University Press, 1971.
Grupp, Stanley E. *The Marihuana Muddle.* Lexington, Mass.: D. C. Heath & Co., 1973.
Hochman, Joel Simon. *Marijuana and Social Evolution.* Englewood Cliffs, N.J.: Prentice-Hall, Inc., 1972.

Johnson, Bruce D. *Marihuana Users and Drug Subcultures.* New York: John Wiley & Sons, 1973.

Kaplan, John. *Marijuana—The New Prohibition.* New York: World Publishing Co., 1970.

Lewis, Barbara. *The Sexual Power of Marijuana.* New York: Peter H. Wyden, Inc., 1970.

Oursler, Will. *Marijuana: The Facts, the Truth.* New York: Paul S. Eriksson, Inc., 1968.

Rowell, Earle Albert, and Rowell, Robert. *On the Trail of Marijuana, the Weed of Madness.* Mountain View, Calif.: Pacific Press, 1939.

Saltman, Jules. *What About Marijuana?* New York Public Affairs Pamphlet No. 436, Public Affairs Committee, July 1969.

Simmons, J. L., ed. *Marihuana: Myths and Realities.* North Hollywood, Calif.: Brandon House, 1967.

Smith, David E., ed. *The New Social Drug: Cultural, Medical, and Legal Perspectives on Marijuana.* Englewood Cliffs, N.J.: Prentice-Hall, Inc., 1970.

Steinbeck, John. *In Touch.* New York: Alfred A. Knopf, Inc., 1969.

To your relief you learn that "locked stacks" have nothing to do with censorship, but only with security; it seems that books about marijuana frequently disappear. Of these thirteen items, the Kaplan, Goode, Grinspoon, and Grupp are out on loan to students, the Simmons is at the Law Library, the Johnson is being cataloged, the Steinbeck is lost, the Lewis (as you expected) has been stolen, and the Rowell is inexplicably charged out to the Women's Gym. You put in recall requests and begin to be glad you started your research early. The Hochman, Oursler, Saltman, and Smith volumes are in, and you take them out. You are disappointed not to get the Kaplan book, which is the only one you have heard about; but luckily you are able to borrow it from a friend. The Simmons, you discover, has appeared in a low-priced paperback edition, which you buy at the campus bookstore. While there you pick up another paperback that looks helpful: *The Marihuana Papers*, edited by David Solomon.

Loaded down with four books from the library and three others that you have bought or borrowed, you are ready to begin. Then, by chance, you discover a few general studies on the drug problem that have detailed chapters on marijuana. Though at this point you feel you probably have more than enough already, you make a note of three of them:

Brecher, Edward M. *Licit and Illicit Drugs.* Boston: Little, Brown & Co., 1972.
Fixx, James F., ed. *Drugs: The Great Contemporary Issues.* New York: Arno Press, 1971.
Laurie, Peter. *Drugs: Medical, Psychological, and Social Facts.* Harmondsworth, Eng.: Penguin Books, 1969.

So you begin to dig in. You are especially pleased with the Brecher book and with the convenience of the *New York Times* reprints in the Fixx book. With an inward guffaw at the appropriateness of Fixx's name to his enterprise, you decide to concentrate first on these two books together with the Kaplan book, since it is relatively recent and bears directly on your subject; and next to spend some time on the Smith and Solomon collections, since they both contain a wide-ranging selection of opinion. The Saltman pamphlet is a perfunctory *Reader's Digest* treatment of the subject; you put it aside. You do the same with the Oursler, which strikes you as melodrama rather than research. At first glance the Simmons seems to offer more entertainment than edification; but since you own the book and since it has a useful glossary, you plan to look further into it.

Figure 1 shows the Library of Congress catalog card for the Kaplan

Figure 1

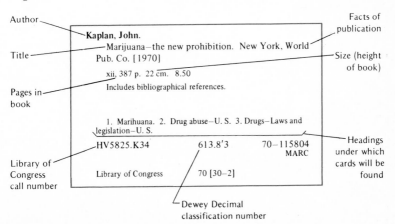

book as it appears in a library card catalog. Some of the items are of interest mainly to librarians; others are of more general interest. For whatever books you intend to use, you should make out your own bibliography card (see pp. 225–226).

Besides the card catalog, you may have occasion to use one or more reference guides. One of the best is the *Bulletin of Bibliography*, a periodical that presents bibliographies on selected subjects and reviews books containing bibliographies—often very amusingly. You find that the October–December 1969 issue of the *Bulletin* has a bibliography entitled "Drugs—A Selective Bibliography for Educators on the Secondary and College Level," compiled by Jean B. Condito, a high school librarian. Most of the bibliography deals with hard drugs, but there is a section on the nonaddictive hallucinogens, including marijuana. This section offers a long and useful list of books, pamphlets, and magazine articles on the subject; many of the books you know of already, but you make notes of some of the articles. A film on marijuana entitled *Assassin of Youth* is also listed, as is a ridiculous propaganda film called *Reefer Madness* that you saw on campus some months earlier.

Another book to check is the annual *Bibliographic Index*, which lists recent bibliographies by subject for a great many subjects. You check from 1966 until the latest Supplement and find only a few of the books you have already listed, but a number of promising magazine articles. In the same category is the *Public Affairs Information Service Bulletin*, which you discover to be a rich mine of bibliographical information, especially for magazine articles. You jot down information on those items that seem promising.

Still another reference guide that can save you time is the *Book Review Digest*. Here, for example, are some entries for the Solomon book as listed in the BRD for 1969:

> "[The book] is the basic reference work on marihuana. . . . Although the nonprofessional will find that some chapters . . . are too technical or jargon-laden for comfort, most chapters are in fairly straightforward prose; and some of the literary selections included are quite entertaining. . . . A good part of this anthology could of course be titled 'The Case Against the Federal Narcotics Bureau.' . . . [The] book convinces one that the Bureau's favorite myths about marihuana . . . are indubitably myths. But [Mr. Solomon] doesn't make the case as airtight as it could be made. . . . All my objections to Mr. Solomon's book are ultimately

quibbles. The important fact is that it is by far the best guide to its subject." Ned Polsky

Book Week p5 Ja 15 '67 1400w

"The compiler of [this anthology] quotes out of context and changes the emphasis in some of the sources he uses. . . . [His] book is frequently repetitious and contains contradictory statements. The general philosophy seems to be that since alcohol is so much more dangerous than marihuana, marihuana should be made legal. . . . Since there is considerable doubt among the authorities about the active principles and potential dangers of marihuana, since inaccuracies and misplaced emphases abound, and since most of this material is already available, this book should be bought by only the most comprehensive collections."

W. K. Beatty

Library J 92:130 Ja 1 '67 400w

"[This] book was put together by David Solomon, whose qualifications are limited to the fact that he is a former editor at *Esquire*, *Playboy*, and *Metronome*, and his bias is plainly evident. . . . Bolstering [his] familiar argument are 400-plus pages of statements, essays, papers, adulatory fiction, and documentary evidence, some of which are impressive, some simply a drag. . . . The most comprehensive defense argument comes from the famed 1944 LaGuardia Report, written by responsible scientists and sociologists (though heavily attacked by the A.M.A. at the time)."

Time 89:84 Ja 27 '67 550w

Clearly these reviewers see the volume from their different points of view, the first as a liberal, the second as a librarian, the third as a popular journalist. Of the three, the second impresses you as the most level-headed; the first seems too extravagant in his praise, the third too given to personal attack. You think Beatty's review might come in useful, so you make out a tentative bibliography card for the *Library Journal*, Volume 92, page 130, for January 1, 1967; "400w" means 400 words.

Suppose now that you are trying to decide whether the Solomon book or Grinspoon's *Marihuana Reconsidered* is better for your purposes. You find these two reviews of the Grinspoon book in the BRD for 1971:

"By the time anyone closes this volume, he will be ready to agree that legalization is a logical course and that moderate use of pot is no more

wicked than a bottle of wine with dinner. At the same time, he will close the book with relief. Dr. Grinspoon is a professor of psychiatry at Harvard Medical School, and his book comes equipped with all the cumbersome apparatus of academic writings and some of the most flat-footed prose that ever escaped from a doctoral thesis. . . . The volume is exhaustively and exhaustingly thorough. No one is going to read it for thrills. That very solidity and stuffiness is what makes [this book] so potent a weapon in the hands of those who want marihuana legalized."
Edward Edelson

Book World p1 My 30 '71 1350w

"Dr. Grinspoon's study, which I'm sure will reap all the scholarly plaudits in the papers that matter, reconsiders mostly the myths and sensations surrounding pot in the past, the unfairness of laws governing its use, and the weed's voluminous history. Beyond that, he tells one more than one wants to know about grass (even if one were a user). . . . [Here is the] nub of the pot problem: the weed is an adjunct, forcing tool and instrument of initiation for a lifestyle that generally rejects or seeks to bring down 'ordered life as we know it.' . . . Pot is symptomatic of [young people's] lack of interest in straight society. Mindful of that, I judge Grinspoon's book a scholarly gesture rather than an illuminating study." S. K. Oberbeck

Nat R 23:597 Je 1 '71 1750w

You have an interesting difference of opinion here. To the bookseller Dr. Grinspoon is exhaustively (in two senses) convincing; to the writer for the conservative *National Review* Dr. Grinspoon is hardly better than a propagandist. Which can you believe? At this point the striking difference of opinion is what impresses you most; since that difference may be important to you later, you make out two more bibliography cards.

Finally, in an idle moment you look up the lost Steinbeck book just to see what it was about. When the book shows up later, you are glad to have had this preview of it. Here is the entry from the BRD:

"The son of the famous John Steinbeck III allowed himself, at twenty-one, to be drafted and sent to Southeast Asia. He was eager for 'a paradise of potential crystallized experience.' He took a good look, fell in love with the people of Vietnam [and] turned dovish. . . . The most extraordinary part of the book he has written concerns his experiences with and observations on the extensive use of marijuana by American troops in Vietnam. . . . The young Steinbeck displays an extraordinary talent for storytelling, a keen sense of issues, and a granite ability to keep his disenchantment cool. He emerges from his first book as a kind of literary Sidney Poitier. If Stanley Kramer made a movie about a hippie, he would undoubtedly be someone like Steinbeck." Lee Israel

Book World   p 5   F 9 '69   550 w

Later you discover that John Steinbeck IV was arrested on a marijuana charge in October 1967, and again in September 1974. You record this information on a card; it may be useful later, or again it may not. Every good job of research yields superfluous notes, but the experienced researcher would rather have too many than too few, and will even take notes on points seemingly tangential to his central topic. Though by this time you are ready to agree with Dwight Macdonald about the flood of "verbal pomposity, elaboration of the obvious, repetition, trivia, low-grade statistics, tedious factifications, drudging recapitulations of the half comprehended, and generally inane and laborious junk" encountered by the conscientious researcher, you are also impressed by the devices available to you for cutting a clean path through the junk to solid ground.

PERIODICALS

You have learned by now that widespread interest in marijuana dates from about 1965. You decide, therefore, to concentrate mainly on newspaper and magazine articles published since that year. There are three main periodical indexes, the first of which is not usable in your present research:°

Poole's Index to Periodical Literature (indexing many nineteenth-century periodicals)

Reader's Guide to Periodical Literature (covering popular magazines from 1900 to the present)

Social Sciences and Humanities Index, known until April 1965 as *International Index to Periodical Literature* (listing articles in a wide range of scholarly journals)

° There are vast numbers of other indexes and reference books as well. A good list of such books appears in Constance M. Winchell, *Guide to Reference Books*, 7th ed. (1951). And nearly every college library has a reference librarian who specializes in helping people find information.

Remember that the *Reader's Guide* covers only popular magazines. You must consult the *Social Sciences and Humanities Index* for more scholarly articles.

Consulting the *Reader's Guide*, you find five articles listed under "Marijuana" in the four years from March 1963 until February 1967. In the next seven years, from March 1967 until February 1974, you find 226 articles listed. Several of them strike you as worth looking up:

Great marijuana hoax   A. Ginsberg   Atlantic   218:104+   N '66

America's social frontiers: why not smoke pot?   Cur   95:39–41   My '68

Politics of pot   J. Sterba   Esquire   70:58–61+   Ag '68

Crackdown   Nation   208:293–4   Mr 10 '69

Grass and the brass   D. Sanford   New Rep   162:11–12   Ap 25 '70

Adolescent marijuana use: role of parents and peers   D. Kandel   bibliog. il.   Science   181:1067–70   S 14 '73

Marihuana: deceptive weed, by G. G. Nahas. Review   Nat R   25:1312   N 23 '73   S. Brauth

Decriminalization of marijuana: dealing with the reality, not the symbol   T. E. Price and R. Hargraves   Chr Cent   91:822–3   S 4 '74

In these abbreviations the first item is the title, the second the author or authors (omitted for anonymous articles), the third the periodical title, the fourth the volume or issue number followed by the page or pages, the fifth the date. Journal abbreviations are spelled out in a separate section of the *Guide*.

In the *Social Science and Humanities Index* you find only thirteen articles listed under "Marihuana" in the nine years between April 1965 and March 1974, but three of them look to be worth reading.° The entries read:

° It is a good idea to check both guides. The *Reader's Guide* has more on some subjects, the *Social Science and Humanities Index* more on others. For example, on "Imagery," listed in both indexes, the *Reader's Guide* for 1966–67 refers you to "Figures of Speech," where only one entry is listed; the *Social Science and Humanities Index* for the same period has 24 entries under "Imagery," plus cross-references under "Figures of Speech" to "Metaphor," "Synecdoche," "Clichés," and "Shakespeare."

Beyond the pleasure principle   R. Coles   Part R   34:415-20   Sum
    '67
Multiple drug use among marijuana smokers   E. Goode   Soc Prob
    17:48-64   Sum '69
Marijuana use, social discontent and political alienation: a study of
    high school youth   J. W. Clarke and E. L. Levine   Am Pol Sci
    R   65:120-30   Mr '71

You then ask the reference librarian what other indexes might be
useful. She suggests *Psychological Abstracts,* an annual collection of
résumés of new books and articles in various psychological categories.
Checking the indexes, you find no mention of marijuana until 1969.
The index entries read as follows:

Avoidance and visual discrimination, monkey, 2280

Marijuana psychosis, case report, 16127

Marijuana use and legalization, political controversy, 14269

Since the effect of marijuana on monkeys seems rather specialized for
your purposes, you decide to ignore the first abstract. You are curious
about the second, which summarizes an article in the *Canadian Psychiatric Association Journal,* 1969, Vol. 14, No. 1, pp. 77-79, about a
"30 yr. old white male's acute psychotic reaction to 1 year daily use
of marijuana." This seems odd, since you have always heard that
marijuana was relatively harmless; later you discover that psychotic
reactions to marijuana are in fact very rare. The third reference deals
with an article by Erich Goode in the *Journal of Health and Social
Behavior,* 1969, Vol. 10, No. 2, pp. 83-94, entitled "Marijuana and
the Politics of Reality." This strikes you as worth investigating, and
later you discover with pleasure that the article is reprinted in the
Smith book.

Now you remember the articles you listed for future reference
from Jean Condito's bibliography in the *Bulletin of Bibliography,* the
Bibliographic Index, and the *Public Affairs Information Service Bulle-
tin* (see p. 218). Some of the same articles are listed in the *Reader's
Guide,* but others are from journals that you have not yet run across.
Two that interest you are listed as follows:

Brill, H. "Case Against Marijuana," *Journal of School Health*, 522-3, Oct. 1968

Der Marderosian, A. H. "Marijuana Madness," *Journal of Secondary Education*, 43:200-5, May 1968

These references make you wonder whether you should not consult some reference guide to educational articles. The reference librarian refers you to the *Education Index*, and further suggests that you consult the current list of international medical literature in the *Index Medicus*, paying particular attention to British articles, since the British, she thinks, are less convinced than the Americans that the drug is harmless. Though you did not initially intend to investigate the medical side of the subject, you are becoming convinced that you cannot ignore it. You find nothing new in the *Education Index*, but the *Index Medicus* lists a number of promising titles:

Potted Dreams.   Brit Med J   1:133-4   18 Jan 69
Cannabis: a short review of its effects and the possible dangers of its use.   Leonard BE.   Brit J Addict   64:121-30   May 69
Runaways, hippies, and marihuana.   Kaufman J. et al.   Amer J Psychiat   126:717-20   Nov 69

While looking at British articles you run across the *British Humanities Index*, but find, over a three-year period, only six articles listed. Two look interesting, but you are not convinced that they are indispensable for your purposes. Besides, you are beginning to feel overwhelmed.

What are you going to do with all this material? First of all, note that it is not as much reading as it may seem to be. Your eighteen selections from all these sources come to less than a hundred pages all told. Add fifty pages for other articles you will find as your investigation deepens, and you will still probably be spending less time reading and pondering periodical articles than you did discovering them—and noting their whereabouts.°

Another thing that lightens your burden is an increasingly sure sense of priorities and possibilities, of what you want to get out of

---

° You may run across still other articles in your reading of daily newspapers and magazines, or as the result of conversations.

your reading. After your initial period of floundering, things are beginning to fall into place. You tentatively decide, so far as possible, to get your hard facts from books and your expressions of opinion from periodical articles and other short papers. You don't know whether or not this is a good working strategy, but you decide to give it a try.

BIBLIOGRAPHY CARDS

As you gather lists of the books and articles you intend to read or consult (or better still, while you are consulting them), you should make out a set of cards to be used in preparing the bibliography for your paper. A card for the Solomon book will read as shown in Figure 2. The entry for this book that ultimately appears in your bibliography will read as follows:

Solomon, David, ed. *The Marihuana Papers.* New York: New American Library, 1968.

Figure 3 shows a sample bibliography card for a periodical article. Volume numbers may be given in roman numerals rather than arabic numbers, but arabic is now usual. One handy style is "164:18 (Apr. 22, 1972)," meaning that the article begins on page 18 of the April 22, 1972, issue of the periodical, which issue will be found in Volume 164 of the bound series on the library. The same style can be used for

Figure 2

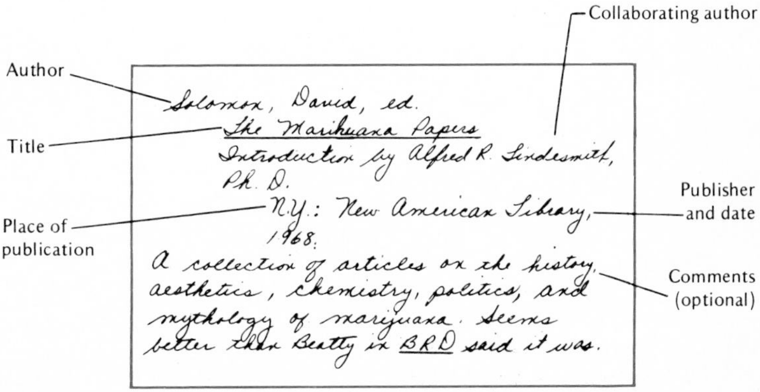

Figure 3

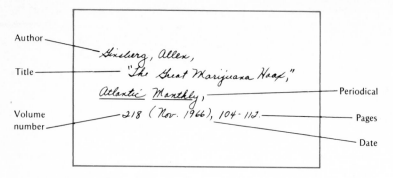

footnotes, in which case the second number is the page cited. Note that whenever the volume number of a periodical is given, "p." or "pp." is omitted before the page citation that follows.

The bibliography for this paper, in final typed form, appears on pp. 244-245. Footnote citations, which differ in form from bibliography entries, are illustrated on pp. 237-243.

NOTE-TAKING

Although there are many ways to take notes, the beginning re-searcher does well to keep his notes on cards.° You will probably take four kinds of notes: (1) quotations from your reading, (2) para-phrases of passages from your reading, (3) statements of fact, and (4) original ideas inspired by your reading—i.e., your own questions about or critical comments on what you read.

In quoting material, make sure you quote exactly and indicate by ellipsis (. . .) any material you omit. Suppose you want to quote a statement from the Ginsberg essay mentioned above. You are not sure you will use it, but it seems promising enough to save for future reference. Your card is shown in Figure 4. Figure 5 shows a card paraphrasing a comment that did not seem worth quoting in full.

° Some teachers recommend using 3 x 5 cards for bibliography entries and larger cards for notes. This system has the virtue of keeping the two kinds of information clearly distinguishable.

Figure 4

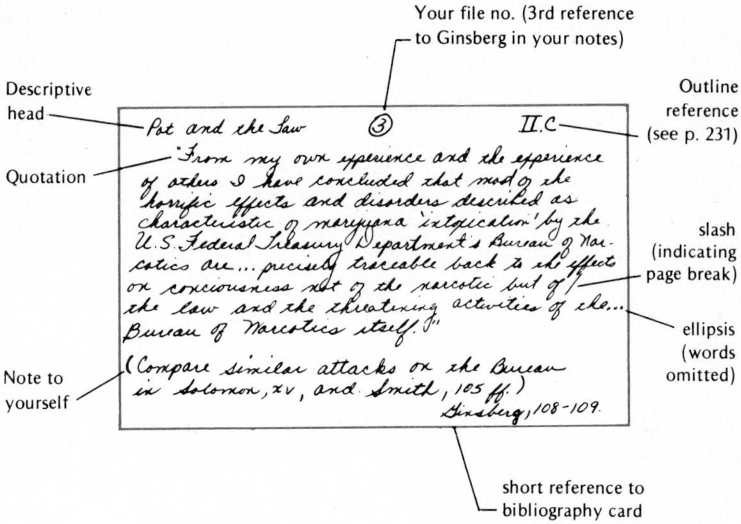

Your file no. (3rd reference to Ginsberg in your notes)

Descriptive head

Outline reference (see p. 231)

Quotation

"From my own experience and the experience of others I have concluded that most of the horrific effects and disorders described as characteristic of marijuana 'intoxication' by the U.S. Federal Treasury Department's Bureau of Narcotics are ... precisely traceable back to the effects on consciousness not of the narcotic but of the law and the threatening activities of the ... Bureau of Narcotics itself."

Pot and the Law ③ II.C

slash (indicating page break)

ellipsis (words omitted)

Note to yourself

(Compare similar attacks on the Bureau in Solomon, xv, and Smith, 105 ff.)
Ginsberg, 108–109.

short reference to bibliography card

Figure 5

Sex and Pot ⑥ III. B

Those "who are comfortable with an unconventional view of sex" would condemn any pot-induced increase in sex as "promiscuous," while "the drug's apostles would cheer society's resurgent interest in the organic, the earthy, the sensual." Goode in Smith, 179

(But there is no evidence that pot leads to promiscuity. See Goode footnote, 179, and Kaplan, 77–81.)

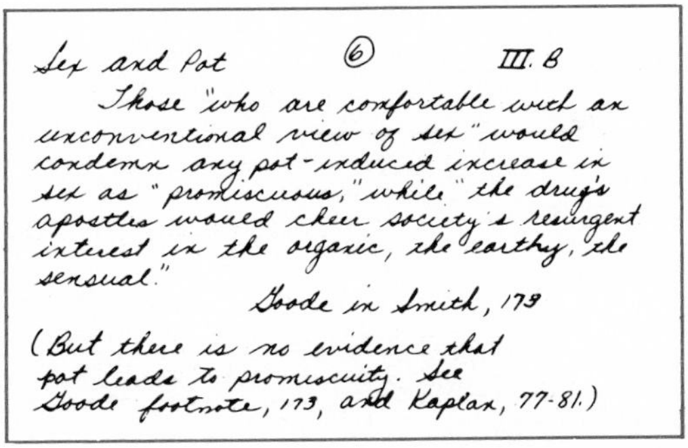

Here Goode's words "who are comfortable with an unconventional view of sex" are put in quotation marks to keep them distinct from your paraphrase. This is important; to take down without quotation marks words or phrases that are in any way unique to the author you are paraphrasing is to risk plagiarism (see pp. 253–258).

In your paper it may strike you as awkward to put "who are comfortable with an unconventional view of sex" in quotation marks, since the phrase is not particularly eloquent; still, the words appear to be carefully chosen, and if you use them you must quote them. An alternative possibility is to paraphrase if a suitable paraphrase can be found. At all events, you should deal with this problem when you get to it, not anticipate it in your note-taking. Since you will ultimately have to give credit in your text or footnotes not only for material quoted verbatim but for paraphrased material as well, and since the credit you give will depend heavily for accuracy and completeness on what you have written on your cards, it only makes sense to bend over backwards to keep things straight in the note-taking stage.

Figure 6 shows a card containing a statement of fact. Since botanical information about marijuana can be found in encyclopedias and in nearly all books on the subject, it requires no special acknowledgment in your paper. You see no immediate use for this information in your outline, but it is so fundamental that you decide to record it anyway for possible use early in your paper.

The fourth kind of card records ideas that come to you as your reading progresses. Maybe you want to argue with something you are reading; maybe you are annoyed by what seem to you contradictions or irresponsible statements; maybe your imagination is fired by a moving argument or appeal. Catch such birds on the wing or they will fly away. Make sure, however, that you also record what you are reacting *to*. In your paper you will need evidence to back up what

Figure 6

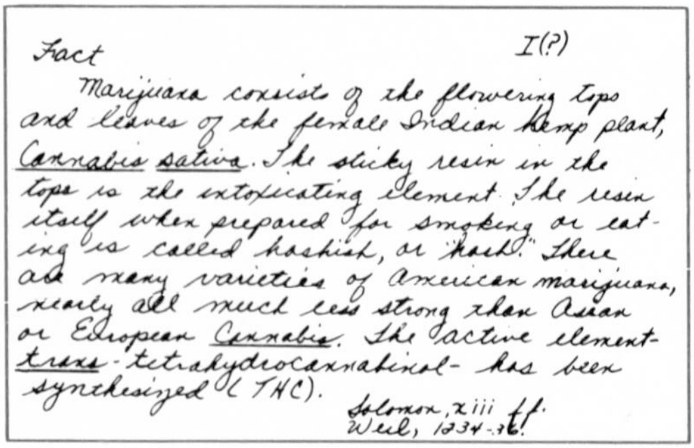

Fact   I(?)

Marijuana consists of the flowering tops and leaves of the female Indian hemp plant, *Cannabis sativa*. The sticky resin in the tops is the intoxicating element. The resin itself when prepared for smoking or eating is called hashish, or "hash." There are many varieties of American marijuana, nearly all much less strong than Asian or European *Cannabis*. The active element-trans-tetrahydrocannabinol- has been synthesized (THC).
Solomon, xiii ff.
Weil, 1234-16.

Figure 7

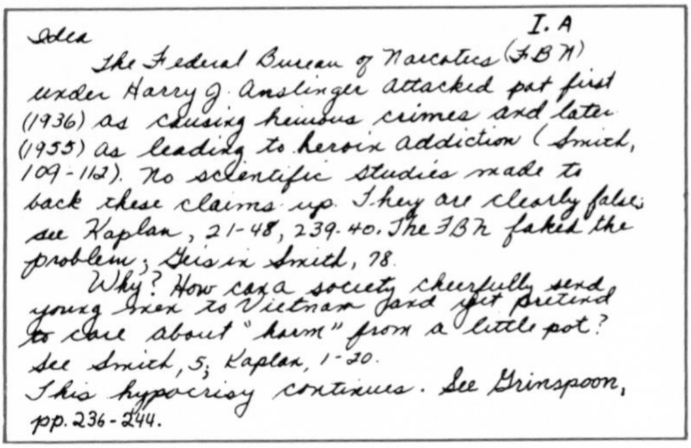

```
Idea                                    I. A
        The Federal Bureau of Narcotics (FBN)
under Harry J. Anslinger attacked pot first
(1936) as causing heinous crimes and later
(1955) as leading to heroin addiction (Smith,
109-112). No scientific studies made to
back these claims up. They are clearly false;
see Kaplan, 21-48, 239.40. The FBN faked the
problem; Grinspoon, 78
        Why? How can a society cheerfully send
young men to Vietnam and yet pretend
to care about "harm" from a little pot?
See Smith, 5; Kaplan, 1-20.
This hypocrisy continues. See Grinspoon,
pp. 236-244.
```

you say, and this evidence will usually be found in the printed passage to which your remarks are a response. Figure 7 shows this sort of card.

Getting your information on these cards straight and complete from the outset will save you at the very least one thankless trip to the library to fill in what you left out and clear up what you got wrong. And it may well spare you more: the confusion of writing weeks later from notes too sketchy to make sense of, or the boredom of hunting in vain for something you remember having seen but did not think to record. Never count on your memory. When you see something you think you may use, write it down and write down where to find it.

PHOTODUPLICATION

Most libraries these days have duplicating machines that students can use for a few cents a page. Though a duplicated page is no substitute for a note card, it relieves you of the worry of accuracy and permits you to write shorter notes. Figure 8 shows a sample photocopied page, Figure 9 a sample note card referring to that page.

INTERVIEWING

The best source of information is the horse's mouth. If you have access to people who can provide you with useful information or

Figure 8

counter-culture, which, while not explicitly opposed to academic pursuits, complements them with a focus on the present, on 'existential' values, on personal experimentation, and on deliberate self-transformation as a way of creating meaning. Participation in this counter-culture provides a powerful support for efforts to explore oneself, to intensify relationships with other people, to change the quality and content of consciousness. It provides a sanctioning context for drug use as one of the pathways of changing the self so as to create meaning in the world.

DRUGS AS A COMMENTARY ON SOCIETY

"It is widely feared that student drug use is a commentary upon American society; words like degeneracy, addiction, thrill-seeking and irresponsibility are eventually introduced into most popular discussions of student drug use. So, too, student drug use is said to be related to the excessive permissiveness of parents, to the laxness of adult standards, to breaches in law enforcement, to disrespect for law and order, and to an impending breakdown of our social fabric.

"Although these particular interpretations of the social implications of drug use are incorrect, drug use *is* importantly influenced by social, political and historical factors. Those students who lust after significance or reject the prevalent values of American society are in fact reacting to and within a societal context. The sense of being locked-off and enclosed in an impermeable shell is related not only to individual psychological states like depression, but to broader cultural phenomena. And the fact that a considerable number of the most able students have become convinced that significance and relevant experience are largely to be found within their own skulls is indirectly related to their perception of the other possibilities for fulfillment in the social and political world. In a variety of ways, then, student drug use is a commentary on American society, although a different kind of commentary than most discussions of youthful 'thrill-seeking' would lead us to believe.

"To single out a small number of social changes as especially relevant to understanding student drug use is to make a highly arbitrary decision. A variety of factors, including rapid social change, the unprecedented possibilities for total destruction in the modern world, the prevalence of violence both domestic and international, the high degree of specialization and bureaucratization of American life, and a host of others are relevant to creating the context of values and expectations within which drug use has become increasingly legitimate.

"But of all the factors that could be discussed, three seem particularly relevant: first, the effect of modern communications and transportation in producing an overwhelming inundation of experience, which I will term *stimulus flooding;* second, the effect of *automatic affluence* in changing the values and outlooks of the young; third, the importance of recent social and historical events in producing a kind of *social and political disenchantment* that leads many students to seek salvation through withdrawal and inner life rather than through engagement and societal involvement.

"Every society subjects its members to pressures and demands that

Figure 9

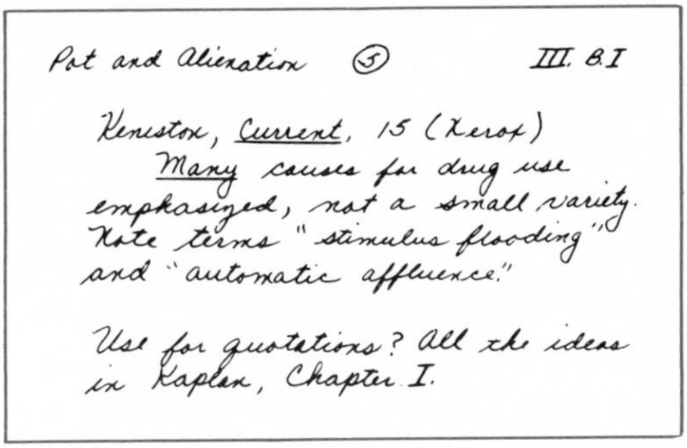
Pot and Alienation (5) III. B.1

Keniston, Current, 15 (Xerox)
Many causes for drug use emphasized, not a small variety. Note terms "stimulus flooding" and "automatic affluence."

Use for quotations? All the ideas in Kaplan, Chapter I.

opinions, by all means use them. If, for example, someone you are writing about or citing as an authority lives nearby, you have nothing to lose and much to gain by asking for an interview. If your request is granted, as it almost surely will be, you have two obligations: to prepare in advance a sensible set of questions, and to tell the interviewee what use you expect to make of his responses. If you would like to tape what he says, get his approval in advance. If you subsequently quote or paraphrase his remarks in your paper, make sure—if possible by checking with the interviewee himself—that you quote him accurately and in context and that you clearly indicate the source of the quotation.

THE OUTLINE

Your teachers have doubtless told you of the importance of an outline when writing—and doubtless you have ignored the advice, since outline-making takes a lot of time and seems to slow your writing down without making the result notably better. You could have been right. But a detailed research paper is different from a book report, short paper, or essay. Moreover, in a long paper the outline is an invaluable guide to your thinking, a check on the validity of your arguments as well as their direction.

All the note cards shown in Figures 4 to 9 carry outline references: numbers tentatively keyed to your emerging sense of the possible structure of your paper, or more often added later when you have a reasonably firm working outline. Early in your reading, you begin to chart your course. You conclude that the marijuana controversy has three critical aspects—the legal, the physical/psychological, and the social/political—and that all three aspects, broad as they are, are relevant to any discussion of marijuana and the generation gap. Since these categories cover a lot of ground, your paper will unquestionably have to be far less ambitious than your outline. That is normal; outlines are made to be trimmed. Think of your outline as a frame of reference for your notes, a way of keeping them in order; and as a way of limiting and focusing your project from the start. So, early on, playing on hunches and sparse knowledge, you jot down the following tentative outline plan:

"*Thesis:* The arguments of the anti-marijuana crusaders that pot (1) causes insanity, (2) leads to crime, and (3) promotes the use of addictive drugs like heroin have been refuted in at least five objective, scientific studies over the past seventy-five years; yet the opposition to pot continues unabated, and the laws in some instances are made more severe. How can we account for this opposition? What can we do about it?"

From this plan you work out a possible outline for your paper, entering references to your reading at appropriate places.

Working Outline

I. Those who have opposed the manufacturing, selling, possessing, or using of pot, especially since the 1930's, have done so on three main grounds:

A. Pot causes insanity and related mental/moral decay
  1. Rowell's claims in *On the Trail of Marijuana,* the film *Reefer Madness,* and other journalistic stories about addiction (Smith, 106-107; Fixx, 344-345; Snyder, 420-427)
  2. The idea of the "dope fiend" and the Dacca reports on "hemp insanity" (Ginsberg, 107; Grinspoon, 254)
  3. Anslinger's letter to the A.M.A. in 1943 (Solomon, xxvii)
  4. Reports of Commissioner Valentine and Mrs. Hamilton Wright (Fixx, 345)

B. Pot causes crime
  1. Anslinger's campaign to spread this idea (Smith, 109; Kaplan, 88-98; Grinspoon, 18-19)

   a. Connection between "hashish" and "assassin" (Smith, 109; Solomon, 32–33)
   b. Anslinger's *The Traffic in Narcotics* and atrocity stories peddled by the Federal Bureau of Narcotics, the New Orleans Commissioner of Public Safety, and others (Grinspoon, 19; Snyder, 426)
   c. Marijuana Tax Act of 1937 (Solomon, xiv–xv; McGlothlin in Simmons, 182–187; Smith, 106)
   2. Testimony before the House Ways and Means Committee, 1937 (Solomon, xxv; Kaplan, 233–234; Smith, 110)

C. Smoking pot leads to shooting heroin
   1. Anslinger's contradictory statements (Kaplan, 234; Smith, 112; Solomon, 55)
   2. The "stepping-stone" theory and the journalistic "argument" (Kaplan, 233; Shick et al. in Smith, 60; Grinspoon, 236–241)

II. The evidence is overwhelming that these assertions are all either exaggerated or downright false

A. There is no evidence that pot causes insanity
   1. Indian Hemp Drug Commission's study of 1894 (Mikuriya, 253; Grinspoon, 125); LaGuardia Report (Grinspoon, 262); 1922 U.S. Army study in the Canal Zone (Laurie, 92–93)
   2. Psychotic and neurotic reactions rare except in already unstable persons (Grinspoon, 253–290; *Psych. Abstr.*, 16127; McGlothlin in Simmons, 179; Keniston, *Current*, 8; Weil et al., 1242)
   3. No long-term mental or physical effects (Arnold in Simmons, 120–121; Stockings in Solomon, 424)
      a. But see literary reports of acute intoxication (Grinspoon, 55–116)
      b. The properties of acute intoxication (Grinspoon, 117–172)

B. There is no established connection between marijuana use and crime
   1. FBN's methodology and "evidence" worthless (Kaplan, 135)

    2. LaGuardia Report's finding of "no direct relationship" between marijuana and crimes of violence, and A.M.A. rebuttal (Solomon, xxvii, 277-410; Lindesmith in Solomon, 57-58; Kaplan, 73; Goode in Smith, 174-75; Grinspoon, 28, 309 ff.)

    3. Negative correlation between marijuana use and aggression generally (Kaplan, 135-36; Smith, 109-110; McGlothlin & West, *Am. J. Psychiat.*, Sept. '68, 372-373; but see Etzioni, 39)

C. There is no proof that pot leads to heroin (Grupp, 101-111; Kaplan, 232-262; Lindesmith in Solomon, 57-58; Oursler, 57; Etzioni, 39; Grinspoon, 236-241)

D. In fact, strong evidence shows that marijuana is nonaddictive and less physically dangerous than alcohol and cigarettes
    1. Indian Hemp Drug Commission's report (Taylor in Solomon, 11)
    2. Dr. Goddard's statement (Etzioni, 38-39; *Time*, Apr. 19 '68, 52, 53; USN&WR, Feb. 5 '68)
    3. Other statements and views (Oursler, xii; Nowlis, 7; in Solomon, xxvii-xxviii, 41, 49, 91-92, 119, 123; Grinspoon, 159-165, 286-287)

III. Then why such strict laws against pot and why are some people so fearful of it?

A. Pot for some is a symbol of a threatening alternative lifestyle; fear of difference (Kaplan, 4-19; Carey in Smith, 96)
    1. Report of the Le Dain Commission, 1970 (Brecher, 457)
    2. Keniston's distinction between "seekers" and "heads" and the threat to the work-ethic (*Current*, Feb. '69, 9, 10)

B. Pot for some represents a political as well as cultural threat
    1. Miscellaneous reactions (Goode, 168 ff.; Kaplan, 5; Grinspoon, 323-343)
    2. Government reactions to government reports:
        a. British reaction to Indian Hemp Drug Commission report (Taylor in Solomon, 11)
        b. U.S. reaction to Canal Zone report (Snyder, 420 ff.)
        c. The Baroness Wooton report of 1968 (Grinspoon, 248)
        d. The Shafer report of 1972 (*Marijuana*, U.S. Print. Off., 1972; Goddard in Etzioni, 38)

    C. Pot symbolizes a struggle for power and authority between the generations (Kaplan, 8-12; Smith, 2; Goode in Smith, 183; Leary in Solomon, 125)

IV. Conclusion: What should be done, if anything?

This is a working outline, not a final one. Clearly, you have far more material than you can use if your paper is to be kept to three or four thousand words; you cannot possibly, for example, go into much detail on all those governmental reports. Still, you have defined your theme and the main direction of your argument. There will be further changes and unexpected difficulties, but your general course is charted.

The outline shown here is neither a pure topic outline nor a pure sentence outline, but a mixture of the two. When you need only a few words to give yourself direction, a topic heading is enough. When you want to remind yourself of some specific detail, a sentence or a parenthesis is more useful. Note that the outline includes possible references to be cited under specific heads. Now is the time to decide what materials you will be using in what sequence—not later, when you will be concentrating on other matters.

Now with your research done (or abandoned) and your outline in shape, you are ready to begin writing.

14

WRITING THE
RESEARCH PAPER

The outline that ends the previous chapter is not the sort of thing you can strike off after an hour's thought, or even after a weekend's reading. It has taken shape in the course of three weeks or more of reading and thought, and perhaps after one or more false starts. It is a distillation of what you know and what you think you know at the time you break off your reading and get ready to start writing.

Your working outline is not necessarily the ideal one for your purposes. Indeed, if your research has been thorough—or even modestly ambitious—your outline will probably cover too much ground for the length of paper you have been assigned. That is exactly what has happened here. Something has to go: at the very least a lot of illustration and detail.

In the following pages we give a paper that could have emerged from the process just described. As we shall see, it departs considerably from the outline in plan as well as content. That is entirely normal; a research paper is a living and creative enterprise, and should be freed, not imprisoned, by an outline. Many different papers might have been written with the same outline as a point of departure.

MARIJUANA: A LOOK AT THE EVIDENCE

In 1973, over 400,000 persons were arrested for the possession of marijuana, "an increase of more than 100,000 over the previous year."[1] Despite some recent unequivocal statements about the harmlessness of the drug, marijuana continues to raise major social and moral issues in America, issues that have been made more complex by prejudice, ignorance, and outright deception.

Over the years a great amount of scientific evidence concerning the effects of marijuana has been collected. The prestigious LaGuardia Report of 1938 concluded that marijuana in moderate doses merely "lessens inhibition"; it "does not evoke responses which would otherwise be totally alien" to the user, "does not lead directly to mental or physical deterioration, . . . and is not a direct causal factor in sexual or criminal misconduct."[2] It has been consistently shown to be nonaddictive.[3] And according to a team of Boston researchers, "Medically, it's quite harmless. It's not like alcohol, which can seriously injure, even kill you."[4] Five major commissions between 1894 and 1972 have delved into the problem, and "remarkable as it may appear, all five of the reports of the investigating bodies are in substantial agreement on substantially all major points of fact."[5]

Scientific concern with the nature of marijuana dates back to the late nineteenth century.[6] In 1894 the Indian Hemp Drug Commission was established by the colonial British government to look into drug traffic in India. The commission's seven-volume report has been called "the most complete and systematic study of marijuana

---

[1] San Jose Mercury, July 22, 1974, p. 7.

[2] The quotations come from a report of the LaGuardia study in the May 1945 issue of Science as quoted in Lester Grinspoon, Marihuana Reconsidered (Cambridge, Mass., 1971), p. 29, and from a summary of the LaGuardia Committee's findings by its chairman, Dr. George B. Wallace, as quoted in David Solomon, ed., The Marihuana Papers (New York, 1968), p. 358.

[3] Edward M. Brecher, Licit and Illicit Drugs (Boston, 1972), p. 451.

[4] Quoted in Jane E. Brody, "Study Finds Marijuana Effects Mild," New York Times, Dec. 14, 1968, reprinted in James F. Fixx, ed., Drugs: The Great Contemporary Issues (New York, 1971), p. 370.

[5] Brecher, p. 453.

[6] Solomon H. Snyder, "What We Have Forgotten About Pot," reprinted in Fixx, pp. 420 ff.

undertaken to date."[7] According to Dr. Norman Taylor, "the inquiry, which lasted nearly two years, was carried through with typical British impartiality."[8] The commission reached the following conclusions:

1. There is no evidence of any weight regarding mental and moral injuries from the moderate use of these drugs.

2. Large numbers of practitioners of long experience have seen no evidence of any connection between the moderate use of hemp drugs and disease.

3. Moderation does not lead to excess in hemp any more than it does in alcohol. Regular, moderate use of ganja or bhang produces the same effects as moderate and regular doses of whiskey. Excess is confined to the idle and dissipated.[9]

It is essentially these facts on which all subsequent investigators have agreed, down to and including the Shafer Commission, appointed by President Nixon, in its report dated 1972.[10]

Yet as consistently as the facts have been affirmed, so consistently have they been ignored or repudiated by government officials and politicians--with one notable exception. In 1967 Dr. James L. Goddard, then head of the Food and Drug Administration, remarked, "Whether or not marijuana is a more dangerous drug than alcohol is debatable--I don't happen to think it is."[11] Goddard was forced to resign his post some months later because of official displeasure with his position.

There are good reasons to believe that marijuana is both physically and psychologically as benign a drug as alcohol or tobacco, yet our official society has gone all-out to suppress it.[12] Why? The question is not an idle one, given the fact that some ten million Americans are legally criminals as a result of smoking marijuana.[13] Per-

---

[7] Tod H. Mikuriya, "Physical, Mental and Moral Effects of Marijuana," International Journal of the Addictions, 3:253 (Fall 1968).

[8] Norman Taylor, "The Pleasant Assassin: The Story of Marihuana," reprinted in Solomon, p. 41.

[9] Ibid.

[10] Marihuana: A Signal of Misunderstanding (Washington, D.C., 1972). See also Bruce D. Johnson, Marihuana Users and Drug Subcultures (New York, 1973), passim.

[11] Quoted in Amitai Etzioni, "America's Social Frontiers: Why Not Smoke Pot?," Current, 95:38 (May 1968).

[12] Peter Laurie, Drugs: Medical, Psychological, and Social Facts (Harmondsworth, Eng., 1969), pp. 90 ff.

[13] Ten million is the estimate of Dr. Stanley Yolles, quoted in Gertrude Samuels, "Pot, Hard Drugs, and the Law," New York Times Magazine, Feb. 15, 1970, p. 4.

haps half to three-quarters of all college undergraduates have smoked at least one joint; and they too are criminals.[14]

But the question of marijuana use is not primarily medical or psychological, nor is it in any profound sense social or moral. Rather, at base, it is political, a question of Us against Them. The waves of students smoking pot at antiwar rallies in the late sixties were acutely aware of this. Their insistence that marijuana was symbolic of an alternative life-style is attested by the Le Dain Commission's 1970 report. This Canadian body of experts stated in part:

In our conversation with [students and young people], they have frequently contrasted marijuana and alcohol effects to describe the former as a drug of peace, a drug that reduces tendencies to aggression, while suggesting that the latter drug produces hostile, aggressive behavior. Thus marijuana is seen as particularly appropriate to a generation that emphasizes peace and is, in many ways, anti-competitive.[15]

Kenneth Keniston draws an illuminating distinction in this regard between "seekers" and "heads." Seekers are antiwar, antipollution, and antipoverty idealists who are not "in any systematic way 'alienated' from American society" but who "have not really made up their minds whether it is worth joining, either." Heads are thoroughly disenchanted with the career-oriented goals of a middle-class America. They are convinced, in Keniston's words, that

American society is trashy, cheap, and commercial; it "dehumanizes" its members; its values of success, materialism, monetary accomplishment undercut more spiritual values. . . . For heads, the goal is to find a way out of the "air-conditioned nightmare" of American society. What matters is the interior world, and, in the exploration of that world, drugs play a major role.[16]

Only in terms like these can we understand the feelings of many people who, like Commissioner Henry L. Giordano of the Federal Bureau of Narcotics, see the attempt to legalize marijuana as "just another effort to break down our whole American

---

[14] The figure for one leading university in 1968 was 69 percent, according to a study by Richard H. Blum and associates cited in John Kaplan, Marijuana--The New Prohibition (New York, 1970), p. 23.

[15] Brecher, p. 457.

[16] Kenneth Keniston, "Students, Drugs, and Protest: Drugs on Campus," Current, 103: 9, 10 (Feb. 1969).

system."[17] As Erich Goode points out, "Marijuana has become a symbol for a complex of positions, beliefs, and activities in which those who use the drug must also be politically radical, sexually promiscuous, and unpatriotic."[18] Kaplan makes the same point in more explicit terms:

In a large portion of our population, then, marijuana is associated with a life-style focusing on immediate experience, present rather than delayed gratification, non-competitiveness and lessened interest in the acquisition of wealth. And even if one is not prepared to use stronger terms, such as irresponsibility, laziness, and a lack of patriotism, there is no doubt that the life-style, like the use of the drug itself, involves a disregard for many of the conventions that the older society regards as dear. It is hardly surprising, then, that many people will wish strongly that the criminalization of marijuana be retained if only as a reminder to marijuana users--and indeed to many who do not use marijuana but who are like users in other ways--that this life-style and these values are less worthy.[19]

Marijuana has not always been the target of such intense opposition. As recently as 1922, a U.S. Army study in the Canal Zone could be completely dispassionate on the subject. "It concluded that marihuana presented no threat to military discipline, and 'there is no evidence that marihuana as grown here is a habit-forming drug in the sense in which the term is applied to alcohol, opium, cocaine, etc. and that no recommendations to prevent the sale or use of marihuana are deemed advisable.' "[20] Indeed until about 1923, according to Roger C. Smith, addiction to narcotics generally (a category in which marijuana was inaccurately included) tended to be regarded as "an unfortunate occurrence, but not really the fault of the individual."[21] How did the change come about? "Owing largely to hysteria generated by a misguided press campaign, drug clinics were closed and the addict was generally considered 'no longer a victim but a threat.' "[22]

---

[17] Hearings . . . Before a Subcommittee of the House Committee on Appropriations, 90th Congress (Feb. 8, 1967), p. 405, quoted in Kaplan, p. 9.

[18] Erich Goode, "Marijuana and the Politics of Reality," quoted in David E. Smith, ed., The New Social Drug: Cultural, Medical, and Legal Perspectives on Marijuana (Englewood Cliffs, N.J., 1970), pp. 168 ff.

[19] Kaplan, p. 5.

[20] Laurie, pp. 92-93.

[21] Roger C. Smith, "U.S. Marijuana Legislation and the Creation of a Social Problem," in David E. Smith, ed., The New Social Drug, p. 108.

[22] Ibid.

The Federal Bureau of Narcotics, directed by Harry Anslinger and staffed largely by former Prohibition agents, supported this new approach. Under Anslinger, "Americans were sold a mythological bill of goods. They were told that marijuana was a 'killer drug' that triggered crimes of violence and acts of sexual excess; a toxic agent capable of driving normal persons into fits of madness and depraved behavior; a destroyer of the will; a satanically destructive drug which, employing lures of euphoria and heightened sensuality, visited physical degeneration and chronic psychosis upon the habitual user."[23] It goes without saying that Anslinger's lurid tales of pot-induced depravity had wide exposure.

By 1936 the country was obsessed with the dangers of marijuana. Early that year a New Orleans police official claimed that the serious crime wave then sweeping the city "was greatly aggravated by the influence of this drug. . . . Youngsters known to be muggle-heads fortified themselves with the narcotic [sic] and proceeded to shoot down police, bank clerks and casual bystanders."[24] In August, New York City's Police Commissioner described marijuana as "an extremely dangerous weed" that "causes temporary insanity."[25] In May 1937, Mrs. Hamilton Wright, a special representative of the Federal Bureau of Narcotics, assured the National Congress of Parents and Teachers meeting in Richmond, Virginia, that marijuana "produced in smokers . . . a temporary sense of complete irresponsibility which led to sex crimes and other 'horrible' acts of violence."[26]

Mayor Fiorello LaGuardia of New York City was not so easily convinced, and in

---

[23] Solomon, p. xv.

[24] Snyder, p. 426.

[25] Fixx, p. 345. This was a widespread belief. For example, a New York Times article of Dec. 29, 1921 (quoted in Fixx, p. 344), states that "marihuana leaves, smoked in cigarettes, produce murderous delirium. Its addicts often become insane. Scientists say its effects are perhaps more terrible than those of any intoxicant or drug."

[26] Ibid. Among the yellow journalism accounts of the day, Laurie (p. 91) cites the following as typical examples: "Marihuana as a Developer of Criminals," "Sex Crazing Drug Menace," and "Exposing the Marijuana Drug Evil in Swing Bands." The contemporary propaganda film Reefer Madness is yet another example of this genre, one that could be viewed with humor were it not for its effectiveness in maintaining repressive anti-marijuana laws.

1938 he asked the prestigious New York Academy of Medicine to look into the problem. The committee's report, generally referred to as the LaGuardia Report, confirmed the findings of all previous scientific investigations:

> In most instances, the behavior of the smoker is of a friendly, sociable character. Aggressiveness and belligerency are not commonly seen, and those showing such traits are not allowed to remain in "tea pads."
> The marihuana user does not come from the hardened criminal class and there was found no direct relationship between the commission of crimes of violence and marihuana. "Tea pads" have no direct association with houses of prostitution, and marihuana itself has no specific stimulant effect in regard to sexual desires.[27]

But the LaGuardia Report came too late to affect the legal status of marijuana. In 1937, thanks to the efforts of Anslinger and his acolytes, Congress passed the Marihuana Tax Act, making the possession, cultivation, sale, or distribution of marijuana a federal offense.

Wartime and postwar problems turned public attention elsewhere for nearly three decades, but in the 1960's the rise of a youth culture reopened the old debate. Marijuana use increased, and the old charges and countercharges were trotted out. The usual reports were commissioned, with the usual results. In England in 1968 a commission headed by Baroness Wooton "confirmed in all substantial respects the findings of the Indian Hemp Drugs Commission and Panama Canal Zone investigations and the LaGuardia Committee report."[28] In Canada the Le Dain Commission in 1970 reached the same conclusion.

In the United States the Presidential Commission of 1972 urged the following reforms on Congress and the Administration:

> Possession of marijuana for personal use would no longer be an offense, but marijuana possessed in public would remain contraband subject to summary seizure and forfeiture.
> Casual distribution of small amounts of marihuana for no remuneration or insignificant remuneration not involving profit would no longer be an offense.[29]

The reception of this report by President Nixon marked a new low in the politicizing

---

[27] Solomon, p. 355.

[28] Brecher, p. 452.

[29] Marihuana: A Signal of Misunderstanding, p. 152.

of the marijuana issue. Before even receiving the document or any official report on its contents, the President announced that he would not accept his own commission's findings!

Will pointing out that there is no established scientific basis for the feeling against marijuana help bring about saner and fairer marijuana laws? On the evidence to date, there is no reason to think so. Like Nixon, most people who are against liberalizing the laws are not, as Erich Goode points out, really worried about marijuana as a <u>cause</u> of anything--a cause of crime or brain damage or heroin addiction or traffic accidents or unwillingness to work. They are worried about it as a thing <u>evil in itself</u>.[30] They tend to present their prejudices and irrational fears in the guise of logical arguments, but in essence their attack on marijuana is a witch hunt.

Such people probably cannot be reached by reason; the best we can do is vote against them when we get the chance. But the climate is changing, and not just because more and more voters have smoked pot without experiencing any heightened propensity to become rapists or drug addicts. It is changing in part because the likes of those Boston researchers have got through to the likes of Dr. Goddard. Prejudice dies hard, but reason dies harder. It may not even take much longer.

---

[30] Goode in Smith, p. 176.

BIBLIOGRAPHY

Allen, James R., and West, Louis Jolyon, "Flight from Violence: Hippies and the Green Rebellion," American Journal of Psychiatry, 125: 364-370 (Sept. 1968).

Brecher, Edward M. Licit and Illicit Drugs. Boston: Little, Brown & Co., 1972.

Etzioni, Amitai, "America's Social Frontiers: Why Not Smoke Pot?," Current, 95:38-41 (May 1968).

Fixx, James F., ed. Drugs: The Great Contemporary Issues. New York: Arno Press, 1971.

Grinspoon, Lester. Marihuana Reconsidered. Cambridge, Mass.: Harvard University Press, 1971.

Grupp, Stanley E. The Marihuana Muddle. Lexington, Mass.: D. C. Heath & Co., 1973.

Johnson, Bruce D. Marihuana Users and Drug Subcultures. New York: John Wiley & Sons, 1973.

Kaplan, John. Marijuana--The New Prohibition. New York: World Publishing Co., 1970.

Keniston, Kenneth, "Students, Drugs, and Protest: Drugs on Campus," Current, 103:5-19 (Feb. 1969).

Laurie, Peter. Drugs: Medical, Psychological, and Social Facts. Harmondsworth, Eng.: Penguin Books, 1969.

Marihuana: A Signal of Misunderstanding. Washington, D.C.: U.S. Government Printing Office, 1972.

Mikuriya, Tod H., "Physical, Mental and Moral Effects of Marijuana," International Journal of the Addictions, 3:250-256 (Fall 1968).

"Potted Dreams," British Medical Journal. 1:133-134 (Jan. 18, 1969).

Samuels, Gertrude, "Pot, Hard Drugs, and the Law," New York Times Magazine, Feb. 15, 1970.

Simmons, J. L., ed. Marihuana: Myths and Realities. North Hollywood, Calif.: Brandon House, 1967.

Smith, David E., ed. The New Social Drug: Cultural, Medical, and Legal Perspectives on Marijuana. Englewood Cliffs, N.J.: Prentice-Hall, Inc., 1970.

    Goode, Erich, "Marijuana and the Politics of Reality," pp. 168-186.

    Messer, Mark, "Running Out of Era: Some Nonpharmacological Notes on the Psychedelic Revolution," pp. 157-167.

    Smith, Roger C., "U.S. Marijuana Legislation and the Creation of a Social Problem," pp. 105-117.

Solomon, David, ed. <u>The Marihuana Papers</u>. New York: New American Library, 1968.

  Allentuck, Samuel, and Bowman, Karl, "Psychiatric Aspects of Marihuana Intoxication," pp. 411–416.

  Ginsberg, Allen, "First Manifesto to End the Bringdown," pp. 230–248.

  McGlothlin, William H., "Cannabis: A Reference," pp. 455–472.

  "The Marihuana Problem in the City of New York," with a Foreword by Mayor F. H. LaGuardia, pp. 277–410.

  Solomon, David, "The Marihuana Myths," pp. xi–xxiii.

  Taylor, Norman, "The Pleasant Assassin: The Story of Marihuana," pp. 31–47.

Steinbeck, John. <u>In Touch</u>. New York: Alfred A. Knopf, Inc., 1969.

Tylden, Elizabeth, et al., "A Case for Cannabis?," <u>British Medical Journal</u>, 3:556 (Aug. 26, 1967).

Weil, Andrew T.; Zinberg, Norman E.; and Nelson, Judith M., "Clinical and Psychological Effects of Marihuana in Man," <u>Science</u> 162:1234–1242 (Dec. 13, 1968).

The paper just presented has several characteristics worth noting. First, it illustrates most of the common problems encountered in handling quoted matter and footnotes. Second, its bibliography includes several publications that are not actually quoted or referred to but that the writer found helpful in shaping his thoughts; though teachers rightly discourage students from padding out their bibliographies with ill-digested or unread material, publications that have influenced the paper may properly be listed even if they have not been cited. Finally, the conclusion of the paper does not merely repeat or recapitulate what the writer has said already but goes on to suggest what the paper means, what message he thinks we should carry away from it. Anyone can summarize facts; what a reader wants is the writer's statement of what they seem to add up to.

FOOTNOTES

Common Abbreviations

In the footnotes and the bibliography of our marijuana paper, we used the conventional abbreviations "ed.," "et al.," and *"ibid."* The first stands for "editor," or more rarely for "edited by," as in *"The Complete Works of Shakespeare,* ed. George Lyman Kittredge"; in its meaning of "editor" it takes the plural "eds." Its most common use is to indicate a man who prepares for publication either an edition of another man's works (as Kittredge did Shakespeare's) or a work by many hands (like the Solomon book on marijuana). As the preceding pages indicate, "ed." should be lowercased and should not be enclosed in parentheses. The same abbreviation also stands for "edition," as in "3d ed." or "rev. ed."

"Et al." is an abbreviation of the Latin *et alii,* "and others"; it may be either roman or italic. The use of "and others" instead of "et al." is also perfectly acceptable. *"Ibid."* is another abbreviation from the Latin; the full form is *ibidem,* "in the same place." (Purists object to "in *ibid."* because this would translate *"in in* the same place," but most professional editors accept the expression anyway.) *"Ibid."* is used to stand for as much of the immediately preceding citation as applies to the present one: thus if note 1 reads *"Paradise Lost,* Bk. 9, lines 115–121," note 2 might read simply *"Ibid."* (meaning that the identical passage is being cited again), or *"Ibid.*, lines 122–123," or *"Ibid.*, Bk. 10, line 8."

Short Forms

In citing a book or article for the second time when the first citation does not immediately precede, some authorities recommend *"op. cit.,"* an abbreviation of the Latin *opere citato,* "in the work cited"; thus "Smith, *op. cit.*, p. 89." But we prefer a short-title system.

Suppose Smith's book is the only work you cite by anyone named Smith; then your second citation need only read "Smith, p. 89." If you cite more than one work by Smith, say a book titled *The Situation in Southeast Asia* and a magazine article titled "The Hong Kong Refugees," you need give just enough of the title in your next citation to make it clear which of the two works you are citing: Smith, *Situation,* p. 89; Smith, "Refugees," p. 191. Finally, if you cite works by more than one Smith, you should distinguish between Smiths by adding first names or initials: H. E. Smith, p. 89; Margaret Chase Smith, pp. 10–12.

Checklist of Footnote Forms

Here is a brief checklist of the most common footnote forms:

Books

First reference to a book:

[1] Fernand Braudel, *Capitalism and Material Life, 1400–1800,* trans. Miriam Kochan (New York, 1973), p. 202.
[2] Wilhelm Windelband, *A History of Philosophy* (New York, 1958), II, 447.

Immediately following reference to the same page of the Windelband book:

[3] *Ibid.*

To a different page of the same volume:

[4] *Ibid.*, p. 449.

To a different volume of the same work:

[5] *Ibid.*, I, 25-26.

Later references to the Windelband book if it is the only work by this author cited:

[6] Windelband, II, 450.

If other works by this author are cited:

[7] Windelband, *History*, II, 450.

If a work by another author named Windelband is also cited:

[8] W. Windelband, II, 450.

First reference to a book with two or three editors:

[9] Cleanth Brooks, John Thibaut Purser, and Robert Penn Warren, eds., *An Approach to Literature*, 3d ed. (New York, 1952), p. 34.

Notice that "3d ed." is not included in the parenthesis; this is not parenthetical information, but an essential indication of which edition you are quoting from, since page 34 of the first or second edition might be very different from page 34 of the third. If there are four or more authors or editors, it becomes cumbersome to list all the names; it is conventional in this case to use the form "Cleanth Brooks and others," or "Cleanth Brooks et al."

Later references to the same book:

[10] Brooks, Purser, and Warren, p. 80.

First reference to a chapter in a multiauthor volume:

> [11] Bette S. Denich, "Sex and Power in the Balkans," in Michelle Zimbalist Rosaldo and Louise Lamphere, eds., *Woman, Culture, and Society* (Stanford, Calif., 1974), p. 245.

Later reference to the same chapter:

> [12] Denich in Rosaldo and Lamphere, pp. 247-248.

If there are many references to the Denich chapter in close succession, the citation can be abbreviated still further to "Denich, pp. 247-248."

Reference to another chapter in the same book:

> [13] Jane Fishburne Collier, "Women in Politics," in Rosaldo and Lamphere, p. 89.

Reference to an edition of the works of a single author prepared by an editor:

> [14] *The Works of Schopenhauer*, ed. Will Durant (New York, 1955), p. 456.

Even though your concern may be exclusively with what Schopenhauer says and Durant's name may mean nothing to you, it is customary to cite the editor's name so that knowledgeable readers will immediately understand that you are using the Durant edition of Schopenhauer rather than any of the various other English-language editions.

Reference to an encyclopedia article:

> [15] "Etruscan Pottery," *Encyclopedia of Arts and Crafts* (New York, 1970), IV, 239.

Reference to a quotation available to you only in a secondary source:

> [16] Axel Munthe, *The Story of San Michele*, p. 245, quoted in Karl Menninger, *Man Against Himself* (New York, 1938), p. 66.

Articles

First reference to an article in a periodical:

> [17] Ellen Moers, "Mme de Staël and the Woman of Genius," *The American Scholar*, 44:225 (Spring 1975).

Alternatively, "XLIV (Spring 1975), 225" or "44 (Spring 1975), 225." Whichever of these forms you use, stick to it for all articles cited in your paper.

Later references to the same article:

> [18] Moers, p. 229.

This assumes that no other works by Moers are cited in your paper. Otherwise use a short form: Moers, "Mme de Staël," p. 229.

Reference to a book review:

> [19] Joseph Frank, review of *Symbols and Civilization* by Ralph Ross, in *Sewanee Review*, 72:478 (Summer 1964).

Reference to an unsigned article in a newspaper:

> [20] "Black Power vs. 'White Guilt,' " *San Francisco Chronicle*, Oct. 15, 1971, p. 6.

Note that a periodical's dates are in parentheses when they follow a volume number. That is because the volume number is enough to enable the reader to locate the periodical in a library; the date is accordingly extra information, given parenthetically for whatever interest it may be to the reader. Where no volume number is given, the date becomes essential to finding the reference; it accordingly appears between commas, like a volume number, e.g. "*New York Times*, May 11, 1976, p. 12."

Citation in Text

Scientists and social scientists often supply source information in parentheses in the text rather than in footnote form. Thus we find a social scientist writing

> Albanian men are served by women, who then eat separately in the kitchen with the children (Hasluck 1954: 28-29)

where a historian or a literary critic might have spelled out the reference in a footnote:

> [1] Margaret Hasluck, *The Unwritten Law in Albania* (London, 1954), pp. 28-29.

If you use the in-text style, be sure that complete information on all works cited appears in your bibliography.

In-text citation is also convenient for a critical paper on a single work. For example, in a paper devoted wholly to Charles Dickens's novel *Our Mutual Friend*, you need give a full footnote citation only to your first quotation:

> [1] *Our Mutual Friend* (Harmondsworth, Eng.: Penguin Books, 1971), p. 205. All subsequent citations are to this edition.

Thereafter you can supply page numbers as necessary in text:

> The one thing Podsnappery requires is that "everything in the universe . . . be fined down and fitted to it" (p. 175).

The "p." is optional, as is the publisher's name in the footnote, but both seem helpful enough to include.

What to Footnote

If you have trouble with footnoting and need a single central idea to get hold of, it should be the concept of *retrievability*. In the last analysis, the use of parentheses or commas, italics or quotation marks, is a matter of form, a convention to be learned for your own convenience and your reader's, but not the heart of the matter. The basic purpose of footnotes is to tell your reader where you got your information so that he can decide for himself how much faith to put in it. Did you get it from the *New York Times*, May 11, 1976, page 12? Well and good. Your reader can either accept the information as true, dismiss it as biased (if he feels, for example, that the *Times* is generally biased), or look it up for himself to see whether your source really says what you say it says and to find out what else it says at the same time. Had you not footnoted your information, your reader would not have had these options.

In deciding what to footnote, it may help to imagine a skeptical reader, one disposed to question everything you say. He may ask, How do you know the Russian Navy is the world's second-largest? Your footnote is your answer: " 'Red Sails in the Sunset,' editorial in the *Topeka News*, Dec. 10, 1975, p. 28." How do you know that President Nixon was unpopular in Spain? "Letter from my brother, Lt. Eugene Hart, in Madrid, Sept. 20, 1973." Where did you learn that Mao Tse-tung was a lifelong champion of equal rights for women? "See Stuart Schram, *Mao Tse-tung* (New York, 1966), p. 43." Some sources are more trustworthy than others; your readers have the right to judge this matter for themselves.

Finally, make sure you include enough information in your footnote to take your reader straight to the right place if he wants to follow in your footsteps. "*Topeka News*, Dec. 10, 1975" is not enough; the reader may have to search through 50 pages of small type to find the passage you cite. "According to Stuart Schram" is not enough; Schram has written several books, each with several hundred pages, and dozens of articles. Even the citation of your brother's letter—not a recommended thing to do, by the way, but permissible where you have reliable information not readily accessible from more public sources—gains authority from the details. Your brother was a lieutenant, which means that he was not a child and probably not a mere tourist; and he was in Spain during President Nixon's administration, which means that his information is firsthand. "Letter from my brother" alone would tell us none of this.

To repeat, the content of footnotes is more important than their form. Get your information down first. You can learn the conventions of punctuation, italicization, and so on later.

PLAGIARISM

Plagiarism is literary burglary. At its worst it involves an outright intent to deceive, to pass off another's work as one's own. More often, it is the result of carelessness or ignorance. But whether intentional or unintentional (the distinction is often hard to draw), plagiarism is always an error, and a serious one.

Whenever you borrow another writer's words or ideas, you must acknowledge the borrowing. The only exceptions are information in the public domain (Columbus landed in America in 1492; oxygen was originally called phlogiston; oranges grow on trees) and opinions within anyone's range (*Hamlet* is a great play; time flies). Many undergraduates have trouble with this problem. Some react with an overnice conscience and footnote even dictionary definitions. Others change two or three words in a quotation and feel that they have somehow made it their own. The first practice is irritating, the second unethical. The right course is a generous and intelligent consideration of both the reader you are addressing (he will take 1492 on faith) and the writers you are using. When you use their words, their ideas, even their organization or sequence of ideas, say so—in a footnote or in the text. Claim as your own only what properly is your own.

The following examples may help to clarify the difference between legitimate and illegitimate borrowing. Here is part of the paragraph on Thoreau from Vernon Louis Parrington's *Main Currents in American Thought:*

> At Walden Pond and on the Merrimac River Thoreau's mind was serene as the open spaces; but this Greek serenity was rudely disturbed when he returned to Concord village and found his neighbors drilling for the Mexican War, and when authority in the person of the constable came to him with the demand that he pay a due share to the public funds. The war to him was a hateful thing, stupid and unjust, waged for the extension of the obscene system of Negro slavery; and Thoreau was brought sharply to consider his relations to the political state that presumed to

demand his allegiance, willing or unwilling, to its acts. Under the stress of such an emergency the transcendentalist was driven to examine the whole theory of the relation of the individual to the state.

The following examples will demonstrate some representative ways in which this passage, or parts of it, might be misused.°

Inadequate Acknowledgment: Outright Theft

When Thoreau was at Walden Pond or on the Merrimac River he knew considerable peace of mind, but when he returned to Concord this peace of mind was rudely disturbed. He came back to find his neighbors drilling for the Mexican War, a war he thought wrong, and when the constable came to him and demanded that he pay taxes to support that war, he balked. The war to him was a hateful thing, stupid and unjust, waged for the extension of the obscene system of Negro slavery; and Thoreau was brought sharply to consider his relations to the political state that presumed to demand his allegiance. In such an emergency, just how did the individual relate to the state?

In this example the writer has rephrased Parrington's first and last sentences, using some of his own words and some of Parrington's. He has made enough other minor modifications so that no full sentence of the original remains intact. But these trivial exceptions apart, he has copied the original word for word. His intent to deceive is clear, the more so from his inept camouflaging of the first and last sentences. Had the writer put the directly quoted portion in quotation marks (or made it a single-spaced insert quotation) and footnoted it, he would not be guilty of plagiarism. He would have made it clear that he was contributing nothing of his own to the discussion, but was simply inviting us to listen to Parrington. As it is, however, he is passing off Parrington's words as his own, pretending to a knowledge (and style) he doesn't have. This is an inexcusable moral error.

° For simplicity we omit footnotes from the following discussion. A truly adequate acknowledgment to Parrington would of course include a footnote giving his name in full, the title of his book, the city and date of publication, and the numbers of the pages from which the writer's information is drawn.

Inadequate Acknowledgment: Paraphrase

At Walden Pond and on the Merrimac River Thoreau's mind was calm as the open spaces; but this serenity was rudely disrupted when he returned to Concord and discovered his neighbors drilling for the Mexican War, and when the constable, representing authority, came to him and demanded that he pay his share of taxes for the war. He regarded the war as hateful, stupid, and unjust, and waged to extend the slave system, which he opposed. This experience caused Thoreau to reconsider sharply the whole question of the relation between the individual and the state.

This example represents only a negligible improvement on the last. The writer has made more changes in wording than the outright plagiarist, but has contributed no more of his own thinking or wording. Every idea in his paragraph and most of the words and phrases are taken directly from Parrington without acknowledgment. Though the writer has avoided copying whole clauses word for word, he is plainly guilty of plagiarism.

But what is a writer to do in such a case? Clearly it is impossible to enclose a paraphrase in quotation marks, for quotation marks may be used only where an author's words are reproduced exactly and completely. How then can plagiarism be avoided here? The best way is by running acknowledgments in the text, as in the following example.

Adequate Acknowledgment: Paraphrase

According to Vernon L. Parrington, the "Greek serenity" of Thoreau's mind at Walden Pond and on the Merrimac River was rudely disturbed when he returned to Concord and found his neighbors drilling for the Mexican War, and when the town constable, representing authority, came to him asking that he pay his share of taxes for the war. Thoreau regarded the war as stupid, unjust, and designed to extend the slave system, which he opposed. Now his direct experience of its effects, says Parrington, caused Thoreau to reconsider the whole question of the relation between the individual and the state.

In the two sentences in which Parrington's name appears, it is clear that the ideas are his. But what about the other sentence? Has the writer slipped in something of Parrington's as his own? An argument can be made either way; but since in general the writer is being straightforward about his debt, we have little trouble giving him the benefit of the doubt.

Decisions like this are not always easy, since too many phrases like "Parrington says" or "Parrington goes on to point out" make writing graceless. If the claims of honesty and grace conflict, be honest first, but try also to be as graceful as you can. Every last comma need not be acknowledged. In the passage above, for example, only one phrase was placed in quotation marks even though other words—among them *stupid* and *unjust*—were used by Parrington. Since it was inconvenient to quote *stupid* and *unjust* in the exact phrasing used by Parrington, and since it would have seemed fussy to put *stupid* in one set of quotation marks and *unjust* in another, the writer decided that honesty was adequately served by his two general acknowledgments to Parrington. We think he was right.

Inadequate Acknowledgment: Forgetfulness

> When Thoreau returned to Concord, he was shocked to find his neighbors drilling for the Mexican War. It was still worse when the government asked him to pay taxes for a war he didn't believe in, a war he considered hateful, stupid, and obscene. At Walden and on the Merrimac his thoughts had taken on an almost Greek serenity; now he was confronted with the dilemmas of real life. He did not hesitate. Putting aside his transcendental notions, he plunged into an examination of what the individual may legitimately be said to owe the state.

This writer has clearly mastered his material and knows what he wants to say. He has abandoned Parrington's sequence of ideas; he has added his own emphases; and his phrasing is largely his own. But in questions of acknowledgment, "largely" is not enough. Three bits of undigested Parrington remain: "his neighbors drilling for the Mexican War," "hateful, stupid, and obscene," and "Greek serenity." The first of these phrases is neutral enough to make its borrowing forgivable. The other two, and especially "Greek serenity," are not.

Given the writer's general performance, it seems likely that he has unconsciously drawn on his memory for the words in question, or perhaps that he has worked from slovenly note cards. He is nonetheless guilty of dishonest borrowing. At the very least, he should have put "Greek serenity" in quotation marks and acknowledged a general indebtedness to Parrington.

Adequate Acknowledgment: Mature Borrowing

There was a time when writers paid no attention to plagiarism. Chaucer and Shakespeare, for example, borrowed incessantly from other writers without acknowledgment, and never gave the matter a thought. But in the last century or so Western writers have taken an increasingly proprietary attitude toward their own work, and it is now considered common decency to give a writer credit for the use of his ideas, his words, or even the sequence in which his ideas are presented.

Many people who do not write much themselves feel that there is something natural or inevitable in a writer's sequence of ideas—they might feel that Parrington, for example, starting with Walden Pond and ending with the state, was simply recording the sequence established by history. But of course he was doing no such thing. History is written by historians; the shape of past events is the shape of the minds that set down these events. And so it is with the Parrington passage: what makes it useful is not so much its individual ideas and phrases as Parrington's general authority and intelligence.

If, therefore, you begin with Walden Pond and end with the individual and the state—no matter what words you use in between—you must make a bow to Parrington somewhere along the line and thank him for his help. This is not only elementary honesty, but elementary courtesy. Here is such a passage from a student paper:

> Vernon Parrington pictures Thoreau at Walden as knowing a kind of "Greek serenity" that was rudely shaken when he returned to Concord and found his neighbors drilling for the Mexican War. Yet one wonders whether this contrast between the serene recluse and the embattled citizen is a valid one. We know

a lot these days about the hostility implicit in an act, any act, of withdrawal. Parrington seems to be saying that Thoreau was driven by events to take a political position, and in a sense he is right. But was there no political content in his move to Walden?

Here the writer has used Parrington, but not exploited him; Parrington has helped him, and he admits as much in the very act of taking issue with one of Parrington's ideas. Such a writer doesn't want to steal and doesn't have to. The words of others are not some sort of mask or false identity that he puts on to deceive the world; they are elements in his search for truth. Why not honor those who have gone before and done good work? We need all the help we can get. In the search for truth we have too few ideas, not too many; if we are honest, we should let the world know what lights we are following and who lit them.

INDEX TO CURRENT USAGE

The following alphabetical sequence mixes words (e.g. *overall*) and categories (e.g. ANTECEDENT PROBLEMS), following the precedent of the first and greatest dictionary of current usage, Henry Watson Fowler's *Modern English Usage* (1926). We have followed Fowler also in including, as a sort of bonus to browsers, discussions under headings that no one with a problem would ever think to look up, e.g. CLASHING VALUES, JOURNALESE. Owing to space limitations, the present sequence is necessarily superficial. It should be supplemented as necessary by reference to Fowler, preferably in the second edition (1965), which was thoroughly revised and updated by Sir Ernest Gowers; or to Wilson Follett's *Modern American Usage* (1966), the best of several efforts to compile an American Fowler. Another valuable book is *The Complete Plain Words* (1973), a revision by Sir Bruce Fraser of a book originally published by Gowers in 1954.

This section is intended essentially as a supplement to Parts 2 and 3 of the text. It does not relate to the text in any systematic fashion: indeed, some usage questions are discussed only in the text, some only in this section, and some in both places. Since cross-references have been kept to a minimum, users of this section may find it helpful to consult the main Index as well. The abbreviations WNC and AHD stand for *Webster's New Collegiate Dictionary* and *The American Heritage Dictionary of the English Language*.

a, an.   (1) *A* should be omitted after *kind* and *sort*. Not *What kind of a fool do you take me for?* but *What kind of fool*. Not *We thought it must be some sort of a trick*, but *some sort of trick*.

(2) *A half a* is illiterate: either *a half dollar* or *half a dollar*, not *a half a dollar*.

(3) *Historic, historical,* and *historian* are properly preceded by *a*, not *an*; the same goes for *heroic* and *humble*. The use of *an* before these words is an affectation.

(4) Distinctions of number often depend on the proper use of *a*. For example, *a secretary and treasurer* is one person who

handles both jobs; *a secretary and a treasurer* are two people. Such locutions as *a man and woman* and *a hat, coat, and tie,* by leaving out articles after the first, make a false and sometimes puzzling amalgam out of elements inherently separate.

above. As an adjective (*the above figures*), *above* is acceptable, though good writers prefer *the figures above* or *the figures cited above.* As a noun (*The above is just one example of what I mean*), *above* is businessmen's jargon.

ACCENTS, on such words as take them, are essential to correct spelling. To spell a word like *protégé* with one accent or none, or with the wrong kind, is to misspell it. Newspapers are a source of confusion on this point; since their type fonts usually contain no accented letters, they accustom people to seeing words like *communiqué* and names like *Mendès-France* shorn of their accents. The best authority here is a dictionary, preferably not WNC, which permits *emigré* for the correct *émigré* and both *resumé* and *resume* for *résumé.*

actually. The use of *actually* as a mere intensifier in sentences like *I was actually afraid to speak* and *She actually begged him to stop* is rarely effective in making a description more vivid, and may lead to confusion with the proper use of *actually,* which is to contrast the facts with some incorrect prediction or version of them.

ADVERB PROBLEMS. (1) An opening adverbial phrase modifies every verb in the following clause. A problem arises when a conflicting phrase is attached to one of the verbs: thus *In 1966 he taught at Harvard and returned to Yale a year later* has the man returning to Yale simultaneously in 1966 and 1967, an impossibility. Either repeat the subject ("In 1966 he taught at Harvard; *he* returned to Yale a year later") or subordinate the opening phrase to the verb it belongs with ("He taught at Harvard *in 1966* and returned to Yale a year later").

(2) Some adverbs have two forms, one ending in *-ly,* the other indistinguishable from the adjective form, leaving a choice between, for example, *tied tight* and *tied tightly,* or *go slow* and *go*

slowly. There is no fixed rule for making this choice. Use the word that sounds better to you; if neither sounds right, rewrite.

(3) On the proper placement of adverbial phrases, see pp. 89-90 and 160-161.

(4) On comparatives and superlatives of adverbs, see COM-PARATIVE AND SUPERLATIVE.

affect, effect.   The verb *affect* means to influence or concern; the verb *effect* means to bring about or cause. A decision may *affect* your future, or *effect* a change in your way of life; taking some pills may *affect* your blood pressure, or *effect* your recovery. The noun *affect* (pronounced *AFFect*), a technical term in psychology, is rarely encountered; for all noun meanings but this one, the word is *effect.*

all that, in expressions like *I don't consider her all that beautiful,* is nonstandard. Use *that* alone if there is a suitable antecedent, otherwise *especially* or *particularly.*

allude.   An allusion is an indirect reference or hint; for example, you may allude to a raucous Christmas party by asking a participant if he is still full of Christmas cheer, or you may allude to love by invoking Venus or Cupid. *Allude* is misused when the reference is direct, as in *I allude to your speech of February 24* or *I do not understand your allusion to "No. 4 tacks."* Change to *refer* and *reference.*

along with.   A singular noun followed by a phrase beginning *along with* takes a singular verb: *Mark, along with his two brothers, has been seeing Dr. Bennett regularly.*

alternate, alternative.   The adjective *alternate* means alternating with something else (*on alternate Tuesdays / alternately dozed and watched the movie*). The adjective *alternative* means involving a choice (*an alternative recommendation / by mail or alternatively by phone*). Partly by confusion with *alternative,* partly from the influence of the noun *alternate* in the sense of a second-level delegate to a convention, the adjective *alternate* is now widely used in the sense of substitute (*an alternate plan in case of bad weather).* Good writers continue to reserve this meaning for *alternative.*

ambivalent and *ambiguous* are not synonyms.   *Ambivalent* refers to a feeling of simultaneous attraction and repulsion; thus a radical might feel ambivalent about his father's wealth. *Ambiguous* means capable of being understood in two or more possible senses, thus uncertain or obscure; the examples under MORE (p. 283) are ambiguous.

amount is used with singular nouns: *a large amount of money / sand / energy.* With plural nouns use *number*: *a large number of hundred-dollar bills / marbles / successes.* In *Murphy had sold the largest amount of sandwiches,* change to *number.* See also FEWER, LESS.

ANACHRONISMS.   One mark of a good writer is sensitivity to time and history in the choice of words. To say *Louis XIV was a teenager when he assumed full power* is technically correct but jarring: *teenager* is a twentieth-century word. In *Here Donne uses a technique that is one of his trademarks* a great poet is diminished by the clatter of modern merchandising. Difficulties of this sort come down to a matter of connotation and denotation, on which see pp. 99–101.

and.   (1) It is perfectly permissible to begin a sentence with *And.*

(2) The precision of *and/or* may make it useful for legal documents, but its odd appearance and legalistic connotations make it unsuitable for any writing that aspires to please. Use *and* or *or*; if neither works, write *X or Y, or both.*

(3) When a series of two or more elements is referred to by a plural noun, the proper conjunction is *and*, not *or. Or* should be *and* in the following rare lapse by Follett: "Others may be influenced by newspaper shortenings, which produce such unidiomatic phrases as *long-drawn recital, stave attack,* or *put in jail on charge he threatened president.*"

See also BETWEEN (2).

ANTECEDENT PROBLEMS.   (1) An antecedent should be an explicit noun, noun phrase, or noun clause. An antecedent cannot be a verb: *The court tried to subpoena him but he would not accept it* should read *accept the subpoena.* An antecedent cannot be an adjective: the feature story headlined FEMININE IDEAS ON WHERE THEY WANT TO LIVE should have read WOMEN'S IDEAS. This error is particularly common with adjectives of nationality: *a Japanese view of their attack on Pearl Harbor* should read *Japan's attack.* Finally, an antecedent cannot be negative: *Although nothing important happened, it impressed me deeply* should read *I was deeply impressed.*

(2) A pronoun should not precede its antecedent unless its meaning is immediately clear and any other construction would be demonstrably awkward. In *When his first play was performed, Shakespeare was 28 years old,* either reverse the sequence of clauses or change *his* to *Shakespeare's* and *Shakespeare* to *he.*

See also pp. 162–164.

anyplace is nonstandard.   Use *anywhere.*

as.   (1) *As to* should be restricted so far as possible to emphatic constructions like *As to my so-called duplicity, I deny it,* and used sparingly, if at all, as a straight preposition. *A clue as to* is an error for *a clue to; the question as to whether* should be *the question whether; doubts as to* might better be *doubts about.* Use *as to* only when you are convinced that no other preposition will serve your purpose as well.

(2) *As well as* takes the singular: *The doctor, as well as his nurse and his receptionist, is involved.* A∩ *well as* cannot follow *both*: in *I invited both Henry as well as Ann and Bill,* delete *both.*

(3) Prepositional constructions in *as* must be properly related to the rest of the sentence. *As a man of experience, we would welcome your opinion* violates this rule by relating the *as* clause to *we,* an impossibility. See also p. 161.

(4) Sentences requiring two *as*'s cannot get by with one. An *as* has been swallowed at the indicated place in each of the following sentences: *"Old Foxy," as he referred to himself /, had won again. The cheese was as good / or better than Boursault. I thought of Mary not so much as my aunt / as my friend.* Since adding *as* at any of the slashes would be awkward, rewrite: *as he*

called himself, as good as Boursault or better, not as my aunt but as my friend.

(5) Good writers do not use *as* to mean *because*. In *As Jane was ill, we did not go*, change *as* to *since* or *because*.

(6) *As* is not idiomatic with *consider, appoint, name, elect,* and *brand*. In *The senators considered the administration's behavior as an outrage*, delete *as* or change *considered* to *regarded*; in *She was appointed as district chairman in 1961* and *McCarthy branded him as a traitor*, delete *as*.

On *like* and *as*, see pp. 173–174. See also EQUALLY AS.

bad, badly.   The distinction between *bad* and *badly* is not clear-cut. Even good writers occasionally use *bad* as an adverb (*want something bad enough to fight for it*) and *badly* as an adjective (*feel badly about losing*). You are on solid ground, however, if you use *bad* only as an adjective and *badly* only as an adverb: *The victim was not so badly off* / *Sundberg was hurt so badly that he had to leave the game* / *She has been feeling bad ever since.*

because.   *Because* can lead to puzzles when carelessly used with *not*. *She did not go because she was ill* could mean either that she was too ill to go, or that she went (e.g. to the hospital) not because she was ill but for some other reason. Reword to make your meaning clear: *She stayed home because she was ill*, or *Her reason for going was not that she was ill*. See also REASON (1).

between.   (1) *Between* properly takes as its object two elements, or any number of elements thought of as relating or interacting closely, e.g. *The Constitution regulates relations between the states. Among* properly takes as its object more than two elements not thought of as interacting closely, e.g. *The book is about his life among the savages*. This distinction is not always easily made; when in doubt, use *between*.

(2) *Between* must be followed either by a plural noun or by a plural construction in *and*. In *Nonwhite family earnings grew between 1970–1975*, change to *between 1970 and 1975*. In *Between thirty to fifty persons are killed annually in hunting accidents*, change to *Between thirty and fifty* or *From thirty to fifty*.

In *The choice was between going to jail or incriminating Larry,* change *or* to *and.* In *He soaked his foot in ice water between each act,* change to *between acts* or *after each act.* In *differences between the hospital in Akron and Canton,* the *and* is in the subordinate *in* phrase and does not make a true plural out of *hospital;* change to *and the one in Canton.*

biweekly, semiweekly. *Biweekly* means every two weeks, *semiweekly* twice a week. *Biweekly* is often misused for *semiweekly,* and some dictionaries, indifferent to the confusion they are authorizing, accord both meanings full status. The same is true of *bimonthly* and *semimonthly.* For years there are three words: *biennially* means every two years; *biannually* and *semiannually* both mean twice a year, with *semiannually* having the stronger suggestion of every six months. Our advice is to spare your reader confusion by spelling out what you mean: *twice a week, every two weeks,* or whatever.

blond, blonde. Use *blonde* for a woman, *blond* for a man, whether as noun or adjective.

brackets [ ], not parentheses ( ), should enclose words that you insert in a direct quotation from somebody else: *According to Delacorte, "Napoleon [III] was Bismarck's superior in all save persistence."* Newspapers use parentheses—*"That guy (Marichal) has never pitched better"*—because their simplified type fonts have no brackets, not because parentheses are right. If your typewriter lacks brackets, leave space and add them later in ink.

BRITISH SPELLINGS. See VARIANT SPELLINGS (2).

bureaucrat is not a neutral word like *official.* It is a disparaging word with strong connotations of stuffiness and narrowmindedness.

case is often superfluous. *In Mary's case, there were two problems to be solved* might better read *Mary had two problems to solve,* and *In the case of the senior class gift, we tried hard to raise money* might better read simply *We tried hard to raise money for the senior class gift.* Use *case* when you must; avoid it when you can.

CLASHING VALUES. Avoid marrying words with no tolerance for each other's company. Three classes of such pairs may be distinguished: absolutes subjected to comparison or appraisal (*almost unique, more perfect, rather exhaustive*); absolutes with redundant modifiers (*sufficiently adequate, general consensus, dead corpse*); and words of great force qualified by tepid words (*a moderate bonanza, somewhat dreadful, a bit vile*). See also ANACHRONISMS.

classic, classical. *Classical* has connotations of "established," *classic* connotations of "outstanding." Use *classical* for ancient Greek and Roman culture, literary forms of language (*Classical Arabic*), music of the educated European tradition, a curriculum centered on the humanities, or a standard body of knowledge seen as a necessary point of departure (*classical physics, classical military strategy*). Use *classic* where connotations of rank or importance are paramount: *a classic battle, a classic blunder, a classic case of mumps.*

CLAUSE TYPES. Although *clause* and *phrase* are often used interchangeably, we use *clause* in this book to mean a phrase having both a subject and a predicate (*she eats too much / when Larry was in California / that we are safe*).

A clause may be either independent or dependent. An independent clause can stand by itself as a sentence: *She eats too much / It had rained all day and all night.* A dependent clause cannot stand by itself, but is attached to another clause or word by either a subordinating conjunction or a relative pronoun: *when Larry was in California / that we are safe / whose men refused to surrender.* A dependent clause introduced by a relative pronoun (usually *who, whom, whose, which,* or *that,* sometimes implied rather than stated, as in *the woman I love*) is often called a relative clause.

A dependent clause may also be classified as an adjectival, adverbial, or noun clause according to its function in the sentence. In *the place where I was born* the *where* clause is adjectival, modifying the noun *place.* In *I go where he goes* the *where* clause is adverbial, modifying the verb *go.* In *Where Nancy works is where I want to work*, both *where* clauses are noun clauses.

See also CONJUNCTION TYPES.

cohort, in the sense of companion, associate, or crony, is nonstandard.

COMPARATIVE AND SUPERLATIVE. We write *earlier* and *narrower* but not *earnester* or *suddener*; *commonest* and *pleasantest* but not *preciousest* and *carefreest*. How is one to know when *-er* and *-est* are right, and when *more* and *most*?

The best authority is a good unabridged dictionary. *Webster's Third*, for example, lists -ER/-EST after every word capable of taking these endings, and gives full forms where an *e* is swallowed (*later, freest*), where a consonant is doubled (*bigger, reddest*), where the comparative and superlative are irregular (*little, less, least*), and where the suffix form is not clearly dominant (thus for *careful* we find "*sometimes* CAREFULLER . . . CAREFULLEST"). Collegiate dictionaries are less useful. WNC, for example, makes no distinction between *quiet*, which takes *-er/-est*, and *constant*, which does not, and states no preference between *yellower* and *more yellow*. If neither way sounds clearly preferable and you lack access to an unabridged dictionary, use *more* or *most*.

compare. (1) To compare X *with* Y is to appraise or measure X in relation to Y: *I compared my notes with hers.* To compare X *to* Y is to assert a similarity between the two: *You are wrong to compare Mao to Lenin.* The distinction is not always clear; when in doubt, use *with*.

(2) The quantities linked by *compare* should be comparable. In *My allowance was high compared with Sally*, they are not; change to *Sally's*.

compliment, complement. To *compliment* a woman is to say something favorable about her; a compliment is an expression of admiration or esteem. To *complement* a woman is to form with her help a team capable of getting some task done; a complement is something that completes or makes perfect.

compose, comprise. *Compose* means to make up; *comprise* means to be made up of, to consist of. The parts compose the whole; the whole comprises the parts. Since *comprise* is the rarer word and the harder to use correctly, and since its exact meaning is conveyed by the passive use of *compose*—i.e. *comprises* = *is composed of*—why not use *compose* in both senses and forget about *comprise*?

CONJUNCTION TYPES. Conjunctions are words or short phrases that indicate the logical relationship of one word, phrase, or clause to another. Conjunctions are of three types: coordinating, subordinating, and correlative.

Coordinating conjunctions link words, phrases, or clauses of equal status (*Joe* AND *I* / *obscure* OR *hard to find* / *Ann is here,* so *let's go*). The coordinating conjunctions are *and, but, or, for, nor, yet,* and *so.*

Subordinating conjunctions link dependent to independent clauses: WHEN *I was eighteen, you were still a child* / *They finished dinner* BEFORE *Sarah arrived.* The main subordinating conjunctions are *after, although, as, because, how, if, since, that, though, unless, until, when, where, whether, while,* and *why,* to which may be added such compounds as *as if* and *in order that.* When words in this list introduce a phrase instead of a clause (for the difference, see CLAUSE TYPES), they are not conjunctions but prepositions: *because of him* / *how to do it* / *since then.*

Correlative conjunctions come in pairs and introduce pairs of words, phrases, or clauses of equal status. The chief correlative conjunctions are *both . . . and, not only . . . but (also), either . . . or,* and *neither . . . nor*; their proper use is illustrated on pp. 157–158. A fifth correlative pair, *whether . . . or,* is like the others except that the sentence elements introduced by *whether* and *or* need not be strictly parallel.

A fourth type of conjunction is commonly called a conjunctive adverb because it both modifies a clause as an adverb does and links it to a previous clause as a conjunction does. Unlike conjunctions proper, conjunctive adverbs typically start a sentence or follow a semicolon. The main ones are *also, besides, further-*

more, however, indeed, moreover, nevertheless, still, then, there-fore, and *thus.*

See also CLAUSE TYPES.

consensus. Thus spelled (not *-census*). A *consensus* is by definition general, and by definition has to do with matters of opinion or belief. Hence *general consensus* and *consensus of opinion* are redundant expressions.

contact as a verb meaning to get in touch with is nonstandard. As a noun meaning a person one is in touch with, *contact* is appropriate chiefly to spies, detectives, and others whose operations involve secrecy.

contemporary means "at the same time," but at the same time as what? Does *the contemporary view of Hamlet* refer to Shakespeare's contemporaries or the writer's? Unless your context makes your meaning unmistakable, replace *contemporary* with something unambiguous: *the prevailing view of Hamlet in Shakespeare's time* or *the current view of Hamlet.*

continuous, continual, constant. *Continuous* means uninterrupted: a string is continuous; the sound of an ambulance siren is continuous; a movie theater properly advertises "continuous performance." *Continual* means repeated at frequent short intervals: a bad cough may be continual; an executive may be continually interrupted by phone calls. *Constant* is a higher-voltage equivalent of *continual.*

convince. You do not convince a person *to* do something; you convince him *that* he should do it, or you convince him *of* its desirability. If *to* is irresistible, use *persuade* or *prevail on.*

council, counsel; council(l)or, counsel(l)or. A *council* is a group of persons with administrative or other functions. A *counsel* is a lawyer, and *counsel* are lawyers collectively or anonymously (*on advice of counsel*); *counsel* also means advice in general, and *to counsel* means to advise. A *councilor* is a member of a council; a *counselor* is one who gives advice. The teenager at a children's summer camp, though he may be a member of a council, is a *counselor.* The *-llor* forms are permissible but old-fashioned.

criteria is plural; the singular is *criterion.*

crucial has a connotation of finality or decisiveness. It is an absolute word, not to be used either with such comparatives as *more, less,* and *rather* or of relatively trivial matters. Above all, *crucial* should not be overused, as it persistently is by sportswriters and other journalists.

data is plural; the singular is *datum. This data is* is fairly common, but most good writers still write *these data are.*

definite, definitive. *Definite* means specific or unmistakable; *definitive* has the further connotation of unalterably final or defined once and for all. Only when this connotation is present is *definitive* allowable as a dramatic intensifier of *definite.*

delusion, illusion. *Delusion* is a negative word; a person with delusions is typically disposed to act on them in such a way as to harm himself or others. *Illusion* is a neutral word; a person with illusions is merely mistaken or given to wishful thinking.

depends without *on* in such expressions as *It depends what you mean by power* is good spoken English but nonstandard in writing.

different than. Fastidious writers go to great lengths to follow *different* with *from,* and Follett, among others, supports them. It is not clear why. *Different than,* by analogy with *other than,* has been a staple of American spoken English for at least a century, and sometimes offers a brevity that *different from* cannot match. In *He used the word in quite a different sense than he did yesterday,* to require *from* would mean to replace *than he did* with no fewer than eight words: *from the one in which he used it.* Use *different from* where you can; but where it does not work and *different than* does, take the plunge.

discreet, discrete. *Discreet* means prudent; *discrete* means separate, or consisting of unconnected elements. The two words have nothing in common but their pronunciation.

disinterested means impartial, free of emotional interest in the issue at hand. A disinterested judge is not one who finds the case boring, but one who is well qualified to judge it fairly because he has no personal stake in the outcome. To equate *disinterested* with *uninterested* is not only to deprive the world of an expressive word, but to render less accessible a noble idea.

double negative. See NEGATIVE PROBLEMS (1).

due to must still be regarded as adjectival, and must accordingly attach itself to a noun or a pronoun rather than to a verb. In *He could not attend due to illness*, the *due to* phrase improperly modifies *attend*; change to *owing to* or *because of*.

each, every. *Each* as a noun takes a singular verb and a singular noun or pronoun: *Each of the boys has his own car*, not *have*, not *their own car*, not *their own cars*. *Each* and *every* as adjectives take the singular when they precede what they modify: *Every man is his own worst enemy*, not *their own worst enemy*. When *each* follows what it modifies, it takes the plural: *They each are wearing the hats they wore Sunday*. Usage is wearing down these distinctions, however, particularly in the first and second persons. *We each have our own cars* is nominally correct, but *car* is almost universal; *Each of you should write his congressman* is nominally correct, but *your* is far more common. The rule is by now so far eroded that these departures may be considered correct.

   Each and every, being simply an emphatic way of saying *each*, takes the singular despite the *and*: *Each and every one of them was found guilty*. So do compounds of the form *Each (every) X and (each/every) Y*: *Every man and woman here has a college education*. The compounds *everybody, everyone, anybody*, and *anyone* take the singular: *Everybody thinks of himself first / Does anyone want his money refunded?*

each other and *one another* are interchangeable.

e.g. stands for *exempli gratia,* "for example": *spitball pitchers, e.g. Gaylord Perry.* It is never used parenthetically: in *A fence or a railing, e.g., would give the necessary protection,* change to *for example.* It may be followed by a comma or not, at the writer's option. Being slightly pedantic in appearance and connotation, *e.g.* is better suited to footnotes and technical exposition than to the text of an essay. It should not be confused with *i.e.,* which stands for *id est,* "that is": in *the three triumvirs, e.g. Octavius, Antony, and Lepidus,* change to *i.e.*

either. (1) In constructions of the form *either . . . or,* what follows *either* should be parallel and grammatically equivalent to what follows *or;* see the text, pp. 157–158.

(2) *Either . . . or* may be used of three or more alternatives: *Either Heise, Shaw, or Butzaikis had to be traded.* As an adjective, however (*Take either road*), and as a pronoun (*Either is all right with me*), *either* is properly confined to two alternatives.

ELLIPSIS is the deliberate omission of words from a quoted passage. Use three dots, spaced as in the previous entry, to indicate an omission within a sentence. If the omitted material includes one or more periods, use four dots, the first one not preceded by a space. For large omissions, e.g. a paragraph or a stanza of poetry, use three dots centered on a separate line.

employment, like *utilization,* is often simply a ponderous word for *use.* In *The engineers recommended the employment of heavy earth-moving equipment,* change to *the use of* or *using.*

enable is incomplete without a following infinitive, whether active (*His fortune enables him to live as he likes*) or passive (*The new law enabled major improvements to be made*), but preferably active. In *The committee's proposal would enable several changes in the clubhouse rules,* the infinitive is lacking; either add it (*enable us to make* or *changes to be made*) or change *enable* to *make possible.*

enhance is not an exact synonym of *increase,* despite Governor Wallace's trip to Vietnam to "enhance my knowledge of the war." *Enhance* means specifically to increase in desirability, value, or attractiveness, and is properly said of something already to some extent desirable, valuable, or attractive. The word takes an abstract object: not *The simple tiara enhanced her,* but *The simple tiara enhanced her beauty.*

enormity means not great size but outrageousness or an outrage. For the other meaning, if you don't like *enormousness,* try *enormous size.*

enthuse is a verb of recent coinage from *enthusiasm.* Like *emote, burgle,* and other formations of this sort, it has long outlasted the chuckles of its inventor without becoming standard.

equally as. *Equally* cannot tolerate *as:* in *Her behavior was equally as foolish,* either delete *as* or change *equally* to *just.* In a complete *as . . . as* comparison there is no place for *equally:* delete it in *Her behavior was equally as foolish as his.* Constructions in between *equally X* and *as X as* should be resolved one way or the other: in *German wine is equally good, in its way, as French,* change *equally* to *as* or *just as.*

equate takes either *with* (*How can you equate Meyerbeer with Mozart?*) or *and* (*The new salary scale equates men and women*), or a plural resolvable into the equated components (*I equate the two sentiments*). Like BETWEEN, *equate* cannot take a singular: in *He appears to equate "democracy" in its American and Soviet senses,* either change to *equate the American and Soviet senses of "democracy"* or rewrite.

etc. is permissible in formal English to avoid a tedious and easily inferrable elaboration. Good writers, however, disliking its inelegant appearance and lazy-careless connotations, tend to use it chiefly where elegance is no issue, as in footnotes, lists, and tables. Getting rid of *etc.* elsewhere is usually no great trick; many phrases of the form *Castroism, Maoism, etc.* can be simply changed to *such as Castroism and Maoism,* and in the rest *etc.* can almost always be replaced by *and so on* or *and the like. Etc.* after *such as* or *e.g.* is redundant; see SUCH AS . . . AND OTHERS.

every, everybody. See EACH, EVERY.

everyplace is nonstandard. Use *everywhere.*

fabulous is the adjective form of *fable* and means legendary or fictitious. By extension it has come to mean amazing or marvelous, in which sense it has been so badly overused as to have no force or credit left.

fact. Novice writers overuse *the fact that.* They write, for example, *I accepted the fact that I could not learn French* and *His lameness was due to the fact that he had had an accident* where they might better have written *I accepted my inability to learn French* and *His lameness was the result of an accident.* Use *the fact that* as sparingly as you can, and preferably where some fact as such is in question: *What I dispute is not the fact that he lied, but his motive in lying.*

farther, further. *Farther* tends to be used of physical distance: *Chicago is farther from New York than from Washington. Further* tends to be used of abstract distance: *We will go into this further at some later date.* When in doubt, use *further.*

faze, phase. To *faze* someone is to daunt or disconcert him. To *phase* something (often *phase in* or *phase out*) is to plan its occurrence in orderly stages. To write *phase* for *faze* is a foolish error that no one should make twice.

female, feminine. *Female* means simply of the female sex as opposed to the male: thus *female doctor, female children, female rabbit, female hormone. Feminine* means having the characteristics commonly attributed to women as opposed to men: thus *feminine features, feminine pursuits, feminine wiles, feminine sensitivity.* To write *feminine* for *female* can be confusing. What is a *feminine doctor,* for example? One with a high voice?

fewer, less.   *Fewer* is used of countable units: *fewer cows, fewer days, fewer cups of coffee.* *Less* is used of abstract or inseparable quantities: *less air, less salt, less pain.* *More and more power in the hands of less and less people* is wrong; change to *fewer and fewer people.* The same distinction is made between *less than* and *fewer than,* except that *less than* is used with countable units considered as single quantities (*less than five dollars, less than three weeks*) and with countable units in large numbers, where the mass dominates the individual: *less than 10,000 armed guerrillas, less than a hundred hotel rooms.*

firstly, secondly, etc. are old-fashioned; good writers and editors prefer *first, second,* etc.

flaunt, flout.   To *flaunt* something is to parade it or show it off (*She flaunted her new mink wrap / The speaker flaunted his patriotism*); to *flout* something is to ignore or reject it publicly (*Khrushchev flouted the fundamental principles of diplomacy*). The two words have a common connotation of ostentation, but are otherwise opposite in meaning.

forego, forgo.   To *forego* is to go before, to precede. To *forgo* is to go without, to renounce. *Forego* is so commonly written for *forgo* that most dictionaries allow both spellings in that sense; but good writers preserve the original distinction.

former, latter.   *Former* and *latter* may be used, together or singly, only when immediately preceded by exactly two antecedent nouns, pronouns, or noun phrases of more or less equal weight, and then only when it would be awkward to repeat the nouns themselves. The following sentences violate the successive conditions of this rule. *Of the grants made to Oklahoma, Texas, and Louisiana, the largest went to the latter.* (More than two antecedents.) *A notice was sent to her next of kin, and the latter supplied the information.* (Only one antecedent.) *When they would not recognize Lyman's immunity, the latter was forced to resign.* (Antecedents not of equal weight.) *The judge and the court clerk had the same name; the former was apparently the latter's father.* (Better to repeat *judge* and *clerk.*) In general, avoid *former* and *latter*; good writers get along very well without them.

fortunate, fortuitous. *Fortunate* means lucky; *fortuitous* means accidental or unexpected. WNC to the contrary, *fortuitous* should not be used as a fancy way of saying *fortunate*.

fulsome does not mean full or complete, or even somewhat overblown and tending to excess; it means disgusting. Fulsome praise is praise so insincere or excessive as to be downright offensive.

gap. In 1958 a reporter coined the term *missile gap* to characterize an alleged American inferiority to the U.S.S.R. in the number of intercontinental missiles completed and under construction. Although this expression did some violence to the classical idea of a gap as a hiatus or break in continuity, it was apt enough to be given wide circulation. Inevitably there followed a large number of less apt gaps like *communications gap, credibility gap,* and *generation gap,* in some of which the idea of a gap could barely be discerned. *Gap* in this sense is today a vogue word; it could use a rest.

GERUNDS. A gerund is the *-ing* form of a verb used as a noun: *Swimming is fun / I am tired of fooling around / How about frying some eggs?*

(1) Gerunds, like participles, should be attached as closely as possible to their subject (if it appears in the sentence); in *By yelling at the top of their lungs, we finally heard them,* change to *they finally made us hear them.*

(2) An infinitive is sometimes erroneously used where only a gerund is idiomatic. Instead of *The Navy was committed to support the program,* idiom requires *to supporting;* instead of *I confessed to have found the question pointless,* idiom requires *to having found.* Only someone with an excellent sense of idiom will have no difficulty on this point. When in doubt, use the gerund.

good. See WELL, GOOD.

got, gotten.   *Got* is the past of *get*; the past participle is sometimes *got*, sometimes *gotten*. *Gotten* is now the usual choice when a sense of progression is involved: *You have gotten much more cautious lately* / *Grandma has gotten worse again* / *I have gotten to know her better.* In other senses *got* and *gotten* are interchangeable: *I have got to bed late every night this week* / *We had got our feet wet.* As an intensive of *have* (*I've got the tickets* / *George has got to help us*), *got* is the only choice.

hardly.   See SCARCELY.

help.   When *help* is used in the sense of *avoid* or *refrain from*, the correct form is *I cannot help liking her*, not *I cannot help but like her.* The incorrect form, though widely used in speech, is not acceptable in writing. Further, the subject of *help* in this sense should be animate: in *The book could not help becoming a best seller*, change *help* to *miss*.

historic, historical.   (1) *Historic* means historically important or famous (*a historic battle, Calhoun's historic speech*); *historical* is a neutral word meaning of, related to, or based on history (*places of historical interest, a historical novel*).
 (2) *History* and words derived from it take *a*, not *an*.

home, house.   A *house* is a building; a *home* is an abstraction. *Home* means the locus of family life (whether a building, a cave, or what have you), or the family itself, as in *a broken home.* Since *house* has neutral connotations and *home* favorable ones, advertisers have taken to advertising *homes, home furnishings, homewares*, and the like, and addressing themselves to *homeowners* and *homemakers.* The dictionaries have accepted—which is to say, recorded—these new locutions, but in good writing *home* remains inseparable from the idea of people.

hopefully means in a hopeful manner: *She asked hopefully if there was a part for her.* Many writers oppose its extension to mean *it is to be hoped that*, as in *Hopefully the strike will be over by then.* Yet unattached adverbs of this form—e.g. *undoubtedly* for *it is not to be doubted that*—offer such notable gains in conciseness over the phrases they replace that we can only applaud this use of *hopefully*.

however.   (1) When *however* comes at the beginning of a sentence or clause, it can be either a conjunction meaning *but* (*However, the children may feel cheated*) or an adverb meaning in whatever way or to whatever degree (*However the children may feel, we must proceed*). So that the reader may distinguish immediately between these two very different constructions, good writers always use a comma in the first.

(2) *However* should be placed early in the sentence if it is not to lose its force. In *The Secretary of Health, Education, and Welfare and two of his undersecretaries, however, opposed the change*, move *however* to the beginning.

(3) When *however* does not come at the beginning of a sentence or clause, it has the effect of emphasizing the word it follows, and this emphasis must accord with the meaning. In *There was no official reply from the White House; the President, however, unofficially praised the plan*, the emphasis given by *however* seems to contrast the President and the White House, not the official and unofficial reactions. Change to *speaking unofficially, however*, or to *however, the President*.

I, me.   (1) *Me* has all but replaced *I* in the predicate nominative: *It's me / Could it have been me that she saw? / The two people they forgot were you and me*.

(2) People who would never dream of writing *They asked I to help* or *everybody except I* sometimes erroneously write *and I* for *and me* in the same constructions. In *They asked my sister and I to help* and *everybody except Bob and I* both pronouns should be *me*.

-ics.   On whether words like *politics* and *ethics* take singular or plural verbs, see p. 147.

i.e. stands for *id est*, "that is," and may be used as a substitute for *that is* or *namely* in footnotes and wherever else elegance is not an issue. *I.e.* should be distinguished from *e.g.*, which has the very

different meaning "for example." In *The most populous states,
i.e. Illinois, are the richest,* change to *e.g.*

implement as a verb is a vogue word of some thirty years' standing. It
is especially beloved by big businessmen and government officials, perhaps because the scale and complexity of their operations make simple expressions like *carry out* and *put into effect*
inappropriate, perhaps because *implement* suggests the sort of
impersonal, deliberate, and orderly changeover that will disrupt
things least, perhaps out of sheer pomposity. "With *implement,*"
as Follett says, "the layman can sound technical." Good writers
use *implement* rarely, if at all.

imply, infer.   *Imply* means to suggest or hint, *infer* to deduce or
surmise. A politician who is unwilling to announce his candidacy
might *imply* his willingness to run by winking at an interviewer,
from which the interviewer might *infer* that the politician would
announce his candidacy later.

in.   How should we write the adjective *in,* meaning fashionable, to
make its meaning immediately clear? Quotation marks *(the "in"
crowd)* give *in* too much emphasis. A hyphen *(the in-crowd)*
makes it look like part of a compound modifier, as in *an in-depth
analysis.* No punctuation *(the in crowd),* though WNC's solution
and standard for conventional adjectives, gives the reader too
little warning that this *in* is not the usual preposition. There is no
good solution. All we can do is pray that no one comes up with
an analogous use for *of.*

include, including.   *Include* supposes the listing of some members,
but not all, of the whole as in *The jurors included two women.* In
Some of those arrested included schoolteachers, either delete
some of or change *included* to *were.* In *The guest list included
Curtis, Watkins, and others,* change to *Curtis and Watkins.* In
*The four countries to be considered include Syria, Lebanon, Jor-
dan, and Iraq,* change *include* to *are.* What goes for *include* goes
also for *including:* in *Twenty-one poems were read, including
poems by Ginsberg, Patchen, and others,* change to *Ginsberg and
Patchen.*

individual as a noun has only two legitimate uses of any interest: to designate the single organism as distinguished from the species, and to designate the single human being as contrasted with a group, an institution, or the state. The use of *individual* as an exact synonym for *person*, as in *Harry is a well-meaning individual*, is a "colloquial vulgarism" according to the *Oxford English Dictionary* and, in a memorable phrase quoted by Fowler, "one of the modern editor's shibboleths for detecting the unfit."

infer.   See IMPLY, INFER.

input is acceptable as a technical noun in economics and data processing. As a noun meaning contribution or factor (*That was the key input in clearing up the confusion*), and as a verb meaning to enter or insert (*You could input either punched cards or paper tape*), it is a vogue word. An irascible purist cited by Fraser says that "the verbs *to input* and *to output* make him want to upstand and outwalk."

interface, like *input*, has a legitimate meaning: "a surface forming a common boundary of two bodies, spaces, or phases" (WNC), thus by extension the place where or means by which independent systems, notably computer programs, meet and act on each other. Beyond this narrow meaning it is a vogue word and often a vague one as well, as in this example cited by Fraser: *I find myself sitting on a number of interfaces.*

irregardless is nonstandard, a bastard mixture of *irrespective* and *regardless*. Use one or the other of these two standard words.

it's, its.   The first stands for *it is* or *it has*; the second is the possessive. *It's its size that bothers me.*

JARGON is the name commonly given to writing that is ugly and hard to understand. Originally, *jargon* meant the lingo of a particular science or occupation (especially as viewed from outside), and this meaning is still current. Among the jargons of American academic writing today, for example, as seen by its detractors, are that of the social scientists, with their *societal needs, func-*

tional capability, variables associated with organizational effectiveness, and the like. More often, however, *jargon* today refers to the general blend of pompous diction and imprecise reference that has become America's style for ceremonial speech and writing. The mark of jargon in this sense is long words, pat phrases, and lifeless verbs; its function is not to communicate, but to impress or reassure.

JOURNALESE is usually written under deadline pressure and beamed at a mythical average newspaper reader, a dimwit who will look elsewhere for entertainment if his paper is not lively enough.

One mark of journalese is its heavy use of intensives: every difficulty is a *crisis,* every important decision *crucial,* every retrenchment *drastic,* every scientist *brilliant,* every death *tragic,* everything impressive *great.* Another mark is gimmicky noun-verbs like *pinpoint, highlight,* and *trigger,* which give the most prosaic proceedings a factitious liveliness. Headlines, with their premium on short, vivid words, have the same effect: critics do not criticize, they *rap;* a political opponent is a *foe;* a disagreement, however mild, is a *clash.* Activity, conflict, crisis are everywhere. The routine investigation of a Soviet complaint about an American aircraft is rendered seemingly ominous by the headline *Red Charge Spurs Probe.* This "tone of contrived excitement" (Follett) is the essence of journalese. Its characteristic exaggerations and oversimplifications have no place in serious writing.

latter. See FORMER, LATTER.

less. See FEWER, LESS.

let. (1) Either *let* or *leave* may be used with *alone* in the sense of not disturbing or interfering: either *We left him alone* or *We let him alone. Leave* is unacceptable, however, in analogous phrases carrying the sense of allow or permit (*Let sleeping dogs lie / Let him go*) and in the *let us* construction (*Let us face the facts / Let's ask Billy*).

(2) *Let* takes the objective case; in *I begged him to let George and I come along,* change to *George and me.*

lie, lay.   *Lie* means to recline, *lay* to place or put in place. The following sentences exhibit the correct use of *lie* and *lay* and their various forms:

	Lie	*Lay*
Present	I *lie* down.	I *lay* the carpet.
Past	I *lay* down.	I *laid* the carpet.
Perfect	I *have lain* down.	I *have laid* the carpet.
Progressive	I *am lying* down.	I *am laying* the carpet.
Future	I *will lie* down.	I *will lay* the carpet.

like and *as.*   See pp. 173–174.

literally is not a mere intensive. *Bill literally broke his heart over Mary* implies that his heart is now, or was at some time, in two or more pieces. Since this is impossible, *literally* should be omitted. *Figuratively* is no improvement; indeed, since all metaphors are figurative, *figuratively broke his heart* is as senselessly redundant as *literally ate his dinner.*

loan, lend.   Use *loan* as the noun, *lend* as the verb.

-ly.   (1) Avoid piling up adverbs in *-ly*: in *He acted completely honorably,* change *completely* to *altogether* to get rid of the singsong effect.

(2) Avoid forming adverbs in *-lily* from adjectives in *-ly* for the same reason: instead of *He answered surlily,* write *He answered sullenly* or *His answer was surly.*

(3) Avoid coining adverbs in *-edly* from participles in *-ed.* Some adverbs so formed have become unobjectionable by reason of manifest convenience and long use: *allegedly, repeatedly, undoubtedly.* But many assail the brain with a Germanic excess of syllables and components: *undisguisedly, animatedly, disappointedly.* Worst of all, and intolerable to good writers, are *-edly* words in which the *-ed* syllable cannot be given full weight: *satisfiedly, puzzledly, discouragedly.* If an *-edly* word cannot be confidently pronounced, it should not be written.

(4) Do not hyphenate compounds formed by adverbs in *-ly* and participles or adjectives: *the newly married pair,* not *newly-married; the brightly lit room,* not *brightly-lit.*

mad for *angry* is nonstandard.

majority. The *majority* is often an unnecessarily long way of saying *most*, as in *The majority of my friends go to college.*

materialize means to take material or effective form, as in *Our plans for a coffee house never materialized.* It is not properly used as a fancy synonym for *happen* or *occur.* In *Nothing important materialized at the San Francisco conference*, change to *happened* or *was decided.*

mean for is nonstandard in such sentences as *I didn't mean for him to to do all that work* and *She meant for the plan to be taken seriously.* The difficulty can often be repaired by simply dropping *for*; alternatively rewrite with *meant that* or *intended that.*

media is invariably plural. In *The press is generally a more reliable media than television*, change to *medium* or rewrite.

militate, mitigate. *Militate* means to count or have weight, and is used exclusively with *against*: *Three things militated against our accepting the offer.* *Mitigate* means to lessen in severity: *Her pleasure mitigated his grief.* The combination *mitigate against* does not exist.

more can be ambiguous. What is meant, for example, by *The proposal called for more fully integrated restaurants*? More restaurants that were fully integrated, or restaurants that were more fully integrated? What is meant by *We need more unbiased reporting on China*? Only a more carefully chosen wording can tell us.

most for *almost*, as in *Most everybody was there* or *You can come most any time*, is a colloquialism that should never find its way into formal writing.

nauseous, despite its similarity to *bilious*, means sickening or repulsive, not sick or beset by nausea. It is a synonym of *nauseating*, not of *nauseated*, the word for which it is frequently misused.

NEGATIVE PROBLEMS. (1) Though in some languages a negative subject or object reinforces a negative verb, in English two such negatives make a positive. Thus *I didn't see no one* means *I saw someone,* and if that is not your meaning you must write *I saw no one* or *I didn't see anyone.* See also SCARCELY.

(2) Even when negatives do not directly cancel each other, two or more in a sentence may cause readers needless difficulties, as in this conundrum from a student paper: *Denying another the right to not participate in religion is as important as that right itself.* In *Cohen did not consider the chance of failure negligible,* readers will have to pause and sort out the three negatives (*not, failure, negligible*) before they can be sure what Cohen thought. Better to do the sorting for them: *Cohen saw a clear chance of failure.*

(3) A negative noun compound or pronoun is not an acceptable antecedent for a positive pronoun. In *Since no one was home, we left them a note,* omit *them.* In *The police expected no trouble but were prepared for it if it came,* change to *did not expect trouble.*

(4) A negative noun compound or pronoun (e.g. *nobody*) cannot serve as the subject of a verb requiring a positive subject: in *Neither the Yankees nor the Mets gave up, but kept on playing to win,* change the comma to a semicolon and *but* to *both.* See also NEITHER; NOR.

neither. (1) With *neither* use *nor,* not *or.*

(2) *Neither . . . nor* may be used of three or more elements, as in *Neither illness, bad weather, nor financial reverses ever dimmed his good spirits.* As an adjective, however (*Neither one is any good*), and as a pronoun (*Neither will do*), *neither* is properly confined to two elements.

(3) Whatever part of speech follows *neither* should also follow *nor*; see pp. 157–158.

none may take either a singular or a plural verb; see p. 145.

nor. Poetic diction apart, *nor* has only two legitimate uses: as the second (or subsequent) element in the correlative pair *neither . . . nor,* and as a conjunction introducing a clause (*Nor do I agree with Senator Kennedy / There was nothing to say, nor was there anything Jean could do).* The correct word after *not* or *no* is not *nor* but *or.* In *The word does not occur at all in Dickens, nor to my knowledge in Thackeray,* change *nor* to *or*; in *She had received no word from the city desk, nor any other messages,* change *nor any* to *and no.*

not only . . . but also. (1) *Also* is optional in this formula: it is commonly used when the second element is simply added to the first (*We will be seeing not only Dr. Shapley but also the surgeon*) and omitted when the second element is an intensification of the first (*He is not only the fattest man I know, but the fattest man I have ever seen / We drove not only to Southampton, but all the way to Plymouth*). When *also* is used, it need not immediately follow *but.*

(2) The same part of speech that follows *not only* should also follow *but also*; see pp. 157–158.

(3) *Not only* may be used without *but* to get intensive effects, as in *He not only smelled, he reeked.* The comma splice here is intentional.

not un- is a construction that persists despite Orwell's celebrated suggestion that writers cure themselves of it by memorizing the sentence *A not unblack dog was chasing a not unsmall rabbit across a not ungreen field.* This construction may be used sparingly, but only where the positive wording has been considered and found wanting. In *I have not infrequently been bored to tears by his stories,* change to *I have frequently.*

number. A (*large,* etc.) *number of* may take either a singular or a plural verb, depending on context. If the idea of a specific figure or quantity is prominent, the singular is best: *A large number of suicides for 1936 does not fit our theory.* If, by contrast, *a (large,* etc.) *number of* means nothing more specific than *some* or *several* or *many,* use the plural: *A large number of suicides are reported every year.* For borderline cases, the plural is usually better: *An unspecified number of aliens were deported.*

See also AMOUNT.

off.   Good writers never use *off of*. In *somewhere off of the coast of Venezuela* and *jumping off of the garage roof,* change *off of* to *off.*

O.K. and *okay* are unacceptable in formal writing.

one.   (1) Even sophisticated writers sometimes come to grief with the construction *one of those men who,* as in this sentence from a recent novel: *Richard is one of those men who is always bragging about his accomplishments.* The intent of this construction is always to assign an individual to a class; the class here is *men who are always bragging about their accomplishments,* and the novelist's wording should be changed accordingly.

(2) *One or more* conventionally takes the plural: *One or more of them were kept overnight* / *One or more waitresses have been hired since June.* Oddly enough, the more unambiguously plural *more than one* conventionally takes the singular: *More than one example comes to mind* / *More than one has been found wanting.*

(3) *One another* and *each other* are interchangeable.

(4) On the numeral *one* and the impersonal *one,* see p. 145.

only.   A vocal class of purists maintains that the placement of *only* is a matter of high importance: thus *Only Martin heard the crash* means no one else heard it; *Martin only heard the crash* means he did not see it as well as hear it; *Martin heard only the crash* means he heard none of the other noises in question. Strong though this argument seems in principle, going against it rarely produces ambiguity and sometimes makes a better-sounding sentence. Our advice is to put *only* wherever you think it best serves your purposes.

or.   On number and gender problems in sentences having subjects linked by *or,* see pp. 142–144. See also AND (2), (3); EITHER; NOR.

overall is a vogue word for *whole, total, general,* etc. when it is not simply redundant, as in *Harvey's overall speed for the 100-yard dash was 10.0 seconds.* Good writers rarely use the word.

overly, once a perfectly acceptable word, has been displaced by the prefix *over-* (as in *overenthusiastic*) and now sounds bumpkinish to a fastidious ear. It is also superfluous, given the availability not only of the *over-* compounds but of *too* and *excessively.*

pair is usually singular: *The other pair of scissors was broken.* It can be plural (*The more experienced pair tend to share the driving equally*), but never after a number higher than one: *He bought two pairs of pants,* not *pair.*

past, passed. The adjective *past* should not be confused with the verb form *passed.* Either *The time for caution was past* or *The time for caution had passed,* but not *was passed* or *had past.*

per should be avoided except in heavily technical contexts. For *30 miles per hour,* say *30 miles an hour;* for *two new trainees per annum,* say *two new trainees every year;* for *1,800 calories per person,* say *1,800 calories each.* Such expressions as *as per your request* are commercial jargon.

percent, percentage, proportion. *Percent* and *percentage* refer to degree or amount reckoned on a scale of 100: *What percentage of applicants are accepted? Between 70 and 80 percent. Proportion,* as currently used, is a synonym for *percentage* except for the scale of 100: *What proportion of applicants are accepted? Perhaps five out of six.* Do not use *proportion* to mean nothing more than *part;* in *A large proportion of the beef was spoiled,* change *a large proportion* to *much* or *most.*

phase. See FAZE.

phenomena is plural; the singular is *phenomenon.*

PLURAL CONFUSIONS. The plurals of Latin words ending in *-ex, -ix, -um, -us,* and *-a,* and of Greek words ending in *-on,* sometimes take the English endings *-s* and *-es,* sometimes the original Latin or Greek endings (usually *-ices* for *-ex* or *-ix, -a* for *-um* and *-on, -i* for *-us,* and *-ae* for *-a*), and sometimes both. Two questions arise. First, how is one to know which form to use, *indexes* or *indices, appendixes* or *appendices, spectrums* or *spectra, cactuses* or *cacti, formulas* or *formulae, criterions* or *criteria?* Second, how is one to know whether Latin or Greek words ending in *-a* like *agenda, criteria, data, memoranda,* and *phenomena* are singular or plural? Both questions have the same answer: consult a dictionary. The complexities are many: *genus,* for example, does not take *genuses* or *geni* but *genera, stigma* not *stigmas* or *stigmae* but *stigmata.* Patterns are unpredictable and inconsistent: *agenda* and *opera,* for example, once strictly the plurals of *agendum* and *opus,* not only have become strictly singular but have engendered the new plurals *agendas* and *operas,* whereas other words of the same form remain strictly plural and still others (e.g. *insignia*) are both plural and singular. Finally, to compound the confusion, usage is rapidly changing: thus *data,* once strictly the plural of *datum* and still used only as plural by careful writers into the 1960's, is accepted as singular by 50 percent of the AHD's Usage Panel. Only a good and reasonably up-to-date dictionary can steer you through these troubled waters.

Other plural problems are discussed in the text (see Index) and under specific words in this section.

pore, pour.   To *pore over* something is to scrutinize or ponder it; *pour,* as from pitchers, is a completely different word. The common misuse of *pour* for *pore* makes for ludicrous sentences like *Brown spent long hours pouring over proposed press releases.*

possess should not be used as a fancy synonym for *have.* In *Bismarck possessed a keen intellect,* and in *That was all the money I possessed,* change to *had.*

POSSESSIVE PROBLEMS.   (1) On the formation of complicated possessives, see pp. 148–150.

(2) When a name must be added in brackets to a quotation, avoid the intolerable forms *George's [Cook] bat* and *George [Cook]'s bat;* whatever the newspapers may say or do, the only acceptable solution to this problem is *George's [George Cook's] bat.*

(3) *Time* magazine, as part of its effort to minimize wordage, uses such possessive constructions as *at week's end* for *at the end*

of the week and *London's Institute for Strategic Studies* for *the Institute for Strategic Studies in London.* Despite the efficiency of this construction, good writers do not use it.

(4) *A friend of my father* and *a friend of my father's* are both acceptable despite the redundancy of the latter form, in which *of* and *'s* are doing the same job. The double possessive is the only idiomatic form for pronouns (*an old habit of mine / a relative of hers*) and is usually preferable for short personal nouns (*a shirt of Joe's*), but the *'s* is dropped when things get more complex or abstract (*a friend of Macarthur's wife / a friend of the court*).

practically means in practical terms or for practical purposes; good writers do not use it to mean *almost* where the idea of practical application is absent. In *I practically never get to sleep before midnight,* change to *almost.*

precipitate, precipitous.   The first as an adjective means with headlong speed, hence hasty or rash; the second means steep. An action is *precipitate,* a cliff *precipitous.*

prefer takes *to* or *rather than,* not *than.*

PREPOSITIONS.   (1) It is no easy matter to choose a preposition in such sentences as *We succeeded (by) (through) sheer good luck* and *Many men go to pieces (in) (under) such conditions;* and it is too complex a matter to tackle here. The leading treatise on the subject is Frederick T. Wood's *English Prepositional Idioms* (New York: St. Martin's, 1967). A useful list of 67 preposition choices that give many writers trouble appears in Follett, pp. 257–259.

(2) It is nonsense to say that a sentence cannot properly end with a preposition. Winston Churchill, finding a change made on this ground in the proofs of one of his books, allegedly wrote, "This is the sort of impertinence up with which I will not put." Yet the notion persists, leading at times to such painfully unidiomatic sentences as this one, from a 1971 United Press story: *Baker told a reporter Wednesday he expects the Lehi VI to cost*

around $250,000 and that he doesn't know from where the money is coming.

presently is widely used as a synonym of *now* or *at present,* but many writers, with 51 percent support from the AHD's Usage Panel, restrict it to the sense of *soon,* as in *He said he would be along presently.*

principal, principle.   The first is an adjective meaning leading or foremost, a noun designating the top official of a school or an important person in various legal contexts, and a noun designating the money on which interest is calculated. The second is a noun only and means a fundamental truth, law, or assumption. Derivation apart, the two words have in common only their sound; in *My principle worry was Margie,* change to *principal.*

proportion.   See PERCENT.

protagonist means the leading character in a drama or other literary work, and by extension the most conspicuous personage in any affair. It is neither etymologically nor in current correct usage the opposite of *antagonist*; being an absolute word, it cannot properly be qualified by *chief* or *leading*; connoting as it does uniqueness in a given context, it cannot take the plural in respect to that context, i.e. we cannot speak of the *protagonists* of a drama; and it is not a synonym of *advocate* or *champion.* Since the temptation to misuse *protagonist* in all four of these ways is seemingly overwhelming, our advice is not to use it at all.

provided, providing.   If you cannot make do with *if,* the word you want is *provided,* not *providing.* In *They agreed to support Jackson providing he honored his pledge,* change to *provided,* or better still to *if.* The full form *provided that* should be used only where omitting *that* would cause confusion.

quote for *quotation* is nonstandard.

rack, wrack.   *Rack* is right, *wrack* wrong or at best no improvement on *rack,* in all the common expressions in which both are sometimes used, notably *rack and ruin, on the rack, racked by pain, nerve-racking, storm-racked,* and *rack up points.*

rather is a halfhearted word and should never be used with all-out words like *spectacular* or *magnificent.*

re-. To *reform* does not mean to form again; to convey this last meaning without confusion we must write *re-form.* Similarly, we *re-solve* a recurring problem, *re-cover* our furniture, witness a *re-creation* of a historical event. Though correct, these hyphenated forms are irritatingly self-conscious; use an *again* construction if you can.

really is used by clumsy writers either to persuade the reader of the intensity of their response (*I really loved that dog*) or to solicit his agreement to an argument for which no evidence is offered (*We really made a mistake at Yalta*). Usually the strategy misfires and *really* comes through as a bankrupt effort to win the reader's respect or attention on the cheap. Good writers know that it takes more than an adverb to convey intensity of feeling or persuade the unpersuaded.

reason. (1) Generations of grammarians have deplored the *reason is because* construction: in *The reason I phoned was because she asked me to,* they say, *because* must be changed to *that.* The grammatical argument for *that* is impeccable, yet *because* persists and may someday become accepted usage, as it has in the reverse syntax: *Just because Diana likes parties is no reason why Tom should.* Until someday comes, use *that.*
(2) *Reason why,* though deplored by purists, is universal in speech and standard in writing, even when *why* is not followed by a clause: *It won't work, and there are two reasons why.*

regards. Of the constructions *in regards to, with regards to, in some regards,* and *as regards,* only the last is standard. The first two require *regard,* the third *respects.*

respectively is used to relate the individual components of one sequence to their prior counterparts in another sequence: *Jane,*

Lois, and Greta married a soldier, a sailor, and a Marine, respectively. The word is obtrusive and should be used only where it is absolutely necessary. In *With people like my father and mother, poker parties and bridge clubs are a way of life,* it would be gratuitous to add *respectively;* the reader can sort things out for himself.

restive, restless.   The two words are interchangeable according to modern dictionaries, but many writers prefer to restrict *restive* to its more distinctive meaning of balky or unwilling to cooperate.

ring takes the past form *rang: He rang the bell,* not *rung.*

rob, steal.   One *robs* a person, an institution, or a building; what the robber takes he *steals.* In *We would rob as many canapés as we could,* change to *steal* or *filch.*

scarcely, hardly, and *barely* take *when* or *before,* not *than;* in *Scarcely had I got my coat off than the telephone rang,* change to *when.* Double negatives like *without hardly a word of protest* and *couldn't barely find enough money for groceries* are illiterate; use *with* and *could.*

-self, -selves.   (1) *Ourself,* not *ourselves,* is the reflexive pronoun for the imperial or editorial *we: We found ourself last week at a party for Mae West.*

(2) The forms *themself, theirself,* and *theirselves* do not exist.

(3) Never use the reflexive pronoun where the simple pronoun will serve as well. In *My sister and myself arrived early,* change *myself* to *I.*

(4) A reflexive pronoun used to emphasize a preceding noun or pronoun takes no punctuation. In *Lenin, himself, never went that far,* delete the commas.

SENTENCE FRAGMENT.   A sentence fragment is any word or combination of words that is followed by a full stop (period, question mark, exclamation point) and that does not contain an independent subject and predicate: for example, the second, third, and fourth elements in *What did Scott need? A guide who knew the country. What else? Money.* Sentence fragments are perfectly legitimate in expository writing if used with proper respect for three caveats. First, do not use many; the repeated use of sentence fragments, as in some humorous newspaper columns, marks the writer as committed to striving for cheap effects. Second, do not use them in highly formal or abstract writing, where their informality would be out of place. Third, do not separate them unnaturally from a preceding or following sentence of which they logically form part; in *He must have meant Truman. Because Roosevelt would never have said that,* change to *Truman, because.*

SENTENCE TYPES.   Sentences are conventionally classified as simple, compound, complex, or compound-complex, depending on the number and kind of clauses they contain. A simple sentence has a single independent clause and no dependent clauses: *Babies cry / She and I fight all the time / Bert was too smart to put anything in writing / Slaloming pell-mell down the hill, their dark coats and scarves flapping behind them, they looked like a flock of drunken ravens.*

A compound sentence has two or more independent clauses linked by punctuation or a coordinating conjunction: *Sheep eat more, but pigs are fatter / Some were ripe; the others were still green / She is a model, her sister teaches Spanish, and her brother is a senior at Duke.*

A complex sentence has one or more dependent clauses linked to the independent clause by a subordinating conjunction (*because, since, when,* etc.) or a relative pronoun (*who, which, that,* etc.): *When I was young, I loved cake / Things started to happen after George arrived / Erika knew a woman who owned one.* The versatile *that* can be either a subordinating conjunction (*I told Bob that Sam was ready / She said [that] we couldn't go*) or a relative pronoun (*Buy me a doll that cries*); in either case the sentence is complex.

A compound-complex sentence has two or more independent clauses and one or more dependent clauses: *It was afternoon when she left, and the sky was dark / Bill did his best, but before the round ended he had been eliminated / She may be crazy, but I know you aren't.*

See also CLAUSE TYPES; CONJUNCTION TYPES.

service as a verb is best confined to repair or maintenance work on specified equipment or machinery; thus one *services* a television set or a car. Any extension to people (*We serviced over a hundred customers*) or even to abstractions (*The office was serviced twice a day by a man from Vend-o-Mat*) risks drawing a titter because of the word's strong sexual connotations (*This bull services four cows*).

shall, will.   In American usage *shall* is now for the most part restricted to the first person interrogative when a decision or recommendation is requested (*Shall we go? / Shall I tell him or will you?*), and even in these uses *should* is now far more common. In all other uses *will* is idiomatic: *I will be 21 in March / We will be lucky to escape alive / Will you want a picnic lunch?/ Will I be the only girl there?*

should, would.   In American usage *should* means *ought to*. In the conditional, *would* is proper with the first person as well as the second and third: *I would be glad to call on her / Would we be welcome there?*

sic, Latin for "thus," may be added in a quoted passage to verify something that might seem erroneous or unlikely but for the verification: "The official report described her as 'a fourteen-year-old hussy [*sic*] from Kansas City.' " Only pedants add *sic* after an insignificant spelling or typesetting error; rather than distract the reader with such trivia, simply correct the error. The use of *sic* in parentheses as a kind of exclamation point—"The first violinist was a native of Mongolia *(sic)*"—is permissible, but so are peanut-butter-and-ketchup sandwiches.

similar is not an adverb. In *She dresses similar to Lucy*, change to *like* or *rather like*.

sink takes the past form *sank*, not *sunk*: *The ship sank / German planes sank two ships.*

situation is a word that insecure writers love because they think it makes them sound impressive. Sometimes it can be simply dropped: in *It is an awkward situation when no one understands English,* change to *It is awkward when.* Almost always some less pretentious equivalent can be found: in *The situation called for prompt action,* for example, we could change to *They had to act promptly,* and in *if I were in John's situation* to *if I were John.*

so.   (1) Some writers mistakenly use *so* and *such* as synonyms for *very* in sentences like *Ireland is such a lovely country* and *We were so glad to get home.* Whatever their virtues in conversation—"Lydia is *so* beautiful tonight, don't you think, Mr. Palmer?"—the intensive *so* and *such* have no place in writing.

(2) *So* for *so that* is nonstandard; in *They saved money all year so they could have an expensive vacation,* change *so* to *so that.*

some is nonstandard for *somewhat* or *occasionally.* In *Things improved some,* change to *somewhat;* in *He played football some,* change to *played football occasionally* or *played a little football.* The expression *some better* for *somewhat better* is now confined to elderly rustics.

someplace and *someway* are nonstandard; use *somewhere* and *somehow.*

SOUNDALIKES.   Pairs of words that are spelled differently and have different meanings but sound identical or very similar cause many writers grief, especially writers whose vocabulary comes more from conversation and television than from print. Troublesome soundalikes are discussed in this section under AFFECT, AMBIVALENT, COMPLIMENT, COMPOSE, CONTINUOUS, COUNCIL, DELUSION, DISCREET, DISINTERESTED, FAZE, FLAUNT, FOREGO, FORTUNATE, IT'S, MILITATE, NAUSEOUS, PAST, PORE, PRECIPITATE, PRINCIPAL, RACK, and WHOSE.

See also SUFFIX CONFUSIONS (2).

SPELLING.   See SUFFIX CONFUSIONS; VARIANT SPELLINGS.

spring takes the past form *sprang,* not *sprung: They sprang to attention.*

steal. See ROB.

strata is strictly plural; not *every strata of society* but *every stratum* or *all strata.*

structure as a verb, meaning to organize or arrange, is social science jargon, and should be restricted to social science uses: e.g., one might contrast a structured psychiatric counseling session with one carried out by the technique of free association. Beyond this domain, *structure* tends to be vague. What is meant, for example, by *Miss Jones works best in a highly structured situation?* That she needs supervision? That she likes clear rules? That she feels more comfortable in a highly stratified or bureaucratic office than in a more informal work setting?

such and *this* are not synonyms. *Such a man* means "a man of this sort"; *this man* means "the man just mentioned." *Such* should be *these* in *She would eat ice cream or sherbet, but even such desserts she did not enjoy.*

See also SO; SUCH AS . . . AND OTHERS.

such as . . . and others, like *including . . . and others,* is a redundant construction. *Such as* selects one or more items from a class; *and others* asserts that the items selected do not constitute the whole class. Since *and others* tells us nothing that *such as* has not told us already, it is pointless to use both expressions; we should choose one or the other. Change *Confederate generals such as Lee, Jackson, and others* either to *Confederate generals such as Lee and Jackson* or to *Lee, Jackson, and other Confederate generals.*

SUFFIX CONFUSIONS.   Three main kinds of confusion arise with suffixes: (1) choosing the correct word from two or more words with the same root but different suffixes; (2) choosing the correct spelling for a word having a suffix that is spelled different ways for different words; (3) determining whether to double a consonant before a suffix. The solution to all three problems is to consult a dictionary. The rest of this entry will simply document the existence and suggest the extent of these problems.

(1) *Definite* and *definitive, precipitate* and *precipitous, principal* and *principle,* are discussed elsewhere in this section. Other often confused adjective pairs are *unexceptional* (routine) and *unexceptionable* (acceptable without change); *seasonal* (according to season) and *seasonable* (appropriate to the season); *sensuous* (pertaining to gratification of the senses in general) and *sensual* (pertaining to physical, especially sexual, gratification). Still other confusions arise between different parts of speech: *predominate* (verb) for *predominant* (adj.); *populous* (adj.) for *populace* (noun); *callous* and *phosphorous* (adj.) for *callus* and *phosphorus* (nouns). These distinctions are made clearly in your dictionary, where you have only to look them up.

(2) Some variant spellings of same-sounding suffixes are as follows:

First spelling	Second spelling	Third spelling or spelling optional
indispens*able*	indefens*ible*	—
gene*alogy,*	archae*ology,*	—
miner*alogy*	soci*ology*	
resist*ance,*	insist*ence,*	intransig*ence*
veng*eance*	indig*ence*	(*-eance*)
defend*ant,*	superintend*ent,*	depend*ent* (*-ant*),
attend*ant*	resplend*ent*	pend*ant* (*-ent*)
men*tion,*	ten*sion,*	—
preven*tion*	preten*sion*	
interpret*er,*	opera*tor,*	advis*er* (*-or*),
advertis*er*	inspec*tor*	invent*or* (*-er*)
boist*erous*	disast*rous*	dext*rous* (*-erous*)
station*ery,*	statu*ary,*	—
monast*ery*	secret*ary*	
critic*ize,*	advert*ise,*	anal*yze,*
organ*ize*	exerc*ise*	paral*yze*
publ*icly*	diplomat*ically*	frant*ically*
		(*-icly*)
her*oes,*	Ner*os,* larg*os*	zer*os* (*-oes*),
embarg*oes*		carg*oes* (*-os*)

Many, many other examples could be given of suffix confusions of this sort, not to mention confusions extending beyond suffixes, e.g. *questionnaire / millionaire / debonair, proceed / precede / supersede*. No one can find his way through this swamp without a dictionary.

(3) In American usage, the *New Yorker* to the contrary, suffix forms of verbs ending in *-l* and *-r* double the consonant when the last syllable of the verb is accented (*occurred, transferring, rebellious, abhorrent*) but not otherwise (*rivaling, offered, traveler, marvelous*). The *New Yorker* follows British usage in doubling *-l* even where the syllable is unaccented.

See also PLURAL CONFUSIONS.

terrific for splendid, as in *a terrific dinner*, is best left to the very young.

than. (1) A few sentences of the form *I like Mary better than Bob* need an extra verb to be clear: is it *than Bob does* or *than I like Bob?* Most such sentences, however, are clear enough in context to get by without elaboration: *The state chairmen liked Taft better than Eisenhower.* Don't add the clarifying verb unless you have to. If you have to, add it after its subject, not before: *than Bob does,* not *than does Bob,* which has the artificial ring of something never heard in speech.

(2) Pronouns take the objective case in the expression *than whom* and after *other than: Anyone other than her would have turned him down.* Otherwise pronouns following *than* take whatever case they would take if the clause introduced by *than* were spelled out: *I like Mary better than he [does] / I like Mary better than [I like] him.*

See also DIFFERENT THAN; PREFER; SCARCELY.

the. (1) When a possessive precedes a book title (or the equivalent) beginning with *The,* it is permissible to omit *The*: thus "Hardy's *Mayor of Casterbridge,*" "Jonson's *Alchemist* and Shakespeare's *Tempest.*"

(2) In writing the names of magazines and newspapers beginning with *The,* it is permissible to omit *The* for convenience: "his *New Yorker* articles," "a *New York Times* reporter." When *the* is

retained, it should be lowercased and roman rather than capitalized and italic: "as the *San Francisco Chronicle* says," "the *New Republic*'s coverage." The lowercased, roman form is of course inevitable when *the* attaches not to the title but to a following noun, as in "the *Times* editorial."

(3) Some writers tend to omit *the* before abstract nouns followed by *of*: thus *Dismissal of Cox came as no surprise* rather than *The dismissal,* or *Meyers opposed extension of the draft* rather than *the extension.* Headline writing, with its premium on saving space, may be responsible for this trend; but whatever the cause, the result is a kind of pidgin English that grates on the sensitive ear. Do not drop *the* casually in such cases, and when in doubt retain it.

thereof, therein, thereto, etc. are sometimes substituted for the rhetorically weak *of it, in it, to it,* etc., especially at the end of a sentence: *The book was tedious, and he longed to get to the end thereof / Sally knew of the plot but not of Nye's part therein.* However serious the *of it* disease may seem, the pompous and archaic *thereof* cure is fifty times worse. If no other cure for *of it, in it,* etc. can be found, live with the disease.

together with.   A singular noun followed by a phrase beginning *together with* takes a singular verb: *The emperor, together with his ministers and his household, was exiled.*

too.   *Not too* for *not very* in such sentences as *I was not feeling too good that morning* and *Fuentes was not too pleased with the verdict* is nonstandard. A number of alternatives are available, among them omitting *too,* changing *too* to *very,* and switching to the standard idiom *none too.*

tortuous means winding, twisting, circuitous, or devious. It is not related to *torture* except by remote derivation, and has no connotation of physical pain.

total.   *A total of* X takes the singular or the plural according to whether X would take the singular or the plural. Thus *Five hun-*

dred signatures was their goal / *A total of 500 signatures was their goal*; but *Five hundred signatures were obtained* / *A total of 500 signatures were obtained.*

towards is an old-fashioned spelling; use *toward.*

trigger in the sense of touch off, as in *The announcement triggered a three-day strike,* is a vogue word popularized by journalists.

try and, as in *We felt we should try and get Senator Cranston to support us,* though acceptable to the British authorities Fowler and Gowers, is unacceptable to 79 percent of the AHD's Usage Panel. Use *try to.*

type.   (1) *Type* is overused for *kind* or *sort.* Properly used, *type* implies a strong and clearly marked relationship to a well-defined class. Where the relationship is less clear or the class less well-defined, as in *He is the type of person who kicks cats,* change to *kind* or *sort.*

   (2) *Type* without *of,* as in *the type person who* or *this type record player,* is illiterate.

   The suffix *-type* is discussed on p. 105.

underway is an adjective only, and occurs exclusively in such seldom-used technical compounds as *underway refueling*; the adverb is two words, *under way.* In *We had a hard time getting the project underway,* change to *under way.*

unique should not be compared or qualified. Something unique is the only one of its kind. A thing is accordingly either unique or not; it cannot be *rather unique, very unique, more unique* or *less unique* than something else, the *most unique* thing of its kind, or (a choice specimen from a London editor) *unique even by Middle Eastern standards.*

upcoming is a journalist's vogue word; use *approaching.*

use as an auxiliary verb is inflected: *I used to go,* not *use to.*

utilize and *utilization* are ugly and unnecessary synonyms for the verb and noun forms of *use*. In *The committee praised our utilization of Russian and Spanish materials*, change *utilization* to *use*.

VARIANT SPELLINGS.   (1) WNC and most other dictionaries distinguish two kinds of variant spellings: the OR spelling (*orangutan* OR *orangoutan* / *index* n, pl *indexes* OR *indices*) and the ALSO spelling (*fogy* ALSO *fogey* / *learn* vb *learned* ALSO *learnt*). When OR is used, the two spellings are alleged to be of equal status and currency but rarely are in practice, as one can infer from the nonalphabetical order of entries like *orangutan* OR *orangoutan*. When ALSO is used, the second spelling is alleged to have less status or currency than the first. Our advice is always to use the first spelling given in your dictionary.

(2) British spellings like *theatre* and *centre, neighbour* and *honour, criticise* and *analyse*, are no more appropriate to American writing than British terms like *lift* for elevator and *lorry* for truck. The only exception is proper names of British offices and institutions: *Minister of Defence*, not *Defense*; *Labour Party*, not *Labor*. Some American spellings, e.g. *glamour, advertise*, do not follow the customary pattern; when in doubt, consult your dictionary.

See also SUFFIX CONFUSIONS (2), col. 3.

very is overused by young writers. Often it can be simply eliminated without changing the meaning of a sentence or weakening its force, e.g. in *She lived in a very big house in Winnetka* and *I was very sorry to hear of Abe's illness.*

wait on for *wait for* is nonstandard; in *If we had waited on Harry, we would still be waiting*, change *on* to *for*.

ways for *way*, as in *quite a ways from home* or *a long ways to go*, is nonstandard.

well, good.   *Well* is the adverb form of *good*: *He plays golf well / He is good at golf.* Athletes and hayseeds to the contrary, *good* is no adverb; utter if you must such locutions as *He got hit good* and

That old car climbs hills pretty good, but do not commit them to paper.

Well as an adjective, apart from the cast-iron idiom *all's well* and the obsolescent *it is well* (*It is well not to anger him*), implies good health. Thus *she was good* means that she behaved or performed well, *she was well* that her health was good; the same general distinction can be made between *she felt good* (happy) and *she felt well* (healthy), and between *she looked good* (attractive) and *she looked well* (healthy).

what as a pronoun can be either singular (*what bothers me most*) or plural (*what seem to be clouds*), but not both at once. In *What takes longest are the field events,* change *takes* to *take* or *are* to *is.*

where. (1) *At* with *where,* as in *Tom could not remember where the car was at,* is a colloquialism of the South and Southwest; it is not acceptable in writing.

(2) *Where* for *that,* as in *I could see where somebody might think so,* is nonstandard.

who, whom. In classical grammar *who* is the subject (*Who did it? / the woman who was hurt*) and *whom* the object (*Whom did they choose? / the ones whom we had neglected*). But this distinction is breaking down and *who* is increasingly used for *whom,* especially in direct questions: *Who did they choose? / Who did you hear that from?* Only following a preposition is *whom* still unmistakably sovereign; no one yet writes *for who* or *many of who.*

whoever, whomever. The form *whomever* exists, but most writers use *whoever* as both subject and object: *Whoever wants to can sign up / Whoever they invited did not come.*

whose. (1) The possessive pronoun *whose* should not be confused with *who's,* a contraction of *who is,* as in *Who's afraid of the big bad wolf?*

(2) *Whose* may be freely used as the possessive of *which;* whether the antecedent is animate or inanimate makes no differ-

ence, so long as it is clear. *Caves for the treasures of which men have given their lives* is clumsy; change to *caves for whose treasures*.

worst.   *Webster's Third Unabridged* prescribes "if *worse* comes to worst," the AHD "if *worst* comes to worst." Though the Webster version is the more rational, we prefer the AHD version, for which the *Oxford English Dictionary* cites examples as far back as 1594.

wrack.   See RACK.

ACKNOWLEDGMENTS

James Baldwin, *Notes of a Native Son*, Boston: Beacon Press, 1955.

Barton J. Bernstein, "The Cuban Missile Crisis," in Lynn Miller and Ronald Pruessen, eds., *Reflections on the Cold War*, Temple University Press, 1974.

Roy Bongartz, from "Three Meanies," in *Esquire* 74:110 (August 1970). Reprinted with the permission of the publisher.

Dee Brown, *Bury My Heart at Wounded Knee*, New York: Bantam Books, 1970.

Kenneth Burke, "Thomas Mann and André Gide," from *Counterstatement* by Kenneth Burke (Harrison-Blaine, 1931) reprinted with the permission of the author.

Stokely Carmichael, "What We Want," from *Crisis*, Peter Collier, ed., Harcourt, Brace, World, 1969. Used with permission of the Student National Coordinating Committee.

Joyce Cary, *The Horse's Mouth*, New York: Harper & Row.

David Denby, "Dirty Movies—Hard Core and Soft," copyright © 1970, by The Atlantic Monthly Company, Boston, Mass. Reprinted with the permission of the author.

Isak Dinesen, *Out of Africa*, New York: Random House, 1937.

Peter F. Drucker, "Keynes: Economics as a Magical System," in *Men, Ideas, and Politics*, Harper & Row, 1971.

Loren Eiseley, excerpt from *The Immense Journey*, Random House, Inc., 1946.

Peter Elbow, *Writing Without Teachers*, New York: Oxford University Press, 1973.

Henry Watson Fowler, excerpt from *Modern English Usage*, Oxford University Press, rev. ed., 1965. By permission of The Clarendon Press, Oxford.

Charles Frankel, from *High on Foggy Bottom* by Charles Frankel, published by Harper & Row, 1969, and reprinted with the permission of the author.

Sigmund Freud, from "Femininity," quoted in Ernest Jones, *Sigmund Freud: His Life and Work*, London: Hogarth Press, 1953–57.

Sir Ernest Gowers, *The Complete Plain Words*, revised by Sir Bruce Fraser, London: Her Majesty's Stationery Office, 1973.

Lillian Hellman, *An Unfinished Woman*, New York: Bantam Books, 1973.

Seymour M. Hersh, "My Lai: A Report on the Massacre and Its Aftermath," *Harper's*, May 1970.

Julian Huxley, excerpt from *Man Stands Alone*, Harper & Row.

James Joyce, excerpt from *A Portrait of the Artist as a Young Man* by James Joyce. Copyright 1916 by B. W. Huebsch, 1944 by Nora Joyce; copyright © 1964 by the

Estate of James Joyce. All Rights Reserved. Reprinted by permission of the Viking Press, Inc., the Executors of the James Joyce Estate, and Jonathan Cape Ltd., publishers.

John Kaplan, from *Marijuana—The New Prohibition*, copyright © 1970 by John Kaplan, reprinted by permission of The World Publishing Company.

Kenneth Keniston, "Students, Drugs, and Protest: Drugs on Campus," in *The American Scholar* and reprinted from *Current*, February, 1969, with the permission of the author.

Oscar Lewis, *The Children of Sanchez*, New York: Random House, 1961.

Dwight Macdonald, from *Against the American Grain* by Dwight Macdonald, copyright Random House, Inc., and reprinted with the permission of the publisher; and from "Purging the University," in *Newsweek*, July 13, 1970, with the permission of the publisher.

Norman Mailer, excerpt reprinted by permission of G. P. Putnam's Sons from *The Presidential Papers* by Norman Mailer, © 1960, 1961, 1962, 1963 by Norman Mailer.

Edwin Newman, adapted from *Strictly Speaking*, Indianapolis: Bobbs-Merrill, 1974.

Oregon Journal, newsbreak reprinted in *The New Yorker*, July 16, 1966.

George Orwell, *Down and Out in Paris and London*, New York: Harcourt, Brace & World, 1961.

George Orwell, excerpt from "Politics and the English Language," *Shooting an Elephant and Other Essays*, Harcourt, Brace & World, Inc., and Martin Secker & Warburg, Ltd.

The Oxford English Dictionary, reprinted with the permission of the Clarendon Press, Oxford, England.

V. L. Parrington, excerpt from *Main Currents in American Thought*, Harcourt, Brace & World, Inc.

Thomas Pynchon, *Gravity's Rainbow*, New York: Bantam Books, 1973.

Ramparts Magazine, "The Redress of Their Grievances," copyright *Ramparts Magazine*, Inc., 1967. By permission of the editors.

Betty Roszak, "The Human Continuum" in Betty and Theodore Roszak, eds., *Masculine/Feminine*, New York: Harper & Row, 1969.

Mark Schorer, "Technique as Discovery," *Hudson Review*, I (Spring, 1948), as reprinted in *The World We Imagine: Selected Essays by Mark Schorer*, copyright 1968, Farrar, Straus & Giroux, Inc., and reprinted with the permission of the author.

Philip E. Slater, *The Pursuit of Loneliness*, Boston: Beacon Press, 1970.

S. R. Slavson, excerpt from *Reclaiming the Delinquent*, The Macmillan Company (Free Press), 1965.

David Solomon, "The Marihuana Myths," in David Solomon, ed., *The Marihuana Papers*, New York: New American Library, 1968.

Una Stannard, "The Mask of Beauty," in Vivian Gornick and Barbara K. Moran, eds., *Women in Sexist Society: Studies in Power and Powerlessness*, New York: Basic Books, 1971.

Alvin Toffler, from *Future Shock*, by Alvin Toffler, by permission of Random House, Inc.

Gore Vidal, "The Republican National Convention," from *For Our Time* by Gore Vidal, reprinted from *The New York Review of Books* with the permission of the publisher. Copyright © 1968, New York Review, Inc.

George Wald, "A Generation in Search of a Future." Reprinted with the permission of George Wald.

Webster's New Collegiate Dictionary (1973), reprinted with the permission of the publisher.

Webster's Seventh Collegiate Dictionary (1963), reprinted with the permission of the publisher.

"Lee Strout White," *The New Yorker*, May 1936.

Margery Wolf, *Women and the Family in Rural Taiwan*, Stanford, 1973.

Philip Wylie, excerpt from *Generation of Vipers*, Holt, Rinehart & Winston, Inc.

INDEX

INDEX